The Economics of
International Integration

The Economics of International Integration

Third revised edition

Peter Robson

University of St Andrews

London and New York

First published 1980
by the Academic Division of Unwin Hyman Ltd
Second edition 1984, third edition 1987, third impression 1990

Reprinted 1993
by Routledge
11 New Fetter Lane, London EC4P 4EE
29 West 35th Street, New York, NY 10001

© Routledge 1993

Printed in Great Britain by
Biddles Ltd, Guildford and King's Lynn

British Library Cataloguing in Publication Data
A catalogue record for this book is available from the British Library

ISBN 0–415–09880–7 (pbk)

Library of Congress Cataloging-in-Publication Data has been applied for

ISBN 0–415–09880–7 (pbk)

CONTENTS

Contents

LIST OF ABBREVIATIONS

ASEAN	Association of South-East Asian Nations
CACM	Central American Common Market
CAP	Common Agricultural Policy
CARICOM	Caribbean Community
CARIFTA	Caribbean Free Trade Area
CEAO	Communauté Economique de l'Afrique de l'Ouest (West African Economic Community)
CEEAC	Communauté Economique des Etats de l'Afrique Centrale (Economic Community of Central African States)
CEPGL	Communauté Economique des Pays des Grands Lacs (Economic Community of the Great Lakes Countries)
CET	common external tariff
CMEA	Council for Mutual Economic Assistance (Comecon)
DRC	domestic resource cost
EAC	East African Community
EAGGF	European Agriculture Guidance and Guarantee Fund
EC[1]	European Community
ECU	European Currency Unit
ECCM	Eastern Caribbean Common Market
ECOWAS	Economic Community of West African States
EEC	European Economic Community[1]
EFTA	European Free Trade Association
EIB	European Investment Bank
EMCF	European Monetary Cooperation Fund
EMF	European Monetary Fund
EMS	European Monetary System
EMU	Economic and Monetary Union
EPC	effective protection coefficient
ERDF	European Regional Development Fund
ERM	exchange rate mechanism
EUA	European unit of account (now superseded by the ECU)
FDI	foreign direct investment
FTA	free trade area
GATT	General Agreement on Tariffs and Trade
GDR	German Democratic Republic
IBEC	International Bank for Economic Cooperation
IIB	International Investment Bank

List of Abbreviations

IMP	Integrated Mediterranean Programme
LAFTA	Latin American Free Trade Association
LAIA	Latin American Integration Association
LDC	less developed country
MCA	Monetary Compensation Amounts
MNC	multinational corporation
MRU	Mano River Union
NCI	New Community Instrument
OECD	Organization for Economic Cooperation and Development
TNE	transnational enterprise
u.a.	units of account
UDEAC	Union Douanière et Economique de l'Afrique Centrale (Customs and Economic Union of Central Africa)

[1] There are strictly three European Communities: the European Economic Community; the European Coal and Steel Community; and the European Atomic Energy Community. Since 1967 there has been a single Commission and a single Council for all three. The term European Community is in general used to refer to activities undertaken under the Treaty of Rome, and to wider activities of the Communities, unless legal enactments covering the institutions or individual treaties are in question.

PREFACE

Like the editions that have preceded it, this book sets out to provide a concise and systematic exposition of the economics of international integration. At the core of that subject is the theory of customs unions that originated in the writings of Jacob Viner and others forty years ago. But the theory of customs unions, though it remains basic, is only one part of the apparatus that is needed to analyse the issues that arise in contemporary forms of economic integration – of which the European Economic Community (EEC) constitutes perhaps the most developed instance – which go far beyond simple customs unions. This book tries to present a unified approach that reflects both the diversity of economic objectives that underly such initiatives and the wide range of economic policies that have to be considered, and their interaction. An adequate treatment of the issues necessarily draws on the whole range of the main fields of economics. The task of bringing it to bear on the issues in question is not easy, not merely because of the range of material, but also – as with macroeconomics – because of the unsettled state of the theory and the considerable disagreement amongst economists on the way in which economies behave and should be modelled. In most cases only one short chapter could be devoted to major areas. Inevitably this has meant that some issues have been dealt with in a summary fashion and others have had to be altogether neglected. I hope nevertheless that the analytical framework will be useful; that the perspective is dependable; and that those who seek to penetrate more deeply into this subject will continue to find in this book a useful foundation and guide to more specialized literature.

The main emphasis of the book is on principles and on the formulation of an analytical framework for thinking about and analysing the issues of integration that gives proper stress to the diversity of objectives and of policy instruments, and to their interaction. At the same time I have attempted to indicate the bearing of the analysis on events, policy issues and discussions in the European Community (EC) and elsewhere to which, after all, the theories and analyses have largely been a response. No single book could hope to provide an adequate evaluation of the experience and policy issues of the EEC, Comecon, or of the many integration groupings that operate in the Third World. This book certainly makes no claim to do so, although in providing material and comment on these groupings it seeks to indicate some of their leading issues, and the ways in which economic analysis can elucidate them.

Preface

The principal change in this volume as compared with its pre-decessor is that a new chapter has been provided on the difficult area of fiscal integration and budgetary policy. It is hoped that this will provide a useful analytical background for students in connec-tion with the recurrent budgetary debate in Europe which, as these pages were being penned, showed every sign of coming once more to occupy the centre of the European stage. The failure of the Heads of State at Fontainebleau in 1984 to grasp the nettle of reform and to address basic issues adequately is now making itself felt and the brief respite provided by that Agreement is already over. The whole of the book has been updated to take account of recent analytical contributions, empirical evaluations and institu-tional progress. The chapter on common markets in particular has been much enlarged and consideration of the multinational integra-tion of enterprises, partly but not exclusively in an EC context, has been expanded. Full account has been taken of the EC's ambitious programme for establishing a fully unified common market in Europe by 1992.

In the course of preparing the successive editions of this book, I have derived immense benefit and stimulus from discussions not only with academic colleagues but also with 'practitioners' from Brussels to Burkina. It would be quite impossible to acknowledge these obligations adequately here. I therefore limit myself to thank-ing specifically those who have made helpful comments on the third edition. In St Andrews, Mohammed Malek and, in particular, David Cobham have been most helpful. Outwith St Andrews I should particularly like to thank Sylviane Guillaumont, Jacques Pelkmans, Josef van Brabant, Geoffrey Denton, Geoffrey Shackleton and Alan Winters. On the purely technical side, Joan Reed has once more demonstrated her outstanding ability to deci-pher manuscripts, and in that and other ways has provided invalu-able secretarial support.

CHAPTER 1

Introduction

THE SCOPE OF THE SUBJECT

Gottfried Haberler once remarked that we live in 'the age of integration'. If integration is taken to denote a state of affairs or a process involving attempts to combine separate national economies into larger economic regions, the appearance of the world economy today amply confirms the continued aptness of this characterization. All but one of the OECD nations are concerned in arrangements for international economic integration, as indeed are most of the rest of Western European countries. Nearly all of the nations of Latin America and the Caribbean, most of those in Africa, and the more important economies of South East Asia are also members of integration arrangements, as are the countries of the Soviet bloc. Of the larger industrial economies, only Japan, China and India have been unaffected by this phenomenon.

Economic integration is basically concerned with efficiency in resource use, with particular reference to the spatial aspect. Necessary conditions for its fullest attainment include: (1) the freedom of movement of goods and of factors of production; and (2) an absence of discrimination amongst the members of the group. In addition, where resources are allocated by the price mechanism, measures will be required to ensure that the market provides the right signals, and institutions will also be required to give effect to the integrating force of the market. The term *negative integration* was coined by Tinbergen (1965) to denote those aspects of integration that involve the removal of discrimination and restrictions on movement, such as arise in the process of trade liberalization. This he has contrasted with *positive integration*, which is concerned with the modification of existing instruments and institutions and the creation of new ones, for the purpose of enabling the market to function effectively and also to promote other broader policy objectives in the union.

Arrangements for international economic integration in this

sense take a variety of forms. For analytical purposes the principal ones to distinguish are free trade areas, customs unions, common markets and economic unions. Both free trade areas and customs unions involve the tariff-free movement of products within the area; but whereas in a free trade area each country retains its own tariff against the rest of the world, in a customs union a common external tariff (CET) is adopted. In a common market, not only is there a customs union, but in addition labour and capital are permitted to move within the union without restriction, so that factor as well as product markets are integrated. An economic union involves not only product and factor market integration but a high degree of integration of monetary, fiscal and other policies as well. Between common markets and economic unions a spectrum of forms of integration may be envisaged, corresponding to the degree of harmonization of other policies adopted. All such arrangements for international economic integration are nevertheless characterized by three features:

(1)   the suppression, in certain matters, of discrimination among the members;
(2)   the maintenance of discrimination against the rest of the world in various respects;
(3)   the conclusion of agreements among the members that are intended to have a lasting character, and that limit the unilateral use of certain instruments of economic policy.

International economic integration is a means, not an end. What motivates it? In practice, most economic groupings are established or advocated partly for political reasons, whose importance as a factor in understanding the actual progress of economic integration can scarcely be over-rated. Even so, economic analysis is essential to identify and, if possible, to quantify the economic effects and issues, so as to provide a basis for policy makers and others to judge whether and to what extent the economic arguments reinforce or offset the political considerations. It is primarily with the economic factors that this study is concerned. From this point of view the primary economic incentive for states to enter into arrangements for regional integration is the prospect of economic gain, in the shape of an increase in the level or rate of growth of output or of some component of it. For the group as a whole such gains may be derived from a number of sources: increased production arising from specialization according to comparative advantage; increased output arising from the better exploitation of scale economies; improvements in the terms of trade of the group with the rest of the

world; forced changes in efficiency arising from increased competition within the bloc; and integration-induced changes affecting the
quantity or quality of factor inputs, such as increased capital inflows
and changes in the rate of technological advance. Most of these
aspects can be analysed up to a point on the basis of the part of
orthodox trade theory that deals with customs unions.

An adequate theory of international economic integration must
however go beyond customs union theory in three important
respects:

(1) it must take account of intra-union factor movements;
(2) it must address the implications of the integration or harmonization of instruments of national economic policy other
than commercial ones;
(3) it must address the evaluation of integration by reference to
criteria that go beyond that of efficiency in resource
allocation.

A theory of international economic integration must take account
of intra-union factor movements because, ultimately, it is unobstructed factor mobility – factor market integration – that creates an
integrated economy out of separate national economic entities. In
particular, free factor movement within a union will entail important constraints on national policies, by making it difficult or impossible for national authorities to maintain an effectively autonomous
jurisdiction in several key policy areas. The theory must also
address the integration of policies in areas other than commerce
since that will be expressly at issue in many forms of international
integration. Moreover integration in these other fields (for
instance, in the areas of monetary and fiscal policies), although it
may be motivated by different goals, can affect commodity and
factor flows and thus the allocation of resources within and between
member countries as well as having other impacts. For that reason
alone, it would follow that an adequate theory of international
economic integration must embody a broader set of criteria or goals
than that of allocative efficiency, which alone is considered in
orthodox trade or customs union theory. In terms of such an
approach, international economic integration is thus to be viewed
as a state or process that derives its importance from its potential for
enabling its participants to achieve a variety of common goals more
effectively by joint or integrated action than by unilateral measures.
These goals include considerations not only of allocative efficiency
but also of stabilization, growth and international balance. In this
light the theory of international economic integration is concerned,

as Tinbergen has emphasized, with the problem of policy optimization in a broad sense within the integrated area.

The contribution of international economic integration to the
more effectual attainment of policy objectives must evidently be
kept in perspective. Membership of an economic bloc cannot of
itself guarantee a satisfactory economic performance to a member
state, or to the group as a whole, or even a better performance than
in the past, whatever the criteria employed. The static gains from
integration, although they may be significant, can be – and often are
– swamped by the influence of factors of domestic or international
origin that have nothing to do with integration. Moreover, many of
the more fundamental factors influencing a country's economic
performance are dynamic and these are unlikely to be affected by
integration except in the long run. It is clearly not a necessary
condition for economic success that a country should be a member
of an economic community, as is indicated by the experience of
several small countries, although some might have performed even
better as members of a suitable group. Nevertheless, although
integration is no panacea for all economic ills, nor even indispensable to success, there are convincing reasons that are discussed
throughout this book for supposing that significant economic benefits may be derived from well-conceived and well-implemented
arrangements for economic integration.

THE HISTORY OF THE THEORY OF
INTERNATIONAL ECONOMIC INTEGRATION

The branch of economic analysis that deals formally with the economics of international economic integration is of recent origin.
The core of the subject is the theory of customs unions, which is
commonly regarded as having taken shape with the publication of
Viner's pioneering study (1950), although this view neglects
important contemporary contributions by de Beers (1941) and Byé
(1950).

This view of the late origins of customs union theory appears to
be essentially well founded, although it has been questioned by
O'Brien (1976). The pre-Vinerian literature on customs unions in
the twentieth century is certainly sparse, and some of it – for
instance, the contributions of Gregory (1921) and of Haberler
(1936) – appears to justify the view that, before the publication of
Viner's study, economists wrongly regarded customs unions as a
step on the road to free trade. This is not to say that some of the
ideas underlying current orthodoxy cannot be found in earlier

writings. Since sixteen customs unions were formed between 1818 and 1924, it would be surprising if this were not the case, for it is hardly to be imagined that the classical and neoclassical economists would have been wholly blind to their implications. O'Brien has gone further and has contended that the central features of the Vinerian analysis of customs unions, namely, trade creation and trade diversion, were a matter of essentially correct analysis by classical economists in the nineteenth century.

The classical economists certainly discussed at length the effects of preferential commercial treaties such as the Methuen Treaty of 1703 (which admitted Portuguese wines into Great Britain on preferential terms in return for the removal of a prohibition on British woollen exports to Portugal) and the Cobden (Anglo-French) Treaty of 1860. In turn, Adam Smith (1776), Ricardo (1817) and McCulloch (1832) each attacked the Methuen Treaty, essentially on the grounds of its trade-diverting effects. The Cobden Treaty also generated lively debate on its trade effects, and trade diversion was an issue here too. When the German Zollverein, the most notable example of a customs union to be formed in the nineteenth century, was established in 1834, McCulloch and others subjected its provisions to detailed scrutiny in the course of which its trade effects, in particular its diversionary effects, were given particular attention. In a different analytical tradition the German economist List (1885) clearly viewed customs unions as protective devices for promoting infant industries, and in this way he can be said to have anticipated a fruitful stream of modern customs-union theorizing initiated by Johnson (1965) and Cooper and Massell (1965).

Relying on such contributions as these, O'Brien has claimed that:

> . . . all Viner did was to start from the position of the classical economists and of Hawtrey and Lord Robbins, and then simply add to this the logical possibility of some trade creation, depending on the relative height of the pre-union tariff and the common external tariff, and/or the possibility that both countries in the union were producers of the goods in question. (1976, p. 560)

Although this may be strictly true, this simple addition, embodying the concept of trade creation, is crucial to the theory of customs unions, and it is not clear that the classical and neoclassical economists grasped its essence, as opposed to the idea of trade expansion. In any event, the discussions by the classical and neoclassical economists of customs unions were largely incidental to their consideration of broader issues, and the theory was largely implicit.

There is, indeed, no systematic treatment of customs unions in the literature prior to Viner's study, apart from the work of de Beers (himself a pupil of Viner). At the same time, although few economists are likely to wish to challenge H. G. Johnson's judgement that Viner's analysis stands unimpaired as the great theoretical contribution that it really was, Byé must surely share the credit for providing the first major explicit formulation of a systematic theoretical foundation for customs union theory. In any case, however significant the contributions of their forerunners are judged to be, the fact remains that customs union theory is only a part of a theory of international economic integration. Prior to the 1950s there certainly did not exist a body of theoretical literature dealing systematically with the impact of other kinds of policy in the context of integration including monetary, fiscal and regional aspects.

THE PRESENT REACH OF
INTERNATIONAL ECONOMIC INTEGRATION:
A GLOBAL PERSPECTIVE

During the past quarter of a century or so, many arrangements for international economic integration have come into existence. The most important of these blocs is the European Economic Community (EEC), founded in 1957 under the Treaty of Rome by France, West Germany, Italy, Belgium, the Netherlands and Luxemburg. The Community of the original six members was enlarged in 1973 by the accession of the United Kingdom, Ireland and Denmark. In 1981 the second enlargement of the Community began with the admission of Greece. Spain and Portugal were admitted in 1986.

The EEC takes the form of a common market, having a common external tariff and making provision for the free movement of labour and capital. A variety of other national policies is also harmonized in order to make the market effective. These policies have to do principally with agriculture, competition, fiscal matters and regional aids. At the time of the first enlargement the European Community (EC) decided to introduce its own regional policy, which is designed to complement national policies and to contribute to a reduction in economic disparities within the Community. So far, expenditure for regional policy purposes is of a very modest order. In the late 1960s proposals were made to and agreed by the Council of the Communities that envisaged the development of the EEC into a full monetary and economic union by 1980. Little progress has subsequently been made towards this objective partly as a result of the stresses accompanying the EEC's enlargement and the impact of a succession of international monetary and economic crises. However, in March 1979 a European Monetary System (EMS) was established with the principal object of providing a greater measure of monetary stability in the Community.

The European Free Trade Association (EFTA) is a second western European grouping. The formation of a Europe-wide free trade association was originally proposed by Britain in the mid-1950s in order to allow those European countries that, like itself, were not prepared to commit themselves to a common agricultural policy or to other political and economic objectives envisaged in the establishment of the EEC at least to enjoy the benefits of free trade in industrial products. The United Kingdom's proposals proved to be unacceptable to the Six, and the free trade association that was in the end established in 1960 was confined to the United Kingdom and the smaller countries of Western Europe, namely, Switzerland, Austria, Denmark, Norway, Sweden and Portugal. Finland became associated with EFTA in 1961. EFTA is purely a trade grouping and has none of the supranational features of the EEC. Since the enlargement of the EEC by the entry of the United Kingdom, Ireland and Denmark, EFTA's importance has diminished considerably. However, simultaneously with the enlargement, those EFTA countries that were left outside became linked to the enlarged EEC through a series of free trade agreements, aimed at creating a wider European industrial free trade area. As a result, as Curzon has remarked:

> The wheel had come full circle and the solutions proposed in the 1956–58 . . . negotiations were finally adopted after a delay of fifteen years – the important difference being that the United Kingdom was no longer on the free trade side of the fence, but on the economic union side. (1974, p. 34)

By 1984, after more than a decade of transition, these arrangements had become fully effective.

Two other initiatives that are potentially of considerable significance for the scope of integration amongst advanced market economies should also be mentioned at this point. First, there are proposals, initially made by a Canadian Senate Committee in 1982, for the development of the already close and preferential trade relations between the US and Canada into a fully fledged industrial free trade area (Lipsey and Smith, 1985). Secondly, building on NAFTA, the free trade area that has been in force between Australia and New Zealand since 1965, agreement has been reached to develop still closer economic relations between these two countries.

This is expressed in the 1983 Closer Economic Relations Agreement (ANZCERTA) that is in the process of implementation.

The instances of economic integration so far mentioned have all involved advanced market economies. In principle, economic integration need not be confined to advanced market economies. In fact, the planned economies of Eastern Europe have also set up an integration bloc. 'Socialist' integration operates under the auspices of the Council for Mutual Economic Assistance (CMEA), usually referred to in the West as Comecon. This institution was established in 1949 and at present formally includes the USSR, Albania, Bulgaria, Czechoslovakia, the German Democratic Republic (GDR), Hungary, Poland and Romania, together with the non-European countries of Cuba, Mongolia and Vietnam. Its objects are to accelerate economic development and to establish a more rational division of labour among its member countries.

The most numerous instances of international economic integration are to be found outside Europe, in the less developed world. In Africa alone, where fertile ground for integration is provided by the existence of many very small and poor states, eight or nine groupings of this kind have been established. In West Africa, three economic communities exist. The Communauté Economique de l'Afrique de l'Ouest (CEAO) is a purely francophone grouping set up in 1974 by the Ivory Coast, Mali, Mauritania, Niger, Senegal and Upper Volta (now Burkina Faso). The CEAO represents the third attempt of the states that came into being as a result of the collapse in 1959 of the French West African Federation to reconstitute the economic links they had shared before independence. The CEAO countries (except Mauritania), together with Benin and Togo, are also linked in a monetary union. In 1985 Benin was admitted into the CEAO. The Mano River Union (MRU) is a grouping that was established in 1973 between Liberia and Sierra Leone. It involves a customs union and certain other forms of cooperation, including cooperation for the establishment of 'union' industries. In 1980, Guinea acceded to the Union. The third and by far the largest grouping is the Economic Community of West African States (ECOWAS). This bloc, which was set up under the Treaty of Lagos in 1975, is made up of sixteen anglophone, francophone and lusophone countries, and it includes those that are already linked in the CEAO and the MRU. It has ambitious plans for trade liberalization and the establishment of a common external tariff and other forms of cooperation, but implementation has been slow.

Equatorial and Central Africa possess three economic communities as well. The Union Douanière et Economique de l'Afrique Centrale (UDEAC), established in 1964, links the People's

Republic of the Congo, Gabon, Cameroon and the Central African Republic. These countries, together with Chad which was a member of UDEAC until 1968, are also linked in a monetary union of long standing to which Equatorial Guinea has recently acceded. The Communauté Economique des Pays des Grands Lacs (CEPGL) was established in 1976 by Burundi, Ruanda and Zaïre. The most recently formed bloc in this area is the Communauté Economique des Etats de l'Afrique Centrale (CEEAC), which was set up in 1983. It groups together ten states, namely the members of UDEAC and CEPGL together with Chad, Equatorial Guinea and the state of Sao Thomé et Principe. It is the counterpart for Central Africa of ECOWAS.

In East and Southern Africa, several arrangements may be noted. Until its break-up in 1978, one notably effective bloc was the East African Community (EAC). This group included Kenya, Uganda and Tanzania, which had a half-century's history of economic integration based on a customs union, a common market and a common currency. Further south there is the Southern African Customs Union which consists of Botswana, Lesotho, Swaziland and the Republic of South Africa. This was set up in 1969 on foundations that date back to 1910. Two looser arrangements may also be mentioned. A Preferential Trade Area for Eastern Africa was set up in 1981 by fifteen countries. Finally, the Southern African Development Coordination Conference, formally established in 1980, represents a different approach to economic cooperation which does not rest on a formal trade bloc.

In Latin America and the Caribbean, four main regional blocs exist. The Latin American Integration Association (LAIA), set up under the Treaty of Montevideo of 1980, includes Mexico and all South American countries except Guyana, French Guiana and Surinam. It is the successor to the Latin American Free Trade Association (LAFTA), which was established in 1960. The Central American Common Market, set up under the Managua Treaty of 1960, includes Guatemala, Honduras, Costa Rica, Nicaragua and El Salvador. The Andean Group, set up under the Cartagena Agreement of 1969, now includes Colombia, Venezuela, Ecuador, Peru and Bolivia and constitutes a closer grouping of certain members of LAFTA, including some of the least developed members of that group. A Caribbean Community (CARICOM) was set up in 1973 on the foundations of the Caribbean Free Trade Area (CARIFTA) by the English-speaking countries of the area, with the exception of some of the smallest countries of that group and the Bahamas. An important element of CARICOM is the Caribbean Common Market. A special regime exists within it for its less developed members in the shape of the Eastern Caribbean Common Market (ECCM).

In Asia, international economic integration has so far made little progress. In Western Asia the financial and labour markets of the Arab states are closely integrated but this does not rest on a trade bloc and inter-country trade is minimal. Limited arrangements for sectoral industrial integration have been attempted in the past by the now defunct group known as Regional Co-operation for Development, the members of which were Iran, Turkey and Pakistan. In South East Asia, broader arrangements for integration on a sectoral industrial basis have been under consideration by the countries of the Association of South-East Asian Nations (ASEAN), namely, Brunei, Indonesia, Malaysia, the Philippines, Singapore and Thailand, and some trade preferences have been introduced that may foreshadow an eventual move towards closer trade integration.

Most of the Third World groups are examples of negative integration, which had their origins in across-the-board trade liberalization measures. Almost everywhere their operation has been characterized by severe stresses, frequently prompted by controversy over distributional issues. A satisfactory solution to those issues in the shape of positive integration measures involving a coordination of development on an efficient and equitable basis has proved to be elusive, although a variety of *ad hoc* palliatives have been resorted to. The outcome has been dissolution in one or two instances (as in the case of the East African Community, which broke up in 1978) and stagnation in some of the others.

PLAN OF THE BOOK

This book sets out to provide a concise systematic exposition of a basic theory of international economic integration, giving particular attention to the incorporation of important recent contributions that have substantially altered the orthodox perspective. A secondary concern has been to indicate the bearing of the analysis, wherever possible, on current policy issues in the European Economic Community and other groupings.

Chapter 2 analyses the simple economics of customs unions and free trade areas on orthodox assumptions, with particular reference to resource allocation effects. In Chapter 3 some of the restrictive assumptions of the basic analysis are relaxed, specifically by introducing terms-of-trade effects, economies of scale, and product differentiation. Chapter 4 considers how the analysis of customs unions is affected by the introduction of policy objectives other than the maximization of present private income. For this purpose public goods are introduced as a surrogate for those other objectives. This analysis paves the way for a more general theory of customs unions and integration in the context of multiple objectives of policy. Chapter 5 takes account of the fact that not only are policy objectives numerous, but so are the instruments by which those objectives may be attained. Moreover, the tariff is not necessarily the best, or on its own a sufficient, instrument to achieve desired results in any policy area. Countries seeking to integrate their economies into a regional bloc in order to promote efficient resource use or other economic objectives may thus be led to go beyond customs unions and to integrate, or at least to harmonize, other policy instruments. These may include not only those that affect the operation of the market, such as competition, taxation and monopoly policy, but also structural policies that influence the framework within which market forces operate. Chapter 6 discusses the effects of instituting a common market for factors of production and certain issues that arise when production is undertaken by transnational enterprises. Chapter 7 considers the role of the budget in economic groupings, and the fiscal efficiency considerations that bear on the question of the optimal fiscal domains of the member states and the bloc. Chapter 8 discusses tax harmonization, primarily from the standpoint of resource allocation considerations. Chapter 9 considers monetary integration with particular reference to its implications for macroeconomic policy objectives. Orthodox integration theory takes little account of the distributional aspects of integration. Regional policy, the subject matter of Chapter 10, is one means by which regional blocs may attempt to deal with distributional issues, although such policies may also be motivated by other objectives.

The basic issues addressed in the theory of international economic integration are relevant just as much to non-market as to market economies, and to less developed as well as to advanced countries. However, integration arrangements among non-market economies and among underdeveloped countries confront special problems, for in neither of these cases can market forces be relied upon to promote optimal integration. These special problems, illustrated by reference to experience, therefore receive separate discussion in Chapters 11 and 12. Finally, Chapter 13 surveys methods that have been used for measuring the impact of integration on trade flows, income and welfare, and reviews some of the results of empirical studies.

Throughout the book the terms 'economic grouping' and

'regional economic bloc' will be used to refer generally to any of the forms of international economic integration distinguished in this chapter. The terms 'customs union', 'free trade area' and 'common market' refer specifically to those forms of integration. The term 'economic community' is used to refer broadly to groupings that, in addition to operating a customs union or a common market, attempt also to harmonize or integrate a range of other economic policies. It will be apparent that the book is in no sense intended to be a study of the problems and policies of the EEC. Nevertheless, it is hoped that it will provide a basis for understanding a number of the key issues of policy in the Community. With that object in mind, throughout the book, appropriate reference is made to the experience or policies of the European Community.

CHAPTER 2

The Theory of Customs Unions and Free Trade Areas

The essential features of a customs union (CU) are:

- the elimination of tariffs on imports from member countries;
- the adoption of a common external tariff (CET) on imports from the rest of the world;
- the apportionment of customs revenue according to an agreed formula.

Its establishment will generally alter the relative prices of goods in the domestic markets of member countries, with repercussions on trade flows, production and consumption. The theory of customs unions analyses these effects and their implications for resource allocation and for the welfare of a participating country, for the group as a whole and for the world. Since the common external tariff can be set at any desired level, in principle a customs union can establish the tariff, and so union prices, at levels that will maximize the social welfare, however defined, of the participating countries as a group. The effects, and the gains and losses that are the subject of the theory, arise from the impact of the customs union on: (1) the allocation of resources and international specialization; (2) the exploitation of scale economies; (3) the terms of trade; (4) the productivity of factors; (5) the rate of economic growth; (6) economic stability; and (7) the distribution of income.

Orthodox theory is mainly concerned with the first three aspects for a customs union and for trade in final products. The fourth aspect is excluded from conventional economic analysis by assuming that technical progress is exogenous and that production is carried out by processes that are technically efficient. Distributional considerations are for the most part disregarded. The analysis is comparative-static in nature. It is assumed that:

- there is pure competition in commodity and factor markets
- factors are mobile within countries but not between them
- transportation costs are ignored
- tariffs are the only form of trade restriction employed – and for simplicity they are often assumed to be specific in form rather than *ad valorem*
- prices accurately reflect the opportunity costs of production
- trade is balanced (exports equal imports)
- resources are fully employed.

This formidable list of assumptions, which the orthodox theory of customs unions shares with the pure theory of international trade, will also be adopted in this chapter. These limitations are not so damaging for the practical bearing of the theory as might at first appear. Nevertheless, the realities of trade and, in particular, the importance of trade in intermediate products and of product differentiation and intra-industry trade mean that the outcome of integration may significantly diverge from the 'predictions' of orthodox customs union theory.

CUSTOMS UNIONS AND RESOURCE ALLOCATION

The basic theory analyses the effects of customs unions on resource allocation, specialization and welfare, for a member state, for the group as a whole and for the world.

Not all customs unions would have allocative effects. For instance, if the prospective member countries initially enjoyed identical tariff rates on all commodities, and the tariffs were not redundant, no trade effects would follow from the introduction of the customs union if tariffs remained unchanged. Each country in the initial situation would be producing the output for which the domestic supply price equalled the world price plus the tariff. Neither the world price nor the tariff would be affected by the institution of the union, and consequently nothing would change.

For a customs union to have allocational effects it is necessary that the tariff rates of prospective members should differ for at least some products, unless some of the tariffs are ineffective. The resulting harmonization of tariffs gives rise to the allocational effects of the customs union. Harmonization may take the form of averaging, or some other intermediate position between the highest and the lowest rate may be adopted.

The orthodox theory of customs unions analyses the effects of customs unions on resource allocation in terms of the *trade creation* and *trade diversion* that would result.

Trade creation refers to a union-induced shift from the consumption or higher-cost domestic products in favour of lower-cost products of the partner country. This shift has two aspects: (1) the reduction or elimination of the domestic production of goods that are identical with those produced abroad, the goods instead being imported from the partner country; and (2) increased consumption of partner-country substitutes for domestic goods that formerly satisfied the need at a higher cost. The first gives rise to the production effect – the saving in the real cost of goods previously produced domestically; the second gives rise to the consumption effect – the gain in consumers' surplus from the substitution of lower-cost for higher-cost means of satisfying wants. The two together constitute the trade creation effect of the union.

Trade diversion refers to a union-induced shift in the source of imports from lower-cost external sources to higher-cost partner sources. This shift can also be regarded as having two aspects: (1) an increase in the cost of the goods previously imported from abroad, owing to the shift from foreign to partner sources; and (2) a loss of consumers' surplus resulting from the substitution of higher-cost partner goods for lower-cost foreign goods of a different description. Such shifts together constitute the trade diversion effect of a customs union.[1]

The merits of particular customs union situations are then evaluated, using as the sole criterion the relative magnitudes of trade creation and trade diversion. A union that is on balance trade creating is regarded as beneficial to welfare, whereas a trade-diverting union is regarded as detrimental. In this context it is to be emphasized that the magnitudes of trade creation and trade diversion depend not merely on union-induced changes in the volumes of trade from different sources, but also on the associated price and cost changes. The terms 'trade created' and 'trade diverted' are sometimes used to refer to the volume changes alone.

The rest of this section analyses in some detail, and for several alternative cases, the resource allocation and other effects of customs unions, utilizing the methods and spirit of the orthodox analysis. The treatment is not intended to be comprehensive – for that purpose a multitude of cases would have to be examined, which would require a book in itself. The examples chosen nevertheless suffice, both to illustrate the method of analysis and to bring out the essential nature of the central issues.

The simplest analysis that is capable of eliciting the basic issues of customs union theory requires a three-country model, as opposed to the two-country model customarily employed in international trade theory. Accordingly, in the following analysis two countries are assumed to form a customs union, while a third country, which can be taken to represent the rest of the world, is excluded. Little of importance is lost by limiting attention to such a three-country world in the first instance. Returns to scale will be disregarded, and terms-of-trade effects for the union will be excluded by assuming a perfectly elastic supply price for its trade with the rest of the world. Some of the implications of relaxing these two limiting assumptions will be considered in Chapter 3.

Figure 2.1 depicts the demand and supply conditions in the market for an identical product in two countries – H, the home country, and P, the partner country – contemplating the establishment of a customs union. The supply price of the same product from the rest of the world is also indicated. D_H is country H's demand curve for the product, S_H is its supply curve, and $(S_H + M_P)$ is the supply curve in country H of the product originating in the customs union. It combines the supply curve of country H with the supply curve of imports from country P, assuming that the goods of the latter are admitted free of duty. P_W indicates the supply price of the rest of the world's product to countries H and P and is assumed to be constant. Market conditions in country P are similarly shown in the lower figure, D_P being country P's demand curve for the product and S_P its supply curve. The presentation of market conditions in both member countries permits the practically important aspect of tariff harmonization to be explicitly treated. Three cases will be considered, which are distinguished from each other only by alternative assumptions about the pre- and post-union tariff positions.

(1)   Suppose first that prior to customs union a tariff of $P_W T_H$ was in force in country H and one of $P_W T_P$ in country P. In this case the domestic demand of each country would be entirely supplied by domestic production. If a customs union were formed on the basis of tariff averaging so that $CET = \frac{1}{2}(T_H + T_P)$, the new common external tariff would be $P_W CET$; but this would be ineffective, or redundant, since at price $OCET$ supply would be greater than union demand. Price would therefore settle at $OCET'$, where supply would equal demand. Domestic consumption in country H would increase to OQ, and domestic production would decline from ON to OL. Country P would then produce OT, consume OR and export $LQ (= RT)$ to country H.

This situation would for country H be one of trade creation. The saving in cost on the initial domestic production in country H that was replaced by imports (the production effect – Vinerian trade

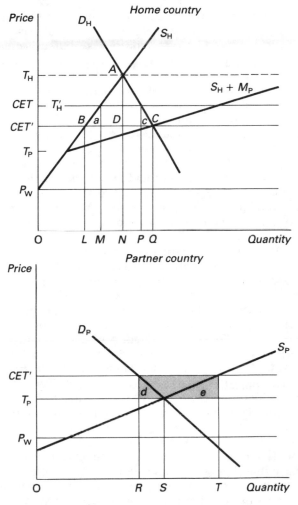

Figure 2.1 The effects of a customs union

creation) would be *ABD*; the gain in consumers' surplus from the substitution of imports for other goods would be *ADC*. The total gain from trade creation would be the sum of these two areas, which would be approximately equal to half of the product of the total change in imports (*LQ*) and the fall in price. The area above S_H marked off by the lines T_H and *CET'* would represent an internal transfer from producers' surplus to consumers' surplus, which for the country as a whole would cancel out.

In the case of country P, which was also initially self-sufficient, the customs union would cause a rise in price. Consumers would suffer a consumption loss equal to d. There would also be a production effect, denoted by e, as additional resources were drawn into the industry to produce an additional amount ST of the product. These costs, however, would be more than outweighed by the extra income earned from the newly created export trade to country H (hatched rectangle). In this case country P would clearly also be in a more favourable position.

As to the rest of the world, its trade with the customs union would be unaffected by the formation of the customs union, being zero both before and after. In these circumstances consideration of the welfare effects of the union could be confined to the countries that constituted it. The formation of the union would result in an improved allocation of resources, and each member would be in a superior position compared with the pre-union situation.

(2)   Alternatively, suppose that while the initial tariff in country P was again $P_W T_P$, in country H it was lower at $P_W T'_H (= P_W CET)$. In this case prior to customs union the initial situation for country P would obviously be as before. In country H, however, domestic demand at the pre-union price of OT'_H would be met partly by domestic production and partly by imports. The quantity consumed would be OP, domestic production would account for OM, and imports from the rest of the world would make up the difference MP. Total tariff revenue would amount to $MP \times P_W T'_H$.

If in these circumstances a tariff-averaging customs union were formed with the common external tariff equal to $P_W CET'$ the effect on country H would be as follows. The amount demanded would increase to OQ as in the first case, and domestic production would fall to OL. There would thus be a saving on production cost, denoted by the triangular area marked a, in respect of the reduction in the initial domestic output and a gain in consumers' surplus, denoted by the triangular area marked c, in respect of the expanded consumption. Together these magnitudes would represent a trade creation effect. However, in addition, the produce formerly imported from the rest of the world would in this case be shifted to a higher-cost source, country P, involving an increase in outlay in respect of the initial import amounting to $MP \times P_W CET'$. This magnitude would represent trade diversion. The magnitudes of trade creation and trade diversion would have to be compared in order to ascertain whether the customs union was beneficial or detrimental for country H. In this specific example it would clearly be detrimental.

The effects on country P of the formation of the customs union would clearly be identical to those that it would experience in the first case: it would thus be in a superior position compared with the pre-union situation. As far as the rest of the world was concerned, its trade with the customs union would be reduced. Since the world supply curve is assumed to be perfectly elastic, the impact of this reduction on the welfare of the rest of the world can be disregarded. However, the reduction of imports from the rest of the world would indicate that the union was, on balance, a trade-diverting one.

(3)   To conclude, a third case may be considered. It will be supposed that the tariff initially in force in country H is $P_W CET'$ giving a tariff-inclusive price of $OCET'$, while in country P the tariff $P_W T_P$ continues to be in force, as in the previous case, giving a tariff-inclusive price of OT_P. It will now be assumed that the common external tariff of the union is established, not by tariff-averaging, but by the alignment of country P's tariff to that of country H, which involves an increase in the average level of protection. The formation of a customs union on such a basis would leave production and consumption of the product in country H wholly unaffected. The effect of the customs union would be to bring about a replacement of its imports from the rest of the world by an identical quantity from country P. This would amount to a case of pure trade diversion from the standpoint of country H and the cost that it would thereby incur would be represented by its loss of tariff revenue. As far as country P is concerned, however, the effect of customs union on the quantity of its exports to country H and the favourable effect on its income would be identical to both of the cases previously considered. As to the rest of the world, since its export supply curve is perfectly elastic, the welfare effect of the reduction in its exports can again be ignored.

In terms of resource allocation effects, this third case is the least favourable of the three that have been considered, since trade creation would be altogether absent. Customs union would result in a deterioration in global resource allocation, accompanied by a redistribution of income from country H to country P.

The three cases just considered involve the analysis of a specific market situation, which might be regarded as a special case. The method of analysis is, however, equally applicable to a large range of other market situations that might be thought to be relevant for customs union analysis. One such case often considered is that in which, in the initial situation, one of the partners already competes in the home country with the rest of the world. No significant points are neglected as a result of the choice adopted here, however, nor are any of the effects considered peculiar to these cases. In other relevant situations the effects produced can be expected to differ in direction and extent but would be similar in kind.

There is, however, a more important point that bears on the generality of the analysis, which must be briefly mentioned. In the interests of simplicity, customs union theory has here been presented in terms of a partial equilibrium analysis that looks at the market for a single product. Is the generality of the analysis limited by this procedure? Specifically, can the analysis be applied to the practically important case of a customs union extending to many products?

The requirement that must be satisfied in order that partial equilibrium analysis should not violate general equilibrium requirements is that the relative prices of all other goods should be unaffected by the changes in the market under consideration, so that the price variable can be interpreted to be the price of the good in question relative to the price index for other goods. Provided that this requirement is met – as effectively would be the case where the market being analysed is so small that changes affecting it would not have significant repercussions on supplies and demands elsewhere in the economy – the approach can be justified. Supply and demand analysis and figures relating to the market for a single product (or sector) can then specifically be given a general equilibrium interpretation, as is sometimes done (Corden, 1974; El-Agraa and Jones, 1980). But a partial equilibrium analysis of a single market cannot appropriately be undertaken on this basis in circumstances in which the relative prices of other goods would be significantly affected. *A fortiori*, it would be inappropriate to seek to arrive at the consequences for an economy as a whole of the formation of a customs union affecting all traded products by simply aggregating the outcomes for particular markets that have been arrived at on partial equilibrium assumptions.

The alternative general equilibrium approach to the analysis of customs unions is well represented in the literature. The earliest post-Vinerian formulations in this vein were presented almost exclusively in terms of an application of the standard two-good general equilibrium model. The first significant advance is represented by the three-country two-product models developed by Vanek (1966) and Kemp (1969). An alternative model first put forward by Meade (1955) deals with three countries and three products. The general equilibrium approach, and more specifically those variants mentioned here, manifests both strengths and weaknesses. In principle, in the interests of symmetry and generality, a three-product approach has substantial merit for the analysis of customs union issues. When more than two products are taken into account however, the analysis becomes highly intricate and can allow only inadequately, if at all, for trade creation and trade diversion and the impact of union on intra-union terms of trade – central features of customs unions that can more easily be given prominence in simpler formulations. The issues – which can only be alluded to here – are explored in Berglas (1979); Collier (1979), where the choice of model is considered; Lloyd (1982), who compares several variants of the three-product approach; and Wooton (1986a).

The analysis of this chapter specifically assumes that the formation of the customs union does not affect the terms of trade of the member countries with the rest of the world. This means, as already noted, that the effect of the customs union on the welfare of the rest of the world can be disregarded. Consequently, a given change in the welfare of the members of the union will mean a *pari passu* change in the welfare of the world as a whole, including the members of the customs union. In principle, the formation of a customs union can make the union in net terms either better off (if the trade creation effect predominates) or worse off (if the trade diversion effect predominates). It is evidently also possible for at least one of the members to be injured in a trade-creating union and, similarly, for at least one member country to benefit in a trade-diverting union. Thus, a trade-creating union can be said to be only *potentially* beneficial to all members. If the distribution of gains and losses among the member countries is not a matter of indifference, then, unless the gains and losses are appropriately distributed, compensatory transfers may be required to ensure that no country loses. In practice, the determination of the structure of the common external tariff is a principal means by which attempts are made to ensure an initially acceptable distribution of gains and losses, but this approach may not be the most efficient way of dealing with the distributional problem.

The Conditions for a Trade-creating Customs Union

A final issue that must be briefly considered is whether any general statements can be made about the circumstances that will determine whether a customs union will be predominantly trade creating rather than trade diverting. If this could be done, it would obviously be very useful. Many economists have offered generalizations; but analytical elaboration has shown that most of these depend on the circumstances of special cases. The few surviving generalizations may usefully be summarized at this point. Some follow directly from the previous analysis, but others could not be demonstrated without carrying the analysis of the present chapter somewhat further. The most helpful statements that can justifiably be made seem to be as follows:

(1)   The larger is the economic area of the customs union, and the more numerous are the countries of which it is composed, the greater will be the scope for trade creation as opposed to trade diversion.
(2)   The relative effects can be related to the height of the 'average' tariff level before and after union. If the post-union level is lower, the union is more likely to be trade creating; if it is higher, trade diversion effects may be more likely.
(3)   Trade creation is more likely the more competitive are the economies of the member states, in the sense that the range of products produced by higher-cost industries in the different parts of the customs union is similar. Likewise, the smaller is the overlap, the smaller will be the possibilities for reallocation, which is the source of trade creation.
(4)   For a specified overlap, trade creation is more likely to predominate the greater are the differences in unit costs for protected industries of the same kinds as between the different parts of the customs union, since these will determine the allocation gains to be derived from free trade among the members.

Intuitively these propositions appear to be reasonable. Nevertheless it must be emphasized, as Viner himself asserted:

Confident judgement as to what the overall balance between these conflicting considerations would be, it should be obvious, cannot be made for customs unions in general and in the abstract, but must be confined to particular projects and be based on economic surveys thorough enough to justify reasonably reliable estimates as to the weights to be given in the particular circumstances to the respective elements in the problem. (1950, p. 52)

This judgement is as valid today as it was in 1950.

THE ECONOMICS OF A FREE TRADE AREA

Although most of the basic theory of market integration is framed in terms of customs unions, a similar analysis may readily be undertaken for free trade areas. Two basic features distinguish a free trade area (FTA) from a customs union:

- the member countries retain the power to fix their own separate tariff rates on imports from the rest of the world;
- the area is equipped with rules of origin, designed to confine intra-area free trade to products originating in, or mainly produced in, the area.

The purpose of rules of origin is to limit *trade deflection*, that is, a redirection of imports through the country with the lowest tariff for the purpose of exploiting the tariff differential. As in the case of a customs union, the formation of a free trade area may be accompanied by trade creation or trade diversion, but there are important differences in the operation of the two alternative forms of integration.

In this section the economics of free trade areas will be briefly analysed. Their effects will be considered first for a single country and then, analogously with the previous section, in such a way as to make explicit the effects on each of the two members of which the free trade area is assumed to be composed. Some comparisons between the relative effects of a customs union and a free trade area will be made for specific situations. For this purpose a tariff-averaging customs union, that is, one in which $CET = \frac{1}{2}(T_H + T_P)$, will again be taken as the basis for comparison. In the light of these comparisons some propositions will be presented on the relative merits of customs unions and free trade areas from the standpoint of their resource allocation effects. It should again be emphasized that the treatment is not claimed to be comprehensive. The technique employed can, however, readily be applied to illuminate the effects of free trade areas in the presence of any alternative assumed market conditions and tariff positions for a particular product.

The Effects of a Free Trade Area from a Single-country Standpoint

Consider two countries, H and P, both of which produce wholly domestically an identical product X, which is subject to a different customs tariff in each country, a lower duty P_wT_P being imposed in country P and a higher duty P_wT_H in country H. Assume that the

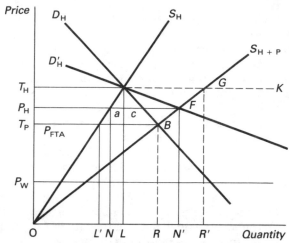

Figure 2.2   The effects of a free trade area on a single country

two countries form a free trade area in which the rules of origin prevent inflows from the rest of the world to country H through country P. Between the markets of countries H and P only the area-origin product enjoys tariff-free movement. This difference in treatment may or may not create a price differential between the area-origin product and non-area product. The effects of such a free trade area will now be analysed with reference to Figure 2.2.

It is assumed for simplicity that country H's tariff before integration is prohibitive, in the sense that it excludes all imports. Country H's supply curve is S_H, its tariff is $P_W T_H$, and its production is OL at price OT_H. Country P's tariff is $P_W T_P$, and its supply curve is horizontally added to that of country H to arrive at curve S_{H+P}. P_W denotes the world supply price.

If a free trade area is formed, the price of the area-origin product in country H can never fall below OT_P so long as the free trade area as a whole remains a net importer. At the same time, the price can never exceed OT_H, which equals OP_W plus $P_W T_H$, country H's protective duty. Consequently, from the standpoint of country H, the effective supply curve of the product, including area and non-area product, is $T_P BFGK$. In a free trade area the amount that country P will be willing to supply will depend on the price, and the price that is obtainable will depend on country H's demand curve.

Two possibilities are considered in Figure 2.2, which correspond to the alternative demand curves D_H and D'_H. If country H's demand for the product were represented by D_H (relatively inelastic at price OT_H by comparison with D'_H), the price in country H would be OT_P, with country P supplying $L'R$ at that price. In this case triangle a would represent trade creation, and triangle c would represent the consumption effect of the reduction in the price of product X in country H brought about by the free trade area.

If, instead, country H's demand were represented by D'_H, the price in country H (OP_H) would be nearer to the upper limit OT_H above which imports would be supplied from the rest of the world. In this case country H would supply its own market to the extent of ON, and country P would supply country H to the extent of NN'. Trade creation would then be denoted by the smaller triangular area below the intersection of D'_H and S_H and above the horizontal line at P_H. In general, in a free trade area country P would supply country H at any price above OT_P, up to its total capacity to supply, making up any consequential shortfall in its domestic market by imports from the rest of the world. In this way the price in country P's market would be kept down to OT_P irrespective of the final price for product X in country H. The induced change in trade flows is termed 'indirect trade deflection' (the substitution by country P of non-area for area products). It cannot be eliminated by the rules of origin of a free trade area. The impact of indirect trade deflection is further clarified for each member in the following section, which analyses the operation of a free trade area from the standpoint of both countries.

A Free Trade Area: Two Countries

Figures 2.3 and 2.4 depict the demand and supply curves in countries H and P for product X. P_W again denotes the world supply price. Before integration, country P has a relatively low tariff $P_W T_P$, giving a tariff-inclusive price of OT_P. In the figures: triangle a represents trade creation (the production effect); rectangle b any excess outlay on the partner product (trade diversion) for the initial import; triangle c the consumption effect in country H, which is positive; triangle d the consumption effect in country P, which is negative; and triangle e the production effect in country P, which may be neutral or negative and is relevant mainly for customs unions. Two illustrative cases will be analysed, and for each a comparison will be made with the alternative of a tariff-averaging customs union.

(1)   In the first case (Figure 2.3) countries H and P are assumed to have similar demand conditions; but country H is a relatively inefficient producer, whereas country P's supply curve is relatively elastic

(a) *Free trade area*

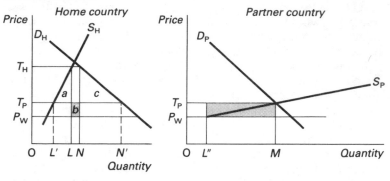

(b) *Tariff-averaging customs union*

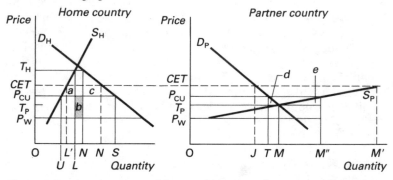

Figure 2.3 A comparison of free trade areas and customs unions – 1
    (a)   Free trade area
    (b)   Tariff-averaging customs union

and competitive, although above world market price P_W for outputs in excess of OL''.

Before the free trade area is formed, country P consumes and produces OM at price OT_P, its tariff keeping out all imports. Country H produces OL and consumes ON, the difference LN being imported at price P_W from the lowest cost source, namely, the rest of the world. Customs revenue in country H is denoted by $LN \times P_W T_H$.

If countries H and P formed a free trade area (Figure 2.3a), area supply at price $OT_P (= OM + OL')$ would clearly be less than area demand at that price $(OM + ON')$, but the difference $(L'N')$ would be less than country P's capacity to supply at that price. In a free trade area that excluded the least cost source of supply, country P would supply country H's market with $L'N'$ $(= L''M)$ at price T_P, leaving an amount equal to OL'' for its home market, its remaining requirement $(L''M)$ being imported from the rest of the world at price OP_W. In this case after integration there would be a single equilibrium price in the free trade area that would be equivalent to the lower of the two member prices before the establishment of the free trade area.

It can be seen that in country H the production effect a (Vinerian trade creation) plus the consumption effect c would outweigh the cost of trade diversion (stippled area b). The difference between the cost of trade diversion, b, and the initial customs revenue represents an internal transfer from the exchequer to consumers and not a loss of real income to the community. In country P the same amount would be produced and consumed as before, at the same price, but government revenue would increase by an amount that equalled the hatched rectangle. This would represent a national income gain to country P. As far as the rest of the world is concerned, its exports would clearly be larger than before $(L''M>LN)$ because of the shifting of country P's supply to satisfy country H's demand. The free trade area would represent an improved position for both countries and also, presumably, for the rest of the world.

This outcome may next be compared with that which would result if instead countries H and P formed a tariff-averaging customs union (Figure 2.3b). In this case it can be seen that union supply at price $OCET$ would be greater than demand, so that the common external tariff would set only the upper limit of the price. The equilibrium price would be OP_{CU} where supply equalled demand $(TM'' = US)$. Once more, trade creation (the production effect a and the consumption effect c) would clearly exceed trade diversion b, although the trade creation effects would be smaller than in the case of the free trade area.

The principal difference between the two alternative situations would arise for country P. In the case of the customs union its consumers would suffer a consumption loss, denoted by d. Although its producers would enjoy a net gain, there would be an adverse production effect, denoted by e. In the case of the free trade area there would be no loss from the production and consumption effects, but there would be a gain in government revenue that was larger than the net gain that would accrue to country P with the customs union. In the case of the customs union, moreover, trade with the rest of the world would be eliminated, whereas it would increase in the alternative of the free trade area.

Taking these considerations into account, the customs union

alternative can be said to be inferior to the free-trade area arrangement. The difference between the two alternatives results essentially from the indirect trade deflection that occurs in the free trade area case, which rules of origin cannot prevent. In limiting cases this may make a free trade area equivalent in its effects to a customs union that takes the lowest pre-union tariff as the basis for the common external tariff. Evidently, if there are transport costs, which have so far been ruled out, the more geographically dispersed are the members of a free trade area, the smaller is likely to be the indirect trade deflection that results.

(2)   A second case will now be considered in which, unlike the first, a price differential would arise for the product in the free trade area. In this case country P's supply is again assumed to be relatively competitive and elastic, but it is now assumed to be incapable of satisfying country H's demand (Figure 2.4).

Before the free trade area is formed, both countries are assumed to have prohibitive tariffs. Country P produces and consumes OM, and country H produces and consumes ON. If a free trade area were formed (Figure 2.4a), country P's supply at price OT_P would be incapable of satisfying the extra demand in country H, and the equilibrium free trade area price in country H would therefore be OP_{FTA} ($L'N = OM'$). At the same time, the price in country P could not rise above OT_P, at which level imports from the rest of the world would be available, so that two equilibrium prices would exist in the area.

In this case country H would experience only a trade creation effect $(a + c)$. Country P would incur no excess costs of consumption or production, but it would enjoy a gain in government revenue, equal to the hatched area, which would represent an increase in its national income.

If instead countries H and P formed a customs union (Figure 2.4b), the common external tariff would be effective, with demand and supply approximately in balance at that level, the price in the union being a little higher than in the free trade area case. Country H would experience trade creation. Country P would benefit, on balance, from its ability to export to country H at a higher price, but at the cost of adverse production and consumption effects, denoted by d and e.

A comparison of these two situations shows that in this second case, just as in the first, the customs union alternative is inferior to the free trade area arrangement. This conclusion appears to be generally valid for the alternatives of a tariff-averaging customs

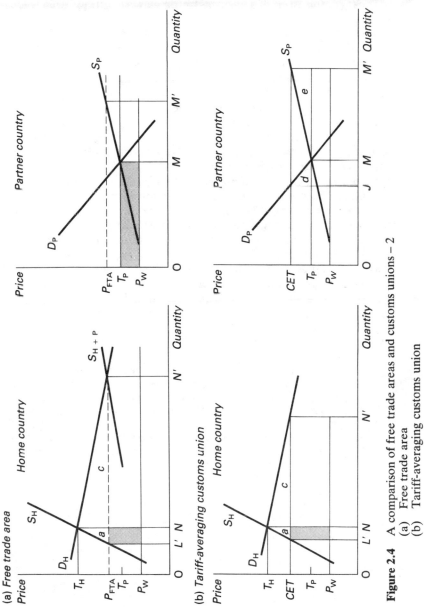

Figure 2.4 A comparison of free trade areas and customs unions – 2
(a) Free trade area
(b) Tariff-averaging customs union

union and a free trade area, irrespective of the particular market conditions assumed.

These comparisons of a customs union with a free trade area refer to trade and tariffs with respect to final products. If, as is possible in a free trade area, tariff disparities also exist on intermediate inputs, these differences may give rise to distortions in the area's pattern of production at that level. If processing costs were identical, production in a free trade area would tend to concentrate on the country whose input tariff was lowest. In general, however, it is not possible to say whether such tariff disparities would encourage a concentration of production of inputs in more efficient or less efficient member countries. In making a comparison of the merits of a customs union with a free trade area, it is clearly necessary to take into account any such production-distorting effects of a non-harmonized tariff at the input stage that might upset the relative advantage of a free trade area in comparison with a customs union.

In conclusion it should be emphasized that, although a free trade area may be shown in this way to be preferable to a customs union in terms of its effects on static allocative efficiency, this result is of limited significance and it provides no case for establishing a free trade area rather than a customs union. The point at issue will be discussed in the course of Chapter 4, where the rationale for establishing a customs union itself will be examined.

NOTE

1   These particular definitions of trade creation and trade diversion are those of Johnson (1962). They differ from those initially employed by Viner (1950), Meade (1955a) and Lipsey (1960), who have used the terms to refer solely to production effects. Johnson's usage has subsequently been endorsed by Viner (1965) in a letter to Corden. It seems preferable in that it rightly emphasizes that there are only two effects at work: the free trade (trade-creating) effect, and the protection (trade-diverting) effect of customs union.

CHAPTER 3

Customs Unions and Free Trade Areas: Broadening the Framework

The last chapter has analysed the gains and losses that may arise from the formation of customs unions and free trade areas as a result of their impact on resource allocation within the group, and between it and the rest of the world. In a less restrictive framework of analysis than was there assumed, other aspects of integration also merit attention. In the first place, if the supply curve of the rest of the world cannot be assumed to be perfectly elastic, potential terms-of-trade effects may need to be considered. The assumption of a perfectly elastic supply curve of imports will often be appropriate for a group of small countries whose importance in world trade is minor, but for a bloc such as the European Economic Community (EEC) it is less likely to be so. Secondly, the enlargement of the market that is brought about by customs union may have a variety of important effects that are disregarded by orthodox theory. These include: (1) effects associated with integration in the presence of economies of scale; (2) effects on the technical efficiency with which given factors are utilized within firms; (3) effects on the rate of growth of output, through the impact of market enlargement on the rate of growth of productivity, technological advance, etc.; (4) effects on output and its rate of growth through the impact of market enlargement on the location of investment and its rate of growth. Thirdly, orthodox customs union theory not only disregards economies of scale but its basic assumption of homogeneous products excludes a consideration of the implications for integration of product differentiation which is a major feature of modern industry and international trade. Economies of scale and product differentiation jointly give rise to the phenomenon of intra-industry trade which in practice constitutes a major element of trade in customs unions. The economic and welfare implications of intra-industry trade in customs unions calls for consideration, although an adequate appreciation can be provided only in the context of a common market, since it is closely bound up with foreign direct investment and the strategies of multinational corporations.

The group of effects of integration that accompany market enlargement are often referred to as its dynamic effects. There is, however, nothing essentially dynamic about economies of scale, even though, as will be seen, it is not possible to define precisely the equilibrium that will be reached when a customs union is formed in the presence of economies of scale without reference to dynamic factors. Some of the other effects that accompany market enlargement can only doubtfully be termed dynamic. The term indeed is not without ambiguity in its usage. For Balassa (1962) it meant the impact of integration on dynamic efficiency, which itself refers to the hypothetical growth rate of national income achievable with given resource use and savings ratio. Thus the dynamic effects of integration refer to the difference between the hypothetical growth rate attainable before and after integration, given resource inputs.

A popular approach to the analysis of these effects has sought to establish a relationship between productivity and market size. However, if such a link exists, this does not mean that integration would necessarily be followed by a sustained increase in the rate of growth of productivity. The integration of national markets may merely result in a once for all increase in productivity levels and the rate of increase in productivity may then return to its former level. Nevertheless, even such a transitional acceleration of productivity growth would permit a continuously higher yearly absolute increase in the standard of living as compared with the pre-integration period. It is clearly helpful however to make a distinction between the static effects that accompany market enlargement and that result at a point in time, and effects that operate continuously and depend on the lapse of time – termed by Corden (1974) 'economies of time' – to which the term dynamic is more properly applied. One example of the latter is the cumulative changes that are part of the process of polarization which is discussed in Chapters 10 and 12.

The various effects of market enlargement on the productive efficiency of firms have been much stressed in relation to the EC. Politicians have repeatedly emphasized the beneficial effects for the industrial efficiency of the EC of what Harold Macmillan once described as the 'bracing cold shower'. Some economists (Pelkmans, 1984) have attempted to embody this effect formally into their analysis of customs unions. Others have argued, on the basis of empirical studies, that the effects that operate through this channel are a much more important source of gains in social product than are the resource allocation gains, based on the assumption of given technical efficiency, that are alone considered by orthodox analysis. Overcoming technical inefficiency through increased competition may, however, have its price in terms of forgone leisure, and a higher work pace, etc., that is, in a loss of non-marketable output of the firm. Any such costs would, in a welfare calculus, have to be weighed against the increase in social product, and – as Scitovsky emphasized long ago (1958) – the cost may outweigh any gain in material goods. Unfortunately, theory does not take one very far in this area, but it is clear that the connection between integration and productive efficiency (static or dynamic) is not a simple one – if only because, as well as the cold shower effect, there is also the 'Turkish bath effect' to consider (Streeten, 1964; Corden, 1970).

The whole issue of these 'dynamic' effects of integration is fraught with difficulty and it is proposed mainly to disregard them from this point in this chapter on the ground that whatever their importance – and it may be very great – economic analysis has not so far shown itself capable of throwing much light on their operation. Accordingly, this chapter will be limited to a discussion of certain modifications to the analysis of the previous chapter that are required when terms-of-trade effects, economies of scale and product differentiation are allowed for. Certain aspects of polarization are discussed in Chapters 8 and 11.

THE TERMS-OF-TRADE EFFECTS OF CUSTOMS UNIONS AND FREE TRADE AREAS

If the possibility of terms-of-trade effects is allowed for, the analysis of the previous chapter may require modification in certain respects. In particular, where terms-of-trade effects arise with respect to the union's trade with the rest of the world, the welfare of the world can no longer be assumed to change *pari passu* with that of the union. One of the most informative analyses of the terms-of-trade effects of preferential arrangements can be found in Mundell (1964).

If the formation of the customs union does not affect the demand for imports from the rest of the world, the union's terms of trade will be unaffected, even if the supply from the rest of the world is less than perfectly elastic. Otherwise, there will be a tendency for the union's terms of trade with the rest of the world to improve. This effect will operate to reduce the loss that any trade diversion imposes, and it may suffice to eliminate it altogether if the fall in the price of the imported product is sufficient.

With respect to free trade areas, the outcome in relation to terms-of-trade effects is less clear. Whereas in a customs union trade with third countries is likely to be reduced after integration unless the average level of tariffs is reduced, in a free trade area imports will not fall below the (low-tariff) partner country's requirements in the pre-free trade area situation, and they may even rise above this on account of the indirect trade deflection that may occur. Consequently, any improvement in the terms of trade will be smaller in a free trade area than in a customs union. Indeed, if indirect trade deflection is very large, it is conceivable that the terms of trade of the free trade area could deteriorate, but this is not a necessary outcome. Where terms-of-trade effects arise, however, a free trade area will inflict less damage on third countries than will a tariff-averaging customs union.

It is possible that members of a customs union may be able to exploit their influence on the terms of trade more effectively than if they imposed tariffs separately. This possible effect, fully recognized by Viner (1950), necessarily involves a corresponding injury to the rest of the world. Other things being equal, the greater is the economic area of the tariff-levying unit, the greater is likely to be the improvement in its terms of trade with the outside world resulting from the tariff.

The possibility that a customs union may provide a larger terms-of-trade gain than would otherwise be possible has been elaborated by Arndt (1968). The difficulty with his analysis, however, is that a conflict of interest is generally implied and, in general, gains arise only if one member country can persuade another to pursue a non-optimal policy in the interests of the former. A possible exception to this might be the case where a customs union was formed solely to impose a common tariff on a particular product that each country continued to import. In this case each country might gain from the action of the others. Although any country could gain still more by not joining, the customs union itself might not be formed unless all agreed to join. The issues then are similar to those that arise in the case of an international commodity agreement in which a group of countries generates gains for itself by increasing the product's price through export restriction. A non-participant would gain still more; but if none participates, no producer will gain.

The terms of trade of a customs union with the rest of the world can be influenced not only by the union's common external tariff but also by the tariffs of other countries. In general, the higher are the tariffs of other countries on the export products of the union, the less favourable will be the terms of trade of the union with the rest of the world. Since the level of foreign tariffs can be affected to some extent by tariff negotiations, this aspect must also be taken into account. In this connection it seems likely that, the larger is the customs union, the greater its bargaining power is likely to be. This consideration has been thought by Viner (1950) to have been historically very important in accounting for the formation of customs unions, and it is one also stressed by Meade (1955a). Although conflicts of interest may obviously arise in this case also in relation to the nature of the concessions to be sought in the course of tariff bargaining, the possibilities of detrimental effects from the standpoint of the individual members of the union, and globally, are perhaps smaller.

ECONOMIES OF SCALE IN CUSTOMS UNION THEORY

The orthodox theory of customs unions presented in the previous chapter assumes that union supply price is increasing. The introduction of economies of scale gives rise to a number of problems and calls for some modification of the basic concepts. This section explains how economies of scale may be taken into account. The economies of scale to be considered are those that are internal to the firm, which result in decreasing unit costs as output expands.

For this purpose we shall consider the case of a single homogeneous product, which is produced in the rest of the world and supplied to countries H and P at constant costs, but which is capable of being produced in countries H and P at declining average costs. Assume that the cost curves of countries H and P for the product are uniformly above import parity price over the relevant ranges and that in the pre-union situation neither country exports to the other. To avoid a number of problems that are not relevant to the point at issue, it is assumed that domestic prices are determined by the cost of imports from the rest of the world plus the tariff. In practice the price of competing imports in the domestic market sets only an upper limit to the price that can be charged by a domestic producer. It might pay a profit-maximizing producer to charge less, but this possibility will be ignored. With respect to tariffs, it is assumed that pre-union tariff rates are fixed at levels designed to make the tariff-inclusive import price just equal to average costs, including normal profit, thus avoiding excess profits to producers. In this case, if there is no domestic production, there will be no tariff. Figure 3.1 depicts demand and cost conditions in the domestic markets of the two countries – H, the home country, and P, the partner country. D_H is the home country's demand curve for the product, and AC_H is the average cost curve. D_P and AC_P are the corresponding demand and cost curves in the prospective partner country. D_{H+P} represents the combined customs union demand curve, P_W represents the constant price at which the product can be imported from W, the rest of the world. Terms-of-trade effects are thus ruled out.

In the pre-union situation, there are three alternative possibilities: production in both countries, in one country only or in neither. Each of these cases may be briefly considered.

(1) If there is initially *production in both countries* the initial equilibrium will be as follows. Prior to the formation of a customs union, the home country H produces and consumes OM, which amount sells domestically at a price OP_H. A tariff of $P_W P_H$ is required to make the industry viable. The more efficient partner country produces and consumes an amount ON at OP_P with a lower tariff $P_W P_P$.

If the two countries form a customs union and production is undertaken wholly by the producer whose cost conditions are more favourable, country P's producer captures the whole market. The average costs of country P's producer when it supplies the whole market will be less than its costs when it supplied only its home market and less than the costs of the former producer in country H when it was supplying its own market. Thus, the union domestic price can be less than the domestic price ruling initially in either country. Consequently, the common external tariff will be less than the initial tariffs, and consumers in both countries will gain from the establishment of the union. The combined requirement of the market, OX_U, would be produced by the partner country at a price OP_{CU}, the required union tariff being $P_W P_{CU}$. Consumption in the home country increases to OM' and in the partner country to ON'. The effect of the customs union can be considered for each country.

Country H's relatively expensive domestic production is replaced by imports from country P, which are cheaper to produce. Hence, there is a movement to a cheaper source of supply, through the opening up of trade between countries H and P – and so an orthodox trade creation gain for country H (using this term in the broader post-Vinerian sense to incorporate consumption effects). This trade creation has two components: the production effect, resulting from the replacement of dearer domestic production by cheaper imports from country P; and the consumption effect, resulting from the increased consumption induced by the lower domestic price. These are measured by areas *a* and *c* respectively.

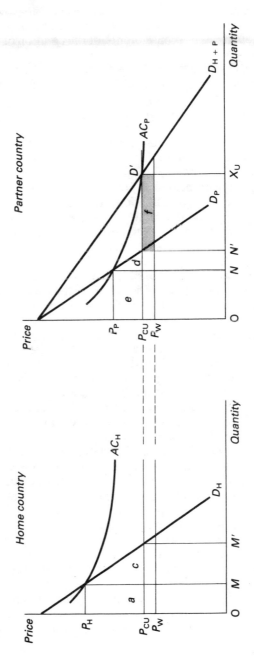

Figure 3.1 A customs union with economies of scale

Country P obtains its domestic supplies at a lower cost of production. This can be called the *cost reduction effect* (Corden, 1972b). Although this is a consequence of the creation of trade with country H, it is not an orthodox trade creation effect since it results, not from a movement to a cheaper source of supply elsewhere, but from the cheapening of an existing domestic source of supply. The cost reduction gain accrues to the consumers of country P. This effect also has a production and consumption component: the production effect is that the original amount of production sold domestically is now obtainable at a lower price; the consumption effect is that, at the lower price, an extra amount is purchased, on which consumers' surplus is obtained. In Figure 3.1, area *e* represents the production component of the cost reduction effect, and *d* represents the gain in consumer's surplus. In addition, country P derives a gain from its sales to the country H at prices in excess of world market prices. This is represented by the hatched area *f*.

(2)   If in the pre-union situation there is *production in one country only*, two main possibilities arise. If the established producer is the more efficient of the two, namely country P, the most probable outcome is that it will capture the whole of the union market. In this case, the pre-union tariff of country H will by assumption have been zero. If country P is to capture country H's market, this must result not from the freeing of trade in the union but from country H imposing a tariff – that is, from the establishment of a common external tariff, which implies an increase in the average level of protection. In this event the price to domestic consumers in country H will rise. The effects for the two countries are then as follows.

Country H replaces its imports from the rest of the world by imports from country P. The latter must be dearer than imports from the rest of the world, since otherwise country P would not have needed the formation of the union to compete in country H's market. Consequently, country H experiences *trade diversion*, a dearer source of imports having replaced a cheaper source. The resultant losses can be divided into production and consumption components. The new lower amount consumed in country H will be obtained at a higher cost than before. In addition there is a loss of consumers' surplus on the reduced amount of consumption induced by the higher price to consumers.

As in the first case, country P obtains its own product at lower cost, so that there is a cost reduction effect, and it again derives gain from its sales to country H at prices in excess of world market prices.

Where there is initial production in only one country and that country is the higher cost producer, (H), the most probable out-come is that the established producer will be driven out of business, giving rise to a production reversal. In that event a further effect has to be recognized. There will be a trade creation gain for H because that country obtains its requirements from a cheaper source, whereas country P loses as a result of the replacement of its cheap imports from the rest of the world by dearer domestic production. The costs of country P's newly established producer when it sup-plies the whole union market must be greater than the cost of imports from the rest of the world, for otherwise it could have become established before the union was formed. Where, as in such a case, imports from the rest of the world are replaced by domestic production, there is an effect that Viner (1950) has termed a 'trade suppression' effect. It is akin to the trade diversion effect in as much as a dearer source replaces a cheaper source, but it differs from it in that the dearer source is a newly established domestic producer, and not a source in the partner country.

(3)   If there is initially *production in neither country*, the establish-ment of the union may permit production in one country – say country P – to begin. Country P's costs will still be above the costs of imports from the rest of the world, excluding duty, for otherwise country P could compete in country H's market prior to the union. In this case the formation of the customs union generates a trade suppression effect for country P and a trade diversion effect for country H.

In the presence of economies of scale, a problem arises that has been hinted at in the last few pages, namely, it is not possible on the basis of a comparative static analysis to predict which of several possible alternative equilibrium positions will be attained in a customs union. For instance, if in the initial situation the product whose production is subject to scale economies is produced in both countries under identical cost conditions, it is to be expected, if the product is homogeneous, that after the union is formed one firm will take over the whole market. However, the analysis cannot indicate which firm it will be. The outcome will depend on dynamic con-siderations including the reaction paths experienced and, in situ-ations in which there is more than one producer in each country, on the nature of oligopolistic competition (Corden, 1972b).

   In this context, one possibility that has received some attention is that the pattern of specialization that results from trade liberaliza-tion when economies of scale are present could be perverse. To illustrate the point at issue, consider the case in which there is initially production in both countries, and suppose that the home country, H, is the higher cost producer in the sense that its cost curve is uniformly above that of its partner. Suppose also that its demand for the product is so much higher than that of its partner that in the pre-union situation its actual unit costs for the larger amount demanded are below those of its partner for the smaller quantity that it is producing. If then, after the liberalization of trade, consumers in P substitute the lower-cost product of country H for their domestic product, the output of H could expand further and its equilibrium price could fall whereas the opposite tendency could occur in P. Ultimately an equilibrium might be attained where H produced the combined requirements of the market at higher unit costs than the same output could have been produced in country P. This is the specific possibility that led Grubel (1967) to argue that trade liberalization would not necessarily produce an optimal pattern of specialization in the group.

Whether or not such perverse outcomes are empirically important, they at any rate seem to depend on different assumptions from those that underly the orthodox model. For instance, in the example considered, it might be thought inevitable that the production must in the long run shift to country P, if there is certainty, perfect knowledge and an absence of transport costs. However, uncertainty and the cost of transporting the product to country H, where most of it is assumed to be consumed, might operate to prevent this outcome. Transport costs must, of course, be taken into account in determining the optimal pattern of specialization. The 'perverse' outcome in question might also be produced if, in a situation in which innovation was proceeding, 'learning by doing' were an important determinant of costs and were related to output. In such an event this 'dynamic' factor in the establishment of comparative advantage might suffice to ensure the survival of the 'higher-cost' industry of country H. It should be noted that the problem in question need not prevent trade liberalization from generating gains from specialization, but might result in those gains being smaller than would be 'technically' feasible.

In a discussion of the same issue in a similar vein, Kojima (1971) has even argued that in the presence of economies of scale, specialization may not occur at all, the price mechanism being ineffective to promote it and equilibrium being stable in the initial situation. Similar issues have been explored in other connections by Meade (1955b).

It can be seen from this analysis that, in the presence of economies of scale, the orthodox concepts of trade creation and trade diversion remain relevant for an evaluation of customs unions, but they require to be supplemented to take account of two other effects, namely trade suppression and cost reduction. However, since those effects are an integral part of the process and are conceptually similar to the ones considered in the orthodox analysis, it is convenient simply to extend the concepts of trade creation and trade diversion to include these phenomena – just as the original Vinerian concepts, once limited to the production effects of customs unions, have been extended to include consumption effects, as explained in the last chapter.

At the same time, the limitations of comparative static analysis in this context and the possible significance of the dynamic factors mentioned above should be borne in mind. If those factors should be empirically significant it would follow that trade liberalization *per se* may not be sufficient to secure the gains from integration. The likelihood of monopolistic behaviour in the presence of persistent and significant economies of scale would strengthen this reservation. Free trade among members of a customs union may then be a necessary condition for securing such gains, but not a sufficient condition. On this and on other grounds discussed in Chapter 4, it may be argued that agreed specialization, involving planning and the supplementation of market forces, may be required to secure the gains from economies of scale in customs unions.

CUSTOMS UNIONS AND INTRA-INDUSTRY TRADE

Irrespective of whether customs union theory incorporates economies of scale on the lines just considered or not, the analysis suggests that the formation of customs unions will give rise to increased inter-industry or inter-sectoral specialization among the member countries. Early empirical studies of the trade effects of economic integration in Western Europe (Verdoorn, 1960; Balassa, 1966; Grubel, 1967) did not wholly bear out these expectations. Instead it was found that although intra-bloc trade expanded markedly following the establishment of the customs union in the EC, much of the expansion took the form of a kind of exchange until then hardly acknowledged in the literature, namely of the same or of similar products, implying a growth of specialization *within* industries. A more recent study (Drabek and Greenaway, 1984) shows that by 1977 such intra-industry trade among the EC countries amounted to more than two-thirds of intra-EC trade, and the more rapid growth of this component relative to inter-industry trade that was noted in earlier studies seems to have continued into the 1970s, albeit at a slower pace.

Orthodox customs union theory clearly cannot encompass the phenomenon of intra-industry trade since a country cannot both import and export the same product. If, however, in addition to incorporating economies of scale into the analysis, the limiting assumption of homogeneous products is also relaxed (so formally recognizing product differentiation and the consumer's demand for variety, which constitute dominant features of modern industry), a plausible explanation for intra-industry trade can be postulated. The existence of similar and therefore competitive, as opposed to complementary, production structures is clearly a necessary condition for intra-industry specialization to arise. If there is also some similarity of demand conditions among the member countries, reflected in overlapping tastes, and if goods are produced with economies of scale, so limiting the amount of product diversity that domestic producers can accommodate profitably, there will be an incentive to horizontal specialization within industries in order to benefit from the economies of large-scale production. Of course, not all intra-industry trade takes the form of final products; indeed, a high proportion takes the form of intermediate goods – a category of trade that, like intra-industry trade, finds no place in orthodox customs union theory either. Intra-industry trade in intermediate products is associated with vertical specialization, and this is best considered in the context of a common market and factor market integration. It will therefore be postponed until Chapter 6, the present chapter being limited to the analysis of product market integration.

Having identified the phenomenon of intra-industry trade and provided an explanation of it, economists have gone on to consider the question of its specific relationship with integration, and other influences, and its possible welfare significance.

It has often been suggested that customs unions and other forms of integration might *a priori* be expected to have a particular impact on intra-industry trade. The importance of this category of trade in the EC has already been noted. However, the fact that in most industrialized countries – even those outside trade blocs – intra-industry trade is also fairly high would suggest that the influence of customs unions on such trade, even if important, could be only one of several such influences.

On what grounds might it be supposed that integration might exert a positive differential impact on intra-industry trade? First, if integration should result in incomes per head in the bloc rising faster than they otherwise would have done, then since the demand for variety is known to increase as income per head rises, trade in differentiated products might be expected to rise faster than other-wise, giving more scope for intra-industry trade. Secondly, customs unions and other forms of integration normally entail a reduction or elimination of non-tariff barriers to intra-union trade – for instance, by the adoption of more uniform industrial standards. Such provi-sions which are not a feature of multilateral trade liberalization arrangements, might be expected to reinforce the intra-industry component of trade expansion in a customs union. Thirdly, a customs union may, as is the case of the EC, be a component of a common market in which factor as well as product markets are integrated. Intra-industry trade may then be generated partly as a result of foreign direct investment conducted by transnational cor-porations that may deliberately adopt a strategy of specializing on the production of particular varieties of their products in their affiliated enterprises within the bloc. But these are possibilities only. The specific character of a customs union and its institutional arrangements will clearly be influential and in principle these might equally well operate to encourage inter-industry as intra-industry trade.

A recent survey of the phenomenon of intra-industry trade (Greenaway and Milner, 1986) that comprehensively reviews a range of documentary and econometric studies in fact finds little evidence, even weak evidence, for the proposition that integration has a positive effect on intra-industry trade at the country level in the EC. However, an earlier study (Drabek and Greenaway, 1984) did conclude that at the industry level some empirical support could be found for the view that intra-industry trade is higher for intra-EC trade. Also, for two groupings of less developed countries, namely the Central American Common Market and LAFTA, Balassa (1979) did establish the existence of a positive regional integration effect on intra-industry trade. In the case of LAFTA at any rate, this is almost certainly attributable to the unique character of the integration arrangements in force there in which a large role was given to the negotiation of so-called industrial complementarity agreements.

A second issue that has received some consideration in relation to intra-industry trade in customs unions concerns its welfare signifi-cance. Clearly there is no reason for supposing that welfare improvements may not arise from integration merely because the specialization that accompanies it largely takes the form of intra-industry rather than of inter-industry trade. Indeed, the oppor-tunities for generating welfare gains from the greater availability of a variety of products and the achievement of scale economies seems on *prima facie* grounds to be considerable. Of course, intra-industry trade expansion, like inter-industry trade expansion, may rest in part on trade that is diverted as well as trade that is created. In orthodox terms, only the latter would be a source of welfare improvement. There seem, however, to be no *a priori* grounds for supposing there would be any systematic difference between the welfare that would be generated by a given amount of trade created through intra-industry trade and the same amount of trade created by inter-industry trade. Ultimately this is an empirical question, but very little empirical material is available that could throw light on this issue.

It is however relevant to mention, from a welfare point of view, that in the opinion of a number of commentators (Balassa, 1966; Aquino, 1978) there are grounds for believing that adjustment to changes in trade policy will be easier when trade expansion takes the form of an increase in intra-industry as opposed to inter-industry trade. Some empirical evidence exists to support this proposition. Costs of adjustment are of course altogether ignored in the comparative static analysis of customs unions, but if they are significant these favourable factors should not be overlooked in a full welfare appraisal of their impacts.

Finally, reference should be made to one other consideration. If account is taken of the existence of monopoly, oligopoly and foreign direct investment, it is possible that some part of intra-industry trade in a customs union may be attributable to the effects of inefficient market sharing by oligopolistic firms operating at sub-optimal scales and outputs. To the extent that these factors operate, intra-industry trade may generate welfare losses and some part of these may be directly attributable to integration. But here again, the institutional arrangements accompanying the customs union – in particular its competition policy – are clearly relevant to the evaluation of possibilities. In any case, if oligopoly is present there is no reason to confine a consideration of its impact on welfare to intra-industry trade alone. In the presence of monopoly and of oligopoly, and of administered prices and markets, many of the resource allocation and welfare conclusions of customs union theory may call for substantial modification. Some of the relevant issues are discussed in Chapter 6, pp. 71–73.

CHAPTER 4

Customs Unions and 'Public Goods'

In Chapters 2 and 3 the basic economic theory of customs unions and free trade areas has been outlined. This chapter is mainly concerned with the implications of a problem that has been implicit in that presentation but that has not been addressed up to this point. On the assumptions of the orthodox model, the basic theory as developed by Viner, Meade and Lipsey fails to provide an economic rationale for the formation of customs unions. This is because, apart from the terms-of-trade argument, the grounds on which it can be shown that customs unions may be superior to a non-discriminatory tariff are precisely those on which customs unions and free trade areas can themselves be shown to be necessarily inferior to free trade.

It might be questioned whether this is a significant issue. The basic model is highly restrictive and it excludes a number of factors that might be expected to motivate the formation of an economic grouping. In any case, even if it should turn out that customs unions would – as Viner suggested – have to be justified on non-economic grounds, their economic effects would still require analysis. The issue, which was initially explored in the mid-1960s (Johnson, 1965; Cooper and Massell, 1965), has nevertheless aroused recurrent interest since that period and it has been taken up again recently (Wonnacott and Wonnacott, 1981, 1984; Berglas, 1979, 1983). The main contribution of the debate has been to suggest fruitful new ways of viewing certain customs union issues, although some of its implications have greater significance for economic communities than for customs unions proper.

THE SUPERIORITY OF FREE TRADE?

The basic issue may be illustrated by reference to Figure 2.1 (p. 17). Suppose that the home country (H) has an initial tariff of $P_wT'_H$. If it enters a customs union with a partner country (P) and they adopt a common external tariff CET', then, as has already been shown, trade creation that is equal to $(a + c)$ will result. However, country H also has the option of unilaterally reducing its tariff to $P_w CET'$ on a non-discriminatory basis. If it were to do so, it would enjoy exactly the same level of domestic production and consumption as in the customs union. The difference would be that, with the non-discriminatory tariff reduction, imports would come from the rest of the world; and this would generate a net gain to country H that was equivalent to the difference in total outlay on imports from the two sources. This net gain would also equal the customs revenue that would be raised if country H were to adopt the lower tariff on a non-discriminatory basis.

In the case of free trade areas it may likewise be shown that, although a free trade area may be superior to a customs union, a free trade area is itself inferior to a non-discriminatory tariff reduction. With respect to the situation depicted in Figure 2.3a (p. 26), for instance, a non-discriminatory tariff reduction to $P_w T_P$ by country H would result in the same amount of consumption and domestic production as in the free trade area case, but again in such a situation import requirements would come from the rest of the world. The additional gain to country H compared with the free trade area option would equal the revenue raised from import duties, which would equal the import duty earned in the free trade area situation by country P. In this particular case the adoption of a free trade area as opposed to a non-discriminatory tariff reduction would merely result in a redistribution of import revenue (equivalent to a national income loss) from country H to country P.

This conclusion is unaffected by the introduction of economies of scale into the analysis. For instance, referring to Figure 3.1 (p. 37), it can be seen that country H would be made just as well off by a unilateral tariff reduction (UTR) to P_{CU} as by entering into a customs union with P with the indicated CET. This would not be the case for the partner country P, but in its case the additional benefit that it would derive from the formation ot the customs union as compared with UTR is obtained entirely at the expense of the home country, which would be still better off if it were to eliminate its tariff altogether.

Within the framework of the orthodox analysis therefore, even when it is extended to incorporate economies of scale, it must apparently be concluded that none of the considerations so far discussed in this book provides an economic rationale for the formation either of customs unions or of free trade areas if the alternative of unilateral tariff reduction is available. If a customs union is beneficial, this is because net trade creation represents a move towards free trade. Free trade would represent a still better position. This is the orthodox point of view, which inevitably follows from its position that any initial tariff (or any other form of intervention in trade) is arbitrary and non-optimal.

The trouble with this point of view, as Johnson has written, is that it:

> . . . puts the economist in opposition to dominant strands in the actual formulation of international economic policy, which have to be treated by definition as 'irrational' or 'non-economic'. . . . At the same time, the economist is left without a theory capable of explaining a variety of important and observable phenomena, such as the nature of tariff bargaining, the commercial policies adopted by various countries, the conditions under which countries are willing to embark on customs unions, and the arguments and considerations that have weight in persuading countries to change their commercial policies. (1965, p. 257)

One instructive approach to the resolution of this dilemma has been to seek an economic rationale for the formation of customs unions and regional economic groupings in the inclusion of 'public goods' in the welfare function. The resulting theory then focuses attention on the implications of this extension – in particular on the question of the relative efficiency from the standpoint of two or more countries acting together of customs unions as opposed to optimal non-preferential tariff systems as a means of providing goods in which an element of 'publicness' is involved, in the sense that the benefits of consuming them do not accrue solely to the purchaser. If, in this context, it could be shown that a customs union may make *both* countries better off relative to individually optimal policies of non-preferential tariff protection, a possible rationale for such unions would have been provided. Approaches along these lines necessarily abandon the single-country single-product analysis of customs unions which is incapable of illuminating the issues.

These issues were first systematically investigated by Johnson (1965) and by Cooper and Massell (1965), who simultaneously and independently have developed an analysis that is relevant for customs unions in which a public good is included in the social welfare function and therefore in the evaluation criteria. Each of these analyses can also be interpreted to apply to a situation where welfare is defined solely in terms of the consumption of private goods and services but where externalities of various kinds give rise to domestic distortions, which have so far been ruled out of the discussion. Johnson was primarily concerned with developing a theory to explain why governments behave as they do in relation to a variety of commercial policies having a protective character. Cooper and Massell, on the other hand, were directly concerned with the customs union issue and more specifically with explaining how membership of a customs union may enable countries to achieve more economically the ends that can be served by protection. Each analysis therefore rests on a prior rational argument for protection of which the case for protecting industry may be regarded as a special case.

THE ANALYSIS OF CUSTOMS UNIONS WITH COLLECTIVE CONSUMPTION

Although the basic point is a simple one, it may be useful to illustrate the issues with a brief example. For this purpose, in contrast to the analysis of previous chapters, it will now be supposed that welfare is generated both by the private consumption of goods and services and by the collective consumption of a variety of public goods that must be provided through government agency at the cost of sacrifices in private consumption. One such good, for instance, might be a level of certain kinds of industrial or agricultural production that was in excess of what would be commercially viable in the absence of protection.

The following analysis allows for such public goods. As in much of the analysis of Chapters 2 and 3, two prospective partners are considered, the home country, H, and the partner country, P. It is assumed that each is producing at least two products in the industrial sector that it is desired to protect. It is also assumed that in the public aspect, the two countries are indifferent between the two industries – or any others – and that industrial diversification is not an object of policy or a source of benefit. The costs and benefits of any customs union are further assumed to arise solely in the course of trade, so that any possibility of redistributing benefits through fiscal transfers is excluded. All of the products of the industrial sector in question are assumed to require protection and therefore cannot be exported to the rest of the world. Thus the level of domestic demand governs the level of sales in each industry.

The gains from customs union can be illustrated in Figure 4.1, which is merely a reinterpretation of Figure 3.1 to apply to two countries and two products. The comments made in Chapter 3 about pricing apply equally here. Curves AC_{H1} and AC_{H2} represent

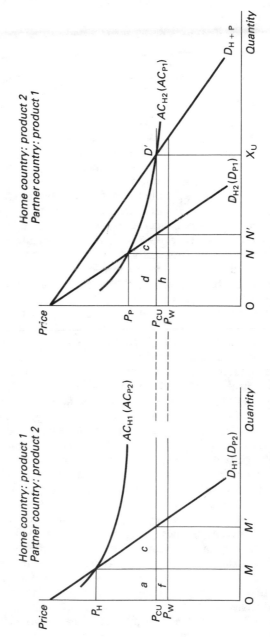

Figure 4.1 A customs union with economies of scale and public goods: the gains from specialization

the average cost curves for the two products produced under conditions of economies of scale in the home country, for which the respective demand curves are D_{H1} and D_{H2}. For simplicity of representation it is supposed that country P's cost curve for industry 2 is represented by the cost curve of country H for industry 1 and that country P's cost curve for industry 1 is represented by country H's cost curve for industry 2. It is assumed that the private domestic demand for each product is the same and identical in each country, so that $D_{H1} = D_{P2} = D_{H2} = D_{P1}$.

In pursuit of its industrialization or public goods objective, it is assumed that prior to customs union country H imposes made-to-measure tariffs on the products of the two industries. This would generate an amount of industrial production equal to OM of product 1 and ON of product 2, the respective tariffs being $P_W P_H$ and $P_W P_P$. The forgone private income compared with importation, which is equivalent to the excess domestic cost of production, is equal to $a + f$ on product 1 and $d + h$ on product 2. Similarly in the pre-customs union situation country P imposes made to measure tariffs and produces OM of product 2 and ON of product 1, the respective tariffs being $P_W P_H$ and $P_W P_P$, the forgone private income being the same as for H.

If the two countries form a customs union and impose a common external tariff of $P_W P_{CU}$ on each product and specialize respectively in product 2 in country H and product 1 in country P, exporting the excess of their domestic production over domestic consumption to the other country, each will be able to satisfy its preference for industrial products or public goods at a smaller cost in terms of forgone national income. In that situation, the right-hand part of Figure 4.1 then depicts the production costs of each product when an amount OX_U of each is produced to satisfy the combined requirements of the market. The gains from union for each country will be identical and can easily be arrived at by a comparison of the relevant areas, as was done in the previous chapter. If the products protected are those that provide the specified amounts of industrial product at the least cost in terms of the combined national income forgone, as we suppose to be the case in this example, the tariff may be termed an *'efficient'* common external tariff.

This convenient outcome, in which an efficient common external tariff results in each country at least achieving its initial industrial production level, is not the only possible one. The industrial cost structure of the two countries may be such that the two least-cost industries are both located in country H. In that event, if a customs union were formed that protected these two industries, country H would produce the whole output of the two goods whose cost and demand conditions are depicted and P would produce none. Such an outcome would not be acceptable to country P since in a customs union it must be assumed to produce at least as much industrial output as in the pre-customs union situation if its preference for industry is to be satisfied. A mutually advantageous customs union might still be feasible if a tariff is chosen that would enable each country to produce at least its pre-customs union or other specified level of industrial production in the cheapest possible way by, for instance, protecting some third industry in the partner country that could produce more economically than the same industry in the home country, even though its costs might be higher than either of the two indicated industries in the home country. Such a tariff may be termed a *'quasi-efficient' common external tariff*.

If, however, all possible industrial products in the partner country are capable of being produced in the home country at lower costs, and if exchange rates are fixed, a simple customs union would not enable the partner country to achieve its public goods or industrialization objective, although opportunities for potential gain from integration could still be present. To achieve those gains, protection within the customs union might be necessary (Cooper and Massell, 1965). This consideration suggests a rationale for the intra-union protective devices found in certain customs unions among developing countries where there is a preference for industry in participating countries, such as the Southern African Customs Union and the West African Economic Community, which effectively rest on a monetary union.

The analysis of this and previous chapters has assumed that the national income effects of customs union on its participants take effect solely through trade. If compensation payments from one country to another are permitted, the analysis becomes much more complex. It is then conceivable that an efficient tariff *could* be chosen, thus maximizing the income gains from the union, even if all industry were located in one country, so long as the other country was compensated for its loss of industry by a sufficiently large income transfer. However, the amount of income compensation required by any country would depend on its particular preference function, and would not necessarily be compatible with the income gains enjoyed by the other country. It is possible, that is to say, that the country gaining industry (and income) would not gain enough to enable it to pay sufficient compensation to its partner to make a fully efficient tariff feasible. In that case, if a customs union is to operate, at best only a quasi-efficient tariff can be adopted. In any event, if one country is to get no industry, it can be concluded that it would presumably need more income compensation than was represented by the excess cost to it of its partner country's products because it could effectively attain that situation by a unilateral move to free trade.

On the approach just outlined the gains to a country from a customs union depend on what happens to both income and industrial output, which in this case is the public good. Does this analysis render irrelevant the classical distinction between trade-creating and trade-diverting customs unions? In their contribution to the discussion Cooper and Massell (1965) have said that 'either trade creation or trade diversion can be good and either can be bad'. Likewise, Johnson has remarked:

> . . . contrary to the standard analysis trade diversion as well as trade creation yields a gain to the partners; in fact, trade diversion is preferable to trade creation, for the preference-granting country, because it entails no sacrifice of domestic industrial production. This reversal of the usual conclusions is due to the presence of the preference for industrial production. . . . (1965, p. 277)

In one sense these are misleadingly paradoxical statements. The source of gain from the formation of a customs union in the presence of a preference for industry is clearly initial potential trade creation as compared with the alternative of autarkic levels of production, initial or planned, for the protected industries. However, for a gain to be enjoyed by each member, trade creation is a necessary but not a sufficient condition. A country will not gain from trade creation unless there is a sufficient expansion of its exports to its partners (which from their point of view may represent trade diversion). Moreover, the reduced opportunity cost of industrial production that intra-union specialization facilitates may, through the substitution effect, induce further industrial development over the initial level, as in the example considered above, which may in some circumstances be a negative factor. In the light of these considerations, the conventional criterion must be judged to be inadequate rather than irrelevant.

PUBLIC GOODS AND THE RATIONALE FOR CUSTOMS UNIONS

In the context of a preference for public goods, it has been suggested in the previous section that the formation of customs unions may be a more efficient means of satisfying that preference than individually optimal non-discriminatory tariff protection. In this way a rationale for the formation of customs unions appears to have been provided. The benefits would, of course, have to be demonstrated in each case, for even in this context a particular customs union may not be beneficial any more than is the case for a customs union in a purely classical framework, as has already been emphasized. However, does the public goods approach, or the recognition of a national economic case for protection satisfactorily dispose of the difficulty raised at the outset?

Simply to demonstrate that a customs union is superior to unilateral tariff policies from an efficiency viewpoint when public goods or other rational considerations motivate protection still fails to provide an economic rationale for the formation of customs unions unless their formation can be shown to represent the best means of encouraging or providing the public goods in question. If governments have the option of providing direct production subsidies, orthodox theory would suggest that these, rather than customs unions, would be the most efficient protective mechanism to use – at least in the specific public goods case considered – on the grounds that they would avoid the consumption costs involved in the imposition of tariffs. This argument is not rebutted by the consideration that subsidies have to be financed by taxation, which will itself impose distortions, since it can be shown that, if optimal tax-subsidy policies are pursued, any such distortions are likely to be smaller than those generated by a tariff (Meade, 1955b; Corden, 1974). On this view, an economic rationale for customs unions, in the sense of a first best case, can be established on public goods grounds only if political or other constraints rule out the use of direct production subsidies.

A variety of institutional factors, and in particular a country's international obligations, do in fact often rule out resort to a range of possibly superior protection policies such as the institution of discriminatory tariff preferences amongst selected partners. Under the provisions of the General Agreement on Tariffs and Trade (GATT) to which most countries adhere, customs unions and free trade areas are the only permissible forms of preferential tariff reduction except in the case of less developed countries. Likewise, the payment of subsidies to make exports feasible to selected partners would encounter obstacles under GATT rules, to say nothing of probable objections from other trading partners. International constraints of these kinds may effectively mean that customs unions may represent the only practicable means of achieving the gains in question. Nevertheless, the view has been expressed that the public goods argument fails to provide a general economic argument for customs unions and that it leaves substantially unimpaired the Vinerian view that customs unions are essentially non-economic institutions (Krauss, 1972).

Stated in these terms the issue is partly semantic. The question of what is non-economic should not, however, be viewed simply in the context of the traditional theory of tariffs. If the concept of public goods is broadly interpreted and the implications for their provision is considered in the framework of a less restrictive model, a public goods rationale for customs unions and other forms of regional and discriminatory international economic integration does not have to rest merely on 'institutional' constraints or on political constraints, but can appeal to significant economic considerations.

It is not disputed that, in relation to the provision of a broad spectrum of public goods that are sought in complex modern societies, there are many considerations deriving from economies of scale and scope, the presence of externalities in a broad sense and, in particular, the implications of structural and policy interdependence, that furnish valid and compelling economic arguments for increasing the size of jurisdictions beyond the boundaries of single countries. In principle, these considerations might suggest a global extension of jurisdiction. In practice, however, integration that finds its justification on such grounds must of necessity be limited to a regional scale and be *ipso facto* discriminatory since organizational, managerial and information costs and the influence of uncertainty – all of which are disregarded by orthodox analysis – will make the optimal jurisdiction well below the global level. At the same time, for many public goods in a broad sense, production subsidies are irrelevant.

Any realistic model must also take account of the fact that states differ widely in their preferences for public goods in general and for specific public goods because of political and social differences and their levels of economic development. This also points to limiting the membership of international groupings to relatively homogeneous states in the interests of an optimal provision of public goods and in particular those that call for the harmonization of a range of economic policies. Most instances of international economic integration are in fact found among groups of countries whose preferences for public goods are relatively homogeneous by global standards.

In this perspective, there can still be little argument with the proposition that there is no general case on public goods grounds for customs unions or wider forms of integration. At the same time, to categorize dismissively the many important factors that may justify regional economic integration as political or non-economic –

or the policy itself as 'second best' – is a needlessly obfuscatory and unconstructive procedure that harks back to the conditions of an extremely restrictive model.

At this point the discussion begins to touch on problems associated with the political economy of forms of integration going beyond customs unions, in which the integration or harmonization of policies other than tariffs is likely to be in issue. Further consideration of these matters is best postponed until later chapters. In conclusion, however, it must be emphasized that a purely comparative static analysis such as has been conducted up to this point, whether of customs unions or of closer forms of economic integration, will fail to capture many considerations that are likely to be important in practice. In the context of the issues referred to in the latter part of this chapter one of the most significant of these is that arrangements for international economic integration do not merely reflect relatively homogeneous preferences for public goods; they may also positively promote their formation. This is a political consideration that has been influential in discussions of integration strategies for Western Europe, and it continues to be an important element in the continuing debate on the progress of the EC.

CHAPTER 5

Beyond Customs Union: the Rationale for the Integration of Other Economic Policies

The last chapter has explained how policy objectives other than the maximization of private income can be introduced into customs union theory in the simplest manner. In fact, not only are the objectives of public policy extremely diverse, but so, evidently, are the policy instruments that may be used to attain them. Tariff policy is not the only instrument available for achieving common allocational objectives nor is it necessarily the most appropriate or, on its own, a sufficient means. The mere elimination of tariffs in a customs union will not necessarily bring about an improved allocation of resources if other policy-induced obstacles to a unified market then become the binding constraints. The gains to be secured from the reduction or elimination of these other obstacles may be as great as, if not greater than, those to be derived from the elimination of tariffs themselves. If states decide to seek the resource allocation gains that may be obtained from market integration, they may thus be induced to seek to expand those gains by the adoption of joint measures that go beyond the institution of a customs union.

Apart from these considerations, it is clear that the elimination of tariffs on intra-group trade can contribute little or nothing to the attainment of wider objectives of economic policy such, for instance, as the promotion of monetary stability or economic convergence. Prompted by the policy implications of the growth in trade and economic interdependence that is fostered by customs unions, member states may be led to pursue these other economic goals in common, and for that purpose to concert or integrate other economic policies in yet other areas. The institution of free movement for factors of production as well as products, involving the creation of a common market, is an obvious step to take on allocational grounds after a customs union has been established. Apart from that, the principal areas of economic policy in which an extension of integration measures is commonly found or advocated are:

- non-tariff policies to unify the internal market;
- structural policies;
- distribution policies;
- monetary and fiscal policies.

The regulation in common of economic policies amongst the members of an economic grouping in these and other fields may be pursued by various means and to various degrees. In its broadest sense, the term integration may be used to refer to any of these approaches, but it is useful to draw a distinction between integration in a strict sense, and harmonization and coordination. In this book, *integration* strictly refers to the assignment of particular economic functions and instruments to the union or community and their exercise at that level rather than at the level of the member states. *Harmonization* is a second level of integration that refers to agreement on the manner in which each member state will exercise or utilize a particular instrument over which it retains control. Harmonization involves the adoption of legislation by the institutions of the community that is designed to bring about changes in the internal legal enactments of member states. *Coordination*, the third level of integration, refers to voluntary and largely unenforceable alignments of national policies and measures in particular fields. The context will normally make clear in which of these senses the term integration is being used.

MARKET POLICIES

It has been seen that a basic rationale for customs unions is to be found in their ability to promote a more efficient allocation of resources in the union. If non-tariff obstacles to trade are not to significantly impede the functioning of the market as an integrated whole, and hinder the beneficial effects of trade liberalization, a variety of measures of positive integration may be indispensable in addition to the negative integration that the institution of a customs union represents.

Some of the most important non-tariff obstacles take the form of technical barriers in the shape of varying safety regulations and industrial standards for machinery and equipment, and varying health regulations in respect of foodstuffs, agricultural products and pharmaceuticals. The fundamental objection to unharmonized industrial standards is that they may make it necessary to produce different products for each member country, thus restricting intra-group trade, making it more difficult to achieve scale economies and, in general, hindering the reduction of costs and prices that it is a major purpose of customs union to bring about. Likewise, if health regulations are not harmonized, trade in agricultural products and foodstuffs may be unjustifiably restricted.

In the EC, despite twenty-five years of harmonization, varying industrial standards constitute one of the biggest remaining obstacles to the creation of a single internal market, and they demonstrably lend themselves to use for covert protection. A not untypical EC case concerns British chocolate. At present this can be sold in only six European countries because it contains a proportion of vegetable oils. British manufacturers wishing to supply other EC markets are therefore obliged to produce another variety that conforms to their requirements, which evidently limits the possibility of exploiting scale economies in manufacture. In motor vehicles, fifteen years after the EC's initial initiative of 1970 aimed at a European-type approval for passenger vehicles, it has still not been fully achieved. Some important advances have nevertheless been made. Notably, the ruling of the European Court of Justice in the 'cassis de Dijon' case lays down that free trade must not be impeded *solely* because an imported product has been manufactured according to specifications that are different from those in force in the importing country. However, a more effective strategy is required if a fully integrated market is to be established in a reasonable time span. The European Council at Brussels in 1985 gave particular emphasis to the completion of the internal market by 1992, and at its request the Commission has prepared a detailed programme (Commission, 1985) which outlines its new strategy for bringing about the removal of technical barriers and other obstacles to a fully integrated market.

Fiscal measures constitute a second area in which a degree of policy integration may be important. Within a customs union, national fiscal systems co-exist through which taxes of diverse forms and rates may be imposed. Subsidies may be similarly diverse. If a customs union is to promote a more efficient use of resources in the presence of diverse national taxes and subsidies, limited measures of harmonization may be indispensable. The theory of fiscal harmonization deals with the question of the extent to which it is necessary or desirable to harmonize tax structures and rates in a union, mainly from the standpoint of optimal resource allocation, although that is not the only relevant goal.

In the context of the EC, the Commission's White Paper on Completing the Internal Market (1985) contains far-reaching proposals on the harmonization of internal indirect taxes, VAT and excises and other measures, including the establishment of a community clearing house for such taxes. All these measures are aimed at eliminating the physical and cost barriers that the maintenance of customs barriers between the member states currently entails.

STRUCTURAL POLICY

Although the removal of technical, physical and fiscal barriers to the working of the internal market may be required to promote efficient resource allocation, other integrated policy measures with a different focus may also be needed. In the presence of economies of scale and the operation of structural factors, a coordinated approach to certain areas of economic policy may be indicated in order to create and maintain an appropriate economic structure or framework within which market forces can function constructively without impairing the attainment of other objectives such as dynamic efficiency and spatial balance. Some issues of structural policy are associated with economies of scale and their implications for competition. By providing additional opportunities for the exploitation of scale economies, product market integration may increase monopolization in industry. To the extent that the effects of monopoly transcend national boundaries, this may point to the need for a competition policy additional to any practised by the member countries themselves. Other structural issues are associated with the operation of secular trends that may render the operation of market forces perverse, inadequate or dynamically unsatisfactory. Yet others are associated with rigidities in adjustment mechanisms, which may create major difficulties for efficiency in resource allocation and use. Again, in a common market, a union-wide coordination of policies may be called for if union interests are to be optimally pursued.

A prime example of a structural policy (though it may have other justifications) is represented by regional policy. Within member states, such policies are developed in response to structural problems that are generated partly by scale economies, partly by secular trends in industrial structures and partly by factor immobility. The creation of a common market normally increases the power of existing central areas to attract economic activity at the expense of peripheral areas. The latter may nevertheless be viable and competitive if, with public support, they can be helped to develop. Left to itself, however, the market may generate perverse adjustments. The choice of areas that should receive public support and the specific forms that it should take are usually regarded mainly as matters for national governmental action. However, once capital and labour have become highly mobile within an economic grouping, it is likely, because of spill-over effects, that a coordination of structural policies on a union scale will ultimately be desirable for the effectual treatment of regional problems. Without a union regional policy the adjustments promoted by market forces may not contribute to overcoming an initial disequilibrium and may indeed exacerbate it.

DISTRIBUTION POLICY

The question of policy integration also poses itself in connection with distributive issues. Integration measures that promote the attainment of allocational and structural efficiency will not necessarily lead to distributionally acceptable results across the market. The operation of market forces alone may well result in a widening of economic disparities among member countries. Integration might even make some member states worse off, according to their perceptions and criteria, than if they were outside the community, even though the community as a whole might enjoy gains. If the community is a significant determinant of the economic performance of the member states, such outcomes may seriously damage the prospects for cohesion of any economic community that lacks a supranational political authority.

To prevent such damage, the harmonization of a number of national policy instruments may be desirable. A harmonization of instruments on distributional grounds will require, not the uniformity that might be aimed at if competition and resource-allocation considerations were alone in question, but rather the introduction of measures of agreed discrimination. Measures such as regionally differentiated industrial development incentives may be used for this purpose, or indeed the structure of the tariff itself may be employed, as has been envisaged in the previous chapter. Any such measures should be designed to deal with distributional constraints and objectives at the least possible cost in terms of resource allocation and other considerations.

Fiscal transfers among the member countries, either directly or through the medium of the community budget, represent an alternative approach to dealing with distributive issues that has the merit that it need not interfere with efficient resource allocation. However, this approach may not represent a feasible solution to what is essentially a political problem, in part because it does not directly contribute to a removal or an amelioration of the underlying causes of difficulty.

FINANCIAL POLICIES

The issue of further policy integration also poses itself in relation to financial (monetary and fiscal) policies. One important argument for moving towards policy integration in these areas is based on the desirability of facilitating the primary resource allocation objectives of economic integration. Neither intra-group trade nor intra-group investment will take place in an optimal way, it may be argued, without a high degree of exchange rate stability, which cannot be assured without a coordination of financial policies. Just as, if not more, important are the arguments for the coordination of monetary and fiscal policies that rest on macroeconomic considerations. As the national economies of member states become progressively interdependent as a result of trade and factor movements, the justification for coordinating their monetary and fiscal policies on macroeconomic grounds becomes increasingly strong since financial measures taken by one country to influence that country's macroeconomic variables are likely to spill over and significantly affect those of other member countries. In these circumstances indeed, unilateral measures of financial policy may be largely ineffective. Financial coordination may be particularly important if there are constraints, such as may be found in a customs union or common market, on the other policies that member states may use domestically to promote external balance. If there should be an agreement to limit exchange rate fluctuations among the members in the interests of promoting intra-community trade and investment, the remaining financial instruments open to a single country may not suffice to enable it to maintain internal and external equilibrium and to faciliate necessary adjustments. Coordinated action by both deficit and surplus countries may be a requisite for bringing about and maintaining a satisfactory equilibrium.

In certain circumstances the weight of argument in favour of policy coordination in the monetary arena might point to full monetary integration involving the establishment of a common currency. In any event, a coordination of financial policies is likely to be very desirable in any union in which a high proportion of external trade is intra-community trade (the proportion is more than 50 per cent in the case of the EEC) and where, for this reason, both economic and policy interdependence can be expected to be considerable.

IS FURTHER POLICY INTEGRATION INDISPENSABLE?

In terms of a political economy approach, the view is often expressed that the formation of a customs union would inevitably entail the extension of policy integration to fields such as those outlined above. From another standpoint the political theory of neo-functionalism (now largely discredited) has arrived at some-what similar conclusions (Webb, 1983). Simply in terms of static equilibrium economic analysis there would be no justification for any such conclusion. It is no doubt the case that the static gains from improved resource allocation in an integrated area can only be maximized if, in addition to product market integration, there is also factor market integration and a harmonization or coordination of certain other policies that directly affect competition and eco-nomic structure. Yet national welfare would not necessarily be enhanced by the adoption of such further measures of integration because the attainment of other 'public goods' objectives, such as domestic or regional balance or of domestic income distribution objectives may be impaired by doing so. To that extent further gains from efficiency in the use of resources have to be balanced against the fuller attainment of other important policy objectives. On such grounds it may be perfectly rational for the member countries of a bloc to wish to confine the scope of their integration mainly to tariff policy and product markets, as would be the case in a simple customs union or free trade area.

It is, of course, self-evident – as has already been stressed – that, even in customs unions and free trade areas, some degree of harmo-nization of other trade and commercial policies and instruments will be indispensable if the basic objectives of the arrangements are not to be frustrated. If quantitative trade restrictions such as quotas are nationally determined, large differences in their scope or structure could undermine the very basis of a customs union by enabling any member unilaterally to alter the degree of *effective* protection enjoyed by an industry or activity, notwithstanding the existence of the customs union. Some degree of harmonization of such measures may thus be indispensable, since they are so closely connected with the purposes of the customs union and are often, indeed, of equiv-alent effect to tariffs. However, the extent to which it would be desirable to go beyond this limited stage, and harmonize other economic policies, should depend on the member states' perceptions of their various policy objectives, on the weight they attach to each, and on the terms on which, in the union, one objective can be traded off against another by political bargaining.

There is, at the same time, one persuasive argument in favour of the view that policy integration that goes well beyond this limited stage is in a sense, inevitable. It is possible that, except in very favourable circumstances, customs unions that fail to concert certain other policies may not constitute a stable long-term equilibrium. A variety of dynamic and structural forces that such unions embody and strengthen may work powerfully either towards a more intimate form of integration, which might approach economic union in the limiting case, or towards separation. Polarization, which is an important determinant of the distribution of the costs and benefits of integration, is one such force, and it may be impossible to regulate it adequately within the confines of a simple customs union. Casual empiricism would suggest that the history of almost every recorded customs union provides support for the view that integration cannot stop there and that the adoption of further measures of policy integration could be said to be inevitable – if the union is to survive. Perhaps, in this respect, the political economy approach emphasizes the right elements.

In an analysis of the economic implications of extending economic integration to policy areas such as those outlined in this chapter, it is convenient to consider the issues in the first instance from the standpoint of a single policy objective or criterion; but a broader basis of appraisal involving multiple goals is ultimately desirable, incorporating considerations of the kinds referred to in this chapter. Thus, for instance, although tax harmonization may be partially evaluated in terms of its beneficial resource allocation effects, its impact on the attainment of other welfare objectives of the separate member countries and of the union itself must also be considered. Likewise, financial integration may be evaluated from the standpoint of its impact on allocational efficiency, but an adequate view of its merits can be formed only if account is also taken of its impact on the macroeconomic objectives of member countries.

The next five chapters of this book discuss in greater detail the more important issues that arise in a progression from a customs union to more developed forms of integration involving the integration of other key economic policies. Chapter 6 discusses the effects of instituting a common market for factors of production and certain issues that arise when production is undertaken by transnational enterprises. Chapter 7 considers the role of the budget in economic groupings, and the fiscal efficiency considerations that bear on the question of the optimal fiscal domains of the member states and the group or union. Chapter 8 discusses tax harmonization, primarily from the standpoint of resource allocation considerations. Chapter 9 considers monetary integration with particular reference to its implications for macroeconomic policy objectives. Finally, regional policy, which has important structural and distributional objectives, forms the subject matter of Chapter 10.

CHAPTER 6

The Theory of Common Markets

The microeconomic theory of international economic integration largely consists of the static theory of customs unions and free trade areas, a central assumption of which is that factors of production are immobile both amongst the member countries and vis-à-vis the rest of the world. A common market, by contrast, involves not only the integration of product markets through the trade liberalization that results from customs union, but also the integration of factor markets through the elimination of obstacles to the free movement of factors within the bloc. The concept of a common market is a fairly new one, probably introduced by the Spaak Report of 1956, but in any case the term was in widespread use from the mid-1950s. The Treaty of Rome itself prescribed the establishment of a common market within twelve years, which would entail 'the abolition, as between Member States, of obstacles to freedom of movement for persons, services and capital'.

In a narrow sense the basic concern of a theory of common markets is with the additional benefits that can be derived by going beyond a simple customs union to the establishment of a common market. At the very least such a market would require the removal of legislative restrictions upon the free movement of factors between the member states, but an effective integration of factor markets would in practice also call for the adoption of positive harmonization measures with respect to the regulation of the markets for labour, capital and enterprise.

At a purely static level, the benefits, if any, to be derived from the superimposition of a common market upon a customs union are allocational gains. If, within a customs union, differences subsist in the marginal social productivity of the different factors in the various member states, a reallocation of factors that equalizes their marginal productivities can increase the income and welfare of the group. A migration of factors from countries where such productivities are relatively low, to those where they are higher, will then be beneficial. This will be accompanied by a tendency for disparities in factor earnings among the different member countries to be reduced.

In orthodox terms the operation of a customs union would itself, through its trade effects, reduce intra-union disparities in factor earnings and marginal productivities. If these effects could be relied upon to equalize intra-union marginal productivities of factors, resources would then be utilized in the most efficient way in the area, and a move from a customs union to a common market would not result in any further increase in allocational efficiency. In terms of that criterion alone therefore, there would be no advantage in establishing a common market.

The conditions required in order that trade alone should equalize marginal productivities are, however, extremely restrictive, and the empirical relevance of the factor-price equalization theorem is generally accepted to be extremely limited. In practice, various reasons such as differences in production functions between member states, or the existence of economies of scale in production, mean that further gains may be anticipated from an advance from a customs union to a common market. These and other sources of gain from factor movement have been analysed in a purely orthodox framework by Meade (1953, pp. 61–73).

In this chapter the principal economic implications of common markets are discussed in a much broader context, although for reasons of simplicity the analysis is conducted entirely in terms of capital flows. The chapter first considers the additional benefits that may be derived by superimposing an integrated factor market upon an existing customs union. It is assumed that the resulting common market chooses an appropriate combined level of capital controls vis-à-vis the outside world so that the possibility of net losses – akin to those that accompany trade diversion – can be disregarded. Secondly it considers the modifications required to the orthodox criteria for evaluating the welfare effects of a customs union in the presence of foreign factors. Thirdly it discusses whether the orthodox analysis of integration calls for qualification where production is carried on by transnational enterprises possessing market power. Fourthly it comments on some dynamic aspects of common markets. It goes on to consider the impact of the European Community on the strategies of transnational enterprises. In conclusion, it briefly considers policy and experience in the EC with respect to the liberalization of the markets for capital, labour and enterprise, and the programme currently under way to 'complete' the common market. The analysis deals mainly with allocational and distributional aspects of the issues. If a complete common market exists, however, and in particular if there is full financial integration (including substantially integrated bond markets), major constraints will be implied for the autonomy of national macroeconomic policies. Likewise, factor mobility will imply major limitations on the effective jurisdictional autonomy of national policies in other areas of policy such as taxation and social security. All of these considerations must be fully taken into account in evaluating both the costs and benefits of the introduction of a common market and the issue of whether a common market can be a stable stage of economic integration. These further aspects are not considered at all in this chapter, but some are briefly discussed in Chapters 7, 9 and 10.

INTEGRATION AND CAPITAL FLOWS

Formal analysis may usefully commence with an application of orthodox partial equilibrium neoclassical analysis of capital flows to the case of a customs union, utilizing for simplicity a two-country model. It is assumed that two countries, H and P, have established a customs union, but that in the pre-common market phase obstacles to intra-regional factor mobility exist, as a result of which the customs union coexists with divergences in the marginal social productivity of capital. Factor supplies in each country are given. A single aggregate product is produced.

Figure 6.1 depicts production conditions in each country. The lines M_H and M_P relate capital stocks in the two countries to the marginal product of capital, given the amount of the other factor, namely labour. Initially, in the customs union phase, the capital stock is assumed to be OM in country H and OQ in country P. In the pre-common market phase, since capital is assumed to be internationally immobile, all capital stock must be nationally owned. Taxation is ignored. In a competitive model, profits per unit of capital equal its marginal product. Hence total profits in country H are $q + t$. Total output is $p + q + r + s + t$, and labour's share is $p + r + s$. In country P similarly, profits will amount to $x + z$, and the share of labour will amount to y. Despite the existence of the customs union, the rewards of capital are different in the two countries, being higher in P, reflecting partly that country's more favourable productive 'atmosphere'.

Let it now be assumed that the two countries decide to superimpose a common market for capital upon the existing customs union, so that obstacles to capital flows between the two countries are eliminated, although existing restrictions are maintained vis-à-vis

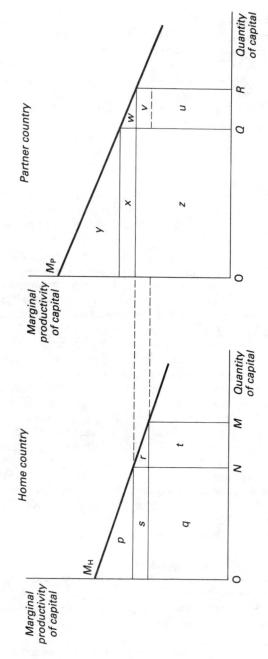

Figure 6.1 The impact of free intra-regional capital flows

the rest of the world. In order to remain initially within the static realm of discourse, it will be assumed that capital continues to be completely immobile vis-à-vis the rest of the world. The total stock of capital of the customs union is thus unaffected by the introduction of the common market for capital.

Following the establishment of the common market, capital will flow from H to P in search of higher rewards and a new equilibrium will be established when the distribution of capital between the two countries is such that its marginal productivity is equal, giving H ON and P OR of the stock.

The outcome is that H's domestically produced product declines to $p + q + s$, but its *national* product, including inward remittances of profit on capital employed in P, namely $v + u$ will increase by $v - r$. In country P *domestic* product increases by $u + v + w$, but *national* product, after allowing for outward profit remittances of $u + v$, increases only by w. In each country the share of labour in national product is altered in favour of owners of capital in country H, and against owners of capital in country P. If intra-market capital flows do not merely entail the application of known and existing technologies in the respective countries (represented by a move along given M_P and M_H curves) but are also accompanied by a significant transfer of new techniques and know-how, as is very often the case, the consequences of intra-group mobility would be more complex and the conclusions of the static neoclassical analysis would need modification. Qualifications on this account (and others) are discussed in MacDougall (1960) and Grubel (1982).

FOREIGN CAPITAL AND THE COSTS AND BENEFITS OF INTEGRATION

Customs unions are rarely, if ever, established in circumstances of complete international immobility of factors. Foreign capital has been an important element in the economies of most of the countries that have sought to establish customs unions and other forms of international integration during the past quarter of a century. How does the presence of foreign capital affect the criteria for evaluating customs unions? At the level of the orthodox neoclassical analysis, the principal qualification is that trade creation and trade diversion then cease to be sufficient indicators of costs and benefits for a member country. Basically this conclusion follows directly from the point just noted, namely that when foreign capital is present the impact of integration on a country's national income is

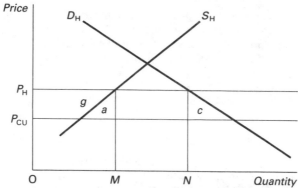

Figure 6.2   The costs and benefits of integration with foreign capital

not identical to its impact on the country's geographical or domestic income.

Whenever foreign direct investment is present in an economy in the shape of foreign enterprises, the effects of integration will be determined partly by its impact on the net economic rents earned by those enterprises from the use of their exclusive assets. These assets include superior technologies, and special administrative and entrepreneurial capacities. These and other factors permit foreign enterprises to produce at lower costs and thus to earn pure or quasi rents even in competitive industries. In a simple partial equilibrium neoclassical analysis, these rents are measured by the producers' surplus. In the presence of foreign rents, a consideration of the gains and losses of integration cannot be limited to the orthodox trade creation and trade diversion effects. *Additional* gains or losses for the host country will arise from changes in the rents earned by foreign companies because these imply a redistribution of income as between the country of origin of the foreign capital and the host country. For instance, in the case of an importable commodity produced by foreign enterprises whose price falls after integration as a result of trade creation, the host country will gain from the reduction in foreign company rents. This additional benefit has been termed by Tironi (1982) the *foreign profit diversion effect*.

Figure 6.2 illustrates the point. S_H and D_H represent the demand and supply curves for an importable produced by country H. Prior to customs union, an amount OM is produced at a price P_H. Assume that if a customs union is formed, the price falls to P_{CU}. If producers are wholly domestic, the gain to country H will be denoted by areas $a + c$, as has been explained in Chapter 2. If, instead, the commodity is produced wholly by foreign enterprise and capital, there will be an additional national gain equal to area g, which represents the reduction in remittable profits, and *mutatis mutandis* for intermediate cases. Area g denotes the *foreign profit diversion effect*.

Similarly, if there are foreign enterprises in the home country that enjoy a regional comparative advantage then, in addition to the standard trade and welfare effects, a further effect termed by Tironi *the foreign profit creation effect*, would have to be taken into account in evaluating the costs and benefits of forming a customs union. This foreign profit creation effect is represented by the additional rents or profits that would, as a consequence of the customs union, be obtained by foreign enterprises from their sales in the host country and their exports to the preferential markets of the partner country. For the host country, the counterpart of these additional rents from home sales is a fall in consumers' surplus, which in this case represents a national income loss from its point of view. At the same time, the additional rents earned on sales to the partner country do not – unlike the cases analysed in Chapter 2 – represent a national gain from the host country's standpoint. For the importing partner country on the other hand, the additional rents earned on its imports by the foreign enterprise in the host country are reflected in the trade diversion that it experiences. This loss is already accounted for in the orthodox analysis and no further adjustment on its account is therefore required.

Typically of course, host countries participate through taxes in rents or profits earned by both foreign and domestic enterprises. On one view indeed, this is the principal benefit derived by a host country from foreign inward investment (MacDougall, 1960), because the host country gains from more advanced technologies and skills imported only to the extent that it can use them without fully paying for them in the form of rents and profit remittances. If a country participates in profits through taxation, the benefit from the foreign profit diversion effect would be reduced to $(1-t)(d)$, where t is the rate of profits tax and d is the profit diversion effect. In the limiting case therefore, where the rate of tax on foreign profits were 100 per cent, the welfare effects of forming a customs union when foreign enterprises are present would be identical to those arising when there are only national enterprises. Similarly, if taxes are paid by a foreign firm that exports to a partner country, then the loss to the host country will be smaller.

TRANSNATIONAL ENTERPRISES AND INTEGRATION

The previous section has explained how the introduction of foreign investment affects the calculation of gain from integration to members of the group, assuming competitive conditions to prevail. In fact, much of contemporary foreign direct investment is undertaken by enterprises that possess a significant degree of market power, and whose operations in many cases are conducted on a multi-country basis. These two characteristics of foreign investment pose a number of important questions for an analysis of integration. The basic question is whether the orthodox analysis linking domestic costs and prices with the direction, composition and extent of intra-group trade and the distribution of its costs and benefits continues to be valid when the operations of such transnational corporations are explicitly taken into account.

This issue is posed in part by the ability of the transnational enterprise (TNE) to bypass the operations of the market, which, in the orthodox model, determines the effects of integration on the efficiency of resource allocation. Within a transnational enterprise the activities of subsidiaries can be regulated as an intra-firm matter in ways that, although they may be optimal from the standpoint of the global interests and objectives of the TNE, are not necessarily so from the standpoint of the individual enterprise considered as a profit-maximizing unit, or from the standpoint of the host country itself. One important aspect of TNE policy from this point of view concerns the prices at which intra-firm transactions take place. These 'transfer prices', which are not market determined, can have an important influence on production, trade flows and the distribution of costs and benefits. At one level, of course, a major source of the TNE's strength is its ability to reduce by 'internalization' the transactions costs that would otherwise be involved in 'arms-length' contractual relationships between independent enterprises. The incentive to engage in 'transfer pricing' will be greater, the greater are the fiscal differences and the impediments to trade and capital movement amongst the countries concerned. The more 'complete' the internal market becomes, the less important this factor is likely to be.

In the simplest of static models with given cost and demand conditions, it can be shown that, if a transnational enterprise is the sole producer of a particular product in an integration group, neither the quantities of goods traded, nor the direction of trade and specialization, need be affected by the phenomenon of transfer prices (Horst, 1973). But when competitors exist, other issues arise. If transfer prices are used for such purposes as to cross-subsidize a subsidiary in order to eliminate local competition, or to maintain a position of market dominance, or to hinder potential competitors from entering, their manipulation must be expected to affect not only trade patterns, but also the character of industrial production, static and dynamic efficiency and the intra-regional distribution of benefits from integration.

The simpler static models that attempt to deal with these issues are certainly open to the objection that they exclude crucial aspects of TNEs' operations. But broader organizational analyses of TNEs sometimes reach similar conclusions. Starting from such approaches, a number of economists (McManus, 1972; Buckley and Casson, 1976; Dunning, 1977) have contended that a transnational's ownership links, which generate economies in transaction costs and benefits from coordination, do not themselves significantly affect the locational distribution of its physical production activities or the scale of its plants – a proposition that Caves (1980, p. 322) has termed the 'separation' theory. These analyses again suggest the conclusion that the international location of production should not, merely as a result of the transnational character of enterprises conducting it, impede the attainment of the pattern indicated by considerations of regional cost minimization.

An important objection to some of these further analyses is that they too disregard the interdependence of enterprises in arriving at their conclusions. Typically, the operations of TNEs take place in an oligopolistic context. In such situations it is well established that patterns of oligopolistic rivalry among TNEs do affect their investment decisions. Knickerbocker (1973), for instance, found that American TNEs had an imitative pattern of behaviour that implies an exaggerated shift of output towards the national markets entered by imitative rivals, and an investment in smaller-scale production facilities, than if no such imitation occurred. In the same way, where TNEs seek to preserve a balance of interest vis-à-vis their rivals, it appears that their investment in production facilities may not serve to minimize costs of production.

In situations of market interdependence and oligopoly it is difficult if not impossible to make *a priori* predictions about the impact of TNEs in the context of integration. It is clearly necessary to be cautious before applying without qualification the resource allocation conclusions of the simple competitive model to sectors in which TNEs dominate. But it should also be borne in mind that often TNEs are in competition with national enterprises, and moreover that, except in a limited range of industries, they may not be dominant (apart from the situation in certain groupings of developing countries). Where that is the case, although the policies of TNEs may influence the outcomes, they need not predominate, and the broad conclusions of the simple models may still hold.

COMMON MARKETS, FACTOR SUPPLIES, DYNAMIC EFFECTS AND CONVERGENCE

Up to this point this chapter has been concerned mainly with the static implications of factor mobility for regional integration.

However, just as the institution of a customs union is likely to affect cost and demand conditions and the supplies of factors and possibly also the rate of growth of the economy partly through dynamic effects, so also may the elimination of restrictions on factor mobility and progress towards a common market. A number of insights into these impacts can be derived from the literature on trade and investment, but strong predictions are few and empirical studies are sparse. In general, the literature suggests that taking these factors into account would merely reinforce the presumed static effects. Starting from different but plausible assumptions however, crucial objections can be made to certain of the qualitative predictions of static neoclassical theory.

In static analysis, the intra-regional movement of factors (here specifically the movement of capital) is seen as an instrument for promoting the convergence of real income. In a growth context also, the intra-regional movement of capital and other factors is orthodoxly viewed as a vehicle for distributing the fruits of technical progress and of productivity growth more evenly throughout a common market. If, however, there is a tendency for those countries whose growth is most vigorous to attract direct investment and other factors from the rest of the economically integrated area, this may produce contrary effects and have adverse consequences for geographical balance. Member states are unlikely to be indifferent to these effects, even if incomes per capita should thereby be rendered more equal, so confronting them with a trade-off between the goals of geographical balance and of income convergence.

Some radical critics of the neoclassical theory argue however, that there is no such trade-off, because the geographical redistribution of factors that is stimulated by the institution of a common market does not contribute to a convergence of incomes, still less to a convergence of growth rates of income. Instead, it is claimed, the impact of economies of scale and of agglomeration effects, together with the progressive adjustments of costs and demands that accompany the interregional migration of factors, will produce self-reinforcing dynamic effects – termed polarization – that accentuate rather than ameliorate regional imbalances of real incomes.

Some empirical support can be found for the existence of such effects, although it is seldom easy to determine to what extent the widening disparities can be attributed to a common market effect rather than to the impact of structural factors that would in any case have produced a similar result even in the absence of a common market – as in the case of Britain's altered position in relation to her partners in the EC. The supposed importance of these dynamic effects constitutes an important part of the general case for instituting a regional policy in a common market.

THE IMPACT OF THE EUROPEAN COMMUNITY
ON THE STRATEGY AND PERFORMANCE OF
TRANSNATIONAL ENTERPRISES

The establishment of the EC, and its later enlargement, has been accompanied by much debate on how the common market would affect (*ex ante*) and has affected (*ex post*) the strategies and performance of multinational corporations (MNCs), which account for a significant and growing share of the Community's output, employment and trade, and on how, if at all, the EC should attempt to influence their operation. In seeking to understand these issues it is necessary to start from the factors that influence the behaviour of multinational enterprises across national boundaries, that is to say, the theory of international production. The factors to be explained are the ability of firms to compete in foreign markets, and the reasons why they would choose to exploit their advantages by foreign production, rather than by exporting to the market or by selling access to their special advantages by means of licensing, etc. This is typically explained in terms of an interaction between the ownership advantages that a firm possesses in the form of its command of technology, the internalization factor, which, because of market failure, may make it advantageous for the firm to use the advantages itself rather than to sell the right to their use to producers in other countries, and the locational factor, which makes it advantageous to combine its assets with factors that are located in foreign countries rather than to serve the market by exports (Dunning, 1977).

A closely related way of looking at the issues distinguishes simply between factors specific to the firm, industry or product, on the one hand, and environmental factors on the other. In the specific context of integration, relevant environmental factors would include: the impact of the negative integration that is brought about by trade liberalization; the impact of more positive harmonization measures in the shape of EC health and industrial standards, patent and trade mark legislation (particularly relevant to the internalization factor); and, lastly, the legislation of member states and their overt or covert practices with respect to such factors as public procurement, capital flows, ownership and acquisition.

The earliest aspect of the subject to be given attention was the impact of the EC through the size of the market, its rate of growth, and tariff discrimination, on the inflow of foreign direct investment from outside the Community, and more specifically from the US. In the quantitative aggregative studies that have been undertaken a strong relationship has commonly been found between the size of the EEC markets and American foreign direct investment (FDI) in the EC (Balassa, 1977). However, the links between the reported changes in FDI and growth are mixed, or weak. None the less the issue cannot be regarded as wholly settled. In a recent survey, Pelkmans (1984) suggests that an industrial economics approach might be more promising.

Apart from the question of the impact of the EC on inflows of FDI into Europe interest in the impact of the EC on multinational strategy and performance has focused on the two issues mentioned above, namely inter-industry and intra-firm plant specialization, and on the employment impact of intra EC foreign direct investment. Of late these issues have been increasingly viewed in the context of innovation and technological change.

The variety of factors at work with respect to decisions on international production and the interaction that is to be expected between firm-specific and environmental variables suggest that any uniform pattern of behaviour with respect to the impact of the EC factor on the strategies and performance of multinational businesses in Europe is hardly to be looked for. And indeed it is the case that few strong generalizations emerge from the more realistic of the models of international business or market structure and foreign trade. *A priori,* however, it is widely supposed that the integration of national economies might be expected to have two opposing effects on the strategy of multinational enterprises in an economic community:

(1) The removal of tariffs and barriers to trade and investment may be expected to result in decreased horizontal integration. Firms producing substantially identical products in plants in different countries should be stimulated to remove duplication if costs differ or if economies of scale are significant, and to concentrate their activities – by divestment – on fewer countries and plants;

(2) The opportunity that integration affords for a better international division of labour might also be expected to stimulate increased vertical integration and perhaps component specialization by MNCs searching for lower costs and scale economies.

One of the earliest systematic studies of these issues was made by

Franko (1976). Using data for the period 1958–71 derived from the Harvard Comparative Multinational Enterprise Project, he analysed the experience of more than eighty of the largest European multinationals – i.e. those with headquarters in the original six member states of the EC. He found little evidence in their conduct of either of the effects distinguished above. On the contrary, despite the fact that tariff barriers in Europe were crumbling during this period, there was a proliferation of international operations in Europe by European multinationals at a rate faster than their rate of growth of foreign production in most other parts of the world. Moreover, particularly high concentrations of foreign subsidiaries in Europe were reported for a number of oligopolistic industries where economies of scale were presumptively very large, such as cans, glass, power turbines, iron and steel, processed foods, industrial chemicals and paints. In the products of these industries, intra-EC trade expansion in the period was relatively low. Only in a very limited number of sectors, such as automobiles, electrical appliances and white goods, were there relatively few acquisitions, even some divestments and an extremely rapid growth of intra-European trade. He concluded that 'reallocation of production did not seem to be a major preoccupation for most Continental firms prior to 1971' and that the behaviour reported is to be explained in terms of efforts by both MNCs and governments to protect existing patterns of activity and investments.

Franko's analysis, which is based on an enumeration of legally incorporated entities, may understate the degree of actual plant closures and product reallocation in the period. Furthermore, his data disregarded the experience of all multinationals with headquarters outside the Six, including the numerically important and, in the case of some industries, dominant US multinationals. Many of these firms – Honeywell, Ford, International Harvester – operate in industries where technology is an important source of competitive strength. In such firms there has been a well-documented tendency, since 1960, for European plants that were previously truncated replicas of their parent companies, each producing similar products for individual national markets without much trade between them, to specialize in particular products and processes for all markets in the region and to trade these products across national boundaries (Dunning, 1983). The formation of Ford (Europe) in 1967, specifically to coordinate and integrate European production, was a major step towards the international rationalization of the motor industry that was undoubtedly stimulated by the progress of the EC.

The numerous studies of the operation of multinational enterprises in Europe that have appeared since the mid-1970s convey a complex picture with respect to the issues that have been singled out for discussion here, and one that cannot be briefly presented. But it is plain that, whatever may have been the case prior to 1970, in the following years 'European' firms – stimulated no doubt in some industries by American MNC behaviour and Japanese competition – have actively sought to rationalize European production, in part by decreased horizontal integration and increased vertical integration and component specialization, although not always with success. Rationalization has been particularly noticeable in the European-owned motor industry, in agricultural machinery and in domestic electrical appliances (refrigerators, freezers, washing machines and driers). In the bearing industry also, significant rationalization took place after 1972, stimulated by the enlargement of the EC and the completion of the EC–EFTA free trade provisions. On the other hand, rationalization has occurred hardly at all in pharmaceuticals, where its progress has been hindered by government controls on the registration of new products and controls over prices (Cantwell, 1987). At the same time, it is clear that frequently European producers based in one country have continued to feel obliged to establish a presence in other countries of the EC – not merely for the purpose of servicing goods imported from headquarters, but also to manufacture. The establishment of such a presence has been attempted in a variety of ways – by acquisition of interests, by mergers and less commonly by the construction of new projects. The experience of the UK's multinationals has been well documented by Stopford and Turner (1985). Their examination of the difficulties encountered by industrial reconstruction initiatives prior to and since 1973 leads them to the conclusion that entry into the European market cannot be achieved by acquisition on a major scale. 'The spirit of the Treaty of Rome does not extend to allowing control of a key national resource to slip into foreign hands, even when those hands are also European.'

One crucial problem in attempting to determine empirically what has been the impact of the EC on multinational strategy, and through it on a variety of variables affecting the incomes and welfare of member states, is to determine, first, what would have happened in the absence of the identified developments, and secondly what part of them is attributable to the presence of the EC. This problem is present in all empirical evaluations of the EC and alternative approaches to its solution are reviewed in Chapter 13. The former issue has been posed most squarely in those studies that have attempted to throw light on the effect of intra-EC direct investment and its employment impact. The *anti-monde* issue is usually tackled in the first instance by reference to the putative relevance of three limiting cases suggested by Hufbauer and Adler (1968). They are:

(1) *The classical case.* This postulates that intra-Community direct investment produces a corresponding net addition to capital formation in the host country but an equivalent decline in the source country so that, overall, capital formation remains unchanged. This implies that intra-Community direct investment is a direct substitute for investment at home and that the output of the investment replaces exports from the source country. Investment in other parts of the Community to take advantage of cheap labour could fall into this category.

(2) *The reverse classical case.* In this case the investment is assumed to be a substitute for investment in the host country and to leave investment in the source country unchanged. This corresponds to the case of defensive investment where restrictions prevent imports into the markets of other Community countries or a presence is required to penetrate them. Without the investment, the source country could not penetrate those markets and would lose it to host country producers.

(3) *The anti-classical case.* In this case, foreign investment is not a substitute for capital investment in the source country and does not reduce investment in host country firms.

These categories can be criticized on account of their rigidity and their static nature and because they ignore market servicing strategies, which concern the decisions with respect to which plants should service which markets and through which channels. Empirical studies of such strategies – which should take account of the significant firm-specific and environmental factors to which reference has been made – illustrate the complexity of these decisions (Buckley and Pearce, 1981). Nevertheless, some anti-monde assumption must be made, and the choice will evidently be crucial to the results reported.

A recent case study (Buckley and Artisien, 1987) that investigates the politically charged question of the impact of intra-EC direct investment on employment in the EC illustrates the issue. The study examines nineteen cases of direct investment by enterprises belonging to more advanced members (France, Germany, the UK) in three less developed members (Greece, Portugal and Spain). The study concludes that the effects on the level of income and employment in the host country were almost invariably positive, but those on the source country were often negative. In itself this study throws no light on the EC effect of multinational behaviour on the level and distribution of employment because it cannot be assumed that this development would not have taken place in the absence of the EC. It is, indeed, highly probable that a large part of the multinational integration that has taken place among enterprises in the EC is to be attributed to the globalization of their operations, and can only be fully understood in the light of the pressures and incentives that have given rise to that phenomenon. Nevertheless, the effect of having intra-EC free trade in force or in prospect is to induce direct investments towards a localization that strengthens *inter*-industry specialization inside the common market. The authors' interpretation of the material suggests that this process has been important.

EC Policy towards MNCs

However MNCs are judged (in terms of private or social efficiency criteria) to have responded to the impact of European integration, it is clear that the outcome has been significantly affected by environmental factors, and in particular by the industrial policies of the member states, and more recently by those of the EC. Many of the factors that impede a more effectual rationalization of European industry geared to the common market are to be attributed not so much to shortcomings of multinational strategies as to a failure on the part of the EC to complete the common market. Some institutional aspects of this issue will be considered in the following section. Here we touch briefly on the question of the EC's MNC policy – perhaps attitudes would be a better term – which has undergone substantial evolution in the past decade.

Initially MNCs as such were not a target of the orthodox instruments of EC policy that impinge on business. These policies (and notably competition policy which intervenes when there is a threat to intra-EC trade) were basically free trade in inspiration and EC actions in the field of company legislation and labour affairs were similarly designed to promote market neutrality and to prevent abuses. Inevitably, however, the importance of the MNCs in the European market and the potential impact of their decisions to invest and divest on individual member states of the EC in terms of employment and income have meant that their operations have attracted particular interest in the actual administration of policy.

None the less, it was not until 1973, with the enunciation of the Commission's action programme with respect to multinationals (Commission, 1973b), that the question of an MNC policy *per se* overtly arose. In that action programme the Commission envisaged controls specifically directed at MNCs (echoing earlier measures proposed by UN and OECD – in those cases largely ineffective). But the Commission's approach to multinationals was not entirely negative; steps were also promised to foster the transnational integration of the member countries' industrial structures. These initiatives and the attitudes they reflected nevertheless appear to have been perceived by the MNCs as a threat. The more aggressive competition policy that was pursued during the 1970s, and the Vredeling draft directive of 1980 (*Bulletin of the European Communities*, Supplement 3, 1980; *Bulletin of the European Communities* 10/1980) aimed at facilitating worker participation and consultation in the affairs of industrial groupings, did nothing to allay those fears.

Whether or not it really was the case that the Commission's attitude towards transnationals at that time was adversarial, it is certainly true that the economic crisis experienced by the EC during the mid-1970s subsequently produced a significant shift of attitudes. From that time it had become plain that the European economy was faced with a severely worsening competitive position vis-à-vis the Third World and the US and Japan. It was widely felt that the problem could not be overcome without a more effectual restructuring of European industry. Within the Commission, an acceptance of this view has been reflected, *inter alia*, in the dominance of a more flexible approach to competition policy that seeks to take greater account of the need not to impede European producers in their attempts to regroup and reorganize in the face of competition, and to facilitate changes in other policy fields designed to speed up institutional changes that could foster such needed development. In the process, business enterprise as a whole, but transnationals in particular, have come to be seen as crucial instruments and allies rather than as adversaries in the achievement of the EC's goals or market integration. The promotion by the EC of transfrontier links in certain key sectors regarded as essential to enable the European economy to withstand the competitive challenge from the US and Japan is an important aspect of this development. It is reflected not only in the initiation and conduct of new projects such as ESPRIT, RACE and BRITE, which presuppose such transnational business links, but also in the new approach to the development of industrial standards and to the harmonization of other areas of policy such as patents and trade marks where

progress will in future be predominantly the responsibility of European business – more and more willingly accepted – and of their
organizations. In the process it seems not unlikely that the former
even-handed treatment of foreign and European transnationals
that has hitherto been a particular feature of EC policy may
undergo modification. In any event, the Europeanization of standards and of patent and trade mark legislation cannot fail to have
important implications for the relative strength and conduct of
European and foreign transnationals.

COMPLETING THE EUROPEAN COMMON MARKET

The European Economic Community is based on the idea of a
common market, and the term itself is used as the colloquial equivalent of the EEC; but in fact there is not yet anything like a full
common market in Western Europe. The pursuit of market integration in Europe may be evaluated in two main ways: first by defining
the measures needed to realize a true common market and comparing them with the prescriptions of the Treaty of Rome; and second
by considering the state of market integration that has been arrived
at by EC decisions and their implementation in member states and
comparing it with the Treaty's prescriptions. From the first point of
view it is indisputable that Treaty prescriptions go a long way in the
direction of the requirements of a full common market, although in
certain respects falling short of an ideal. In this sense a perfect
common market would be a degree of market integration among
member countries in which neither national frontiers, nor residency
nor nationality of economic agents have any differential economic
significance (Pelkmans and Robson, 1987). At the same time, if the
issue is approached from the second point of view, it is equally
indisputable that the actual arrangements of the EC – the *'acquis
communautaire'* – with respect to market integration fall far short of
Treaty requirements. This has led to sometimes exaggerated criticisms of the alleged failure of market integration in Europe, cari-
catured by unsympathetic critics as 'the uncommon market'
(Holland, 1980) or centring on criticisms that the EC has become
merely an area of free trade.

Even today's incomplete common market embodies a number of
respectable achievements. What the EC has accomplished in terms
of market integration is both historically unique – given the absence
of coercion that has accompanied it – and economically significant.
Disillusion derives from the even greater aspirations that the EC

proclaims and its failure to live up to them. Of late, an awareness of the costs involved in maintaining an incomplete common market, in terms of the obstacles it imposes to industrial reconstruction and rationalization, has greatly increased. This partly explains why an appreciation of the achievements of the common market has lately been overshadowed by a lamentation over its omissions and failures.

It is in this context that the Commission's White Paper (Commission, 1985) on completing the common market is to be viewed. This paper represents a plan for a large scale assault on the limitations of the common market with the objective of completing it by 1992. Unlike some other EC initiatives, the plan has not been launched in a political vacuum. It has been embraced by the European Council. The aim of completing the common market has moreover been included in the Single European Act (Lodge, 1986) in a formulation that is stronger than the Rome Treaty, which itself contains no reference to eliminating frontiers in the common market. What progress has been made towards the establishment of a common market in Europe? What remains to be done? What are the Commission's proposals?

The European Common Market: Institutional Progress, Gaps and Plans

If purely physical and administrative obstacles are put on one side, together with the fiscal barriers that will be discussed in Chapter 8, the principal remaining obstacles to an undivided internal market in Europe may be divided into (1) those affecting the movement of products, including both goods and services; and (2) those affecting the free movement of factors – labour, capital and enterprise.

FREE MOVEMENT OF PRODUCTS

With respect to the movement of goods, it has already been noted that a variety of non-tariff barriers associated with 'voluntary' industrial standards and governmental health and safety regulations impede the free movement in Europe and the establishment of a single unified market. Hitherto the Community has utilized Article 100 of the Treaty of Rome in its efforts to bring about a harmonization of technical regulations. This article provides for the issue of directives on the basis of unanimity for the harmonization of national legal provisions that directly affect the functioning of the common market. Progress along this line has been painfully slow, in part because of the need to incorporate detailed technical specifications into directives. Henceforward the two-stage procedure that is envisaged in the 'new approach' of the White Paper will consist of laying down, it is hoped in most cases on the basis of qualified majority voting, only those identical requirements or objectives that are seen to be 'essential' in the interests of health, safety and environmental protection. The tasks of actually laying down the technical specifications necessary to meet the requirements as defined in the regulations, will be left to European standards bodies (CEN, CENELEC, etc.). This approach is calculated to make it much more difficult for harmonization to be resisted by vested interests.

A second area of difficulty in relation to the free movement of goods relates to public procurement. In principle, the basic rules of the Treaty apply fully to the supply of goods to public purchasing bodies, as do the rules relating to the freedom to provide services without discrimination. But whereas member states meet 20–40 per cent if not more of the requirements of private consumption by supplies from another member state, the corresponding ratio for public procurement is probably rather less than 1 per cent, if not zero. Since 1971 public works contracts are supposed to be advertised in the *Official Journal* and contracts awarded to the most economic tender. Since 1978 similar provisions have also applied to supply contracts. Reports prepared by the Commission in 1984 (*Bulletin of the European Communities* 12/1984, 6/1985) and endorsed by the European Parliament suggest that neither the letter nor the spirit of the directives is being adhered to. For instance, according to the Commission, less than a quarter of the public expenditure involved in public contracts in fields covered by the existing directives is advertised in the *Official Journal*. Recession is encouraging the use of national suppliers. The Commission's reports do suggest, however, that an important factor hindering effectual Community-wide competition is the lack of harmonization of technical standards. The Commission has proposed a number of measures to open up this important area of the market, including the broadening of the field of application of the relevant directives to cover certain transport services, energy, water and telecommunications, and the establishment of a public procurement unit to monitor action.

Freedom to provide services across the internal frontiers of the Community is also provided for in the Treaty, but progress has been still slower in this area, not only in relation to traditional services such as transport and insurance and banking, but also in relation to services associated with the development of new technologies such as audiovisual services, information and data processing services and certain forms of telecommunications. The importance of making progress in this area is underlined by the growing role of the service sector in the economies of the EC, where it now accounts for a more substantial share of GDP than industry – and by contrast to that sector is generating a growing volume of employment. Any liberalization of the financial service sector in banking and insurance is necessarily closely linked to the free movement of capital, which is discussed below.

FREE MOVEMENT OF LABOUR

Freedom of movement for workers and the abolition of discrimination by nationality is required by the Treaty of Rome and the provisions for it are formally almost complete except for a limited right of public authorities to reserve posts for nationals. The Treaty provisions on labour mobility have been supported by the adoption of social security provisions that entitle migrants who are nationals of member states to the same benefits as those of nationals of the host countries.

Despite substantial differences in levels of wages and social security benefits among the EC countries, intra-Community labour migration, at least of non-professional workers, has to date been modest. Until the 1970s the main internal source of Community migrants was Italy. Migration seems to have been stimulated largely by the lack of employment opportunities rather than by differences in wage rates and earnings. The principal source of migrants has in fact been non-Community states, such as Turkey, Yugoslavia and Portugal, the latter a member since 1986.

In the field of the professions, and the right of establishment for the self-employed, on the other hand, very slow progress has been made towards freedom of movement. The complexities of harmonizing the requirements for professional recognition have proved to be immense. Considerable freedom has nevertheless been secured for those engaged in medicine and nursing. But the right of establishment for architects and pharmacists was not approved until 1985, after respectively seventeen and fourteen years of discussion!

CAPITAL FLOWS: POLICY AND EXPERIENCE IN THE EC

With respect to the integration of capital markets, the Treaty of Rome commits member states progressively to abolish restrictions on intra-EC capital movements to the extent necessary to secure the proper functioning of the Common Market, including the abolition of discriminatory restrictions based on nationality and place of residence. However, under Article 73, if the movement of capital disturbs the capital market of a member state, the Commission may, after consulting the Monetary Committee, authorize a state to take protective measures. The Council itself may revoke or amend such authorization. In addition, under Article 109, which relates to balance of payments policy, a member state is allowed to take certain measures in the event of a crisis, which could include control of capital movements.

Unlike the Treaty provisions relating to free trade in goods and services, the principle of freedom of capital movements does not apply directly. All progress towards liberalization requires the imposition of Community obligations by agreed adoption of directives by the Council. Two such directives were agreed in 1960 and 1962. They resulted in the removal of restrictions on direct investment, portfolio investment in quoted securities, transactions involving real estate, and certain others. These provisions can only be revoked under the emergency provisions of Articles 73 and 109. Liberalization was also agreed in principle for certain other capital flows, but on certain grounds member states were permitted to seek a dispensation from the applications of EC regulations in those fields. The Commission also attempted to liberalize capital flows by means of a third directive that required each member to permit new foreign issues on its security markets up to a certain percentage of all new public issues, but this directive was not adopted.

At Community level, the position that had been reached in 1962 remained formally unchanged until November 1986 when finance ministers agreed to widen the range of capital movements to be freed from exchange controls. This latest directive, which should come into effect in 1987, is the first element of a three-stage liberalization plan. The directive largely reflects the status quo and the separate easing of exchange controls that has already occurred in a number of member states, several of which – West Germany, the UK, Belgium, Luxemburg, the Netherlands and Denmark – have virtually no controls left. Other members however, such as France, Italy and Ireland, have enjoyed dispensations from existing provisions on grounds of balance of payments difficulties. Although they and other members have also eased their controls recently, they fall short of compliance with the latest regulation and will either have to try to liberalize further or seek a dispensation from the new rules.

Apart from the exchange controls that currently remain, many national legal and administrative regulations obstruct the free operation of a Community capital market, as do differences in national systems of direct taxation. Efforts by the Commission to deal with these national regulations have so far made little progress. Similarly, although a proposal for a directive on the harmonization of corporation tax was made some years ago by the Commission, it has yet to be adopted by the Council.

The Community has thus made some progress towards freeing capital flows and integrating its capital markets but a completely free and integrated market certainly does not yet exist.

ENTERPRISE

Apart from the formal removal of restrictions on foreign direct investment, there is also the question of what positive measures are required if cooperation and integration amongst enterprises in the Community are to be effectual – if there is to be a Community-wide integration of enterprise. In this area the absence of a legal framework for cross-border activities by enterprises and for cooperation amongst enterprises from different member states may have hampered cooperation and the development of joint projects. To overcome this the Commission has proposed to establish a new type of association to be known as the European Economic Interest Grouping, which would be governed by uniform Community legislation, with the object of making it easier for enterprises from different Community states to undertake specific activities. A statute for a European company has also been proposed.

Another important area that impinges on transnational integration and the mobility of enterprise is the differences in trade mark and patent legislation from one country to another. This inevitably has a negative impact on intra-Community trade and prevents enterprises from treating the common market as a single environment for their activities. Proposals are under consideration for a Community trade mark and for the harmonization of national trade mark laws. In the field of patents, a Convention on the Community Patent was signed in 1975 but it has not yet entered in force.

This brief review of the stage reached in progressing towards a complete common market highlights the areas in which progress is needed if the internal market of the EC is to be freed of barriers to its full integration. The Commission's White Paper is an action plan of breathtaking ambition for overcoming those barriers. Its implementation is likely to throw into sharp relief the need for the Community to expand the effectiveness of measures and to develop new policies to assist member states to deal with the acute adjustment problems that are likely to be entailed. Indeed, without such measures, the prospect of full implementation is not only likely to be remote; it would also be undesirable.

CONCLUSION

Even if macroeconomic policy issues are disregarded, an assessment of the effects and of the costs and benefits of factor market integration involves many complex issues. Although important efficiency gains may be secured by a move from a customs union to a common market, the need for an effective regional policy will almost certainly become more acute if structural forces contributing to economic divergence and possible losses for certain member states are to be contained. Moreover, if the presence of monopoly is strengthened by a common market through increased opportunities to exploit scale economies, there may be adverse allocational consequences to take into account, in addition to adverse distributional effects. Above all, if integration significantly expands the role of transnational corporations – at least of those based outside the common market and therefore less amenable to its control – the assessment becomes still more complex, for the maintenance of national sovereignty is likely to be an important policy objective for most member states. In terms of political economy considerations, a neoclassical preoccupation with competitive allocational gains that neglects such crucial aspects of the problem as seen by policy makers is of limited value.

CHAPTER 7

Fiscal Integration

Fiscal integration refers to the role of public finance and of a community's budget in arrangements for international economic integration. The theory of fiscal integration seeks primarily to provide a rationale for the integration of budgetary functions and their appropriate assignment between community and member states in terms of considerations of fiscal efficiency. It thus deals with the question of optimal fiscal domains in economic groupings. At a more practical level, it studies the structure, evolution and impact of actual community budgets. The integration of fiscal functions results in fiscal union, a situation in which the choice of policy targets and the administration of policy instruments are a matter for the community's authority. Fiscal integration in this sense is to be distinguished both from *fiscal harmonization*, which refers to agreement on the manner in which each member state will utilize a particular fiscal instrument over which it retains control, and from *fiscal coordination*, which refers to largely unenforceable and voluntary alignments of national policies in the fiscal arena. The significance of these other forms of fiscal cooperation in practice is often considerable. This chapter deals mainly with fiscal integration. The issues that arise in fiscal harmonization are discussed in Chapter 8.

OPTIMAL FISCAL DOMAINS

Any analysis of fiscal integration confronts the difficulty that, in contrast to the issue of customs and monetary unions, there is no single well-demarcated case to address. A spectrum of workable states of integration can be envisaged that ranges from simple customs unions by way of economic communities up to other forms that approach the status of a full economic union. In each case the degree of fiscal union and the role of the community budget will necessarily vary as a result of essentially political choices about the transfer of authority from the member states to the community over decisions that affect public expenditure and its financing, and, to a degree, as a result of the internal dynamics of the system that is established.

Yet fiscal efficiency is a significant factor in its own right, and in each state of economic integration there will normally exist some degree of flexibility that would permit adjustments to be made on economic grounds. Moreover, economic communities change. In considering their evolution, it is important to appreciate the general considerations that bear on the construction of efficient fiscal structures even though any such analysis must perforce largely disregard significant non-economic and non-fiscal factors.

In order to analyse the issues of fiscal integration in these terms, it is useful to start by considering what fiscal functions are performed through national budgets. In both unitary states and federations the national budget is a crucial instrument of national economic management whose size and structure reflects the nation's varied political, social and economic objectives. The budget affects an economy in a variety of ways that in practice cannot be separated, but for analytical purposes it is convenient to distinguish three distinct impacts that are bound up with three separable objectives of public policy. These concern: (1) the allocation of resources; (2) the redistribution of incomes; and (3) macroeconomic objectives.

The allocation function of a budget has to do with the provision or encouragement through the budget of 'public goods'. These are goods or services not effectively provided by the market either because of the characteristics of the good itself or because of imperfections in the market mechanism. The redistribution function is concerned with the use of tax and expenditure policies to alter the regional or personal distribution of incomes that is brought about by the market. The macroeconomic function of the budget refers to its use to achieve objectives in the field of price stability, external equilibrium and perhaps employment and economic growth, although these last two are seen nowadays as more a matter for structural policies.

In international economic groupings, the same three fiscal functions either must be performed at the level of the member states that carry them out prior to integration, or they must be assigned wholly or partly to institutions of the community, together with any additional functions necessitated by its creation.

The principles put forward in the literature of public finance (Musgrave 1969) to determine the efficient assignment of fiscal responsibilities amongst different tiers of authority appeal to one or more of three principal phenomena that are employed as criteria, namely: economies of scale; externalities and spillovers; political homogeneity. In a more complete analysis other criteria would have to be considered (Oates, 1972, 1977; Forte, 1977), of which the need for democratic control is obviously important.

The general bearing of the three indicated criteria on the assignment of fiscal responsibilities and so on fiscal integration can be stated very simply. If significant technological or pecuniary economies of scale or of size are generated when certain public activities are jointly conducted, there may be a *prima facie* case on efficiency grounds, in the absence of sufficiently powerful countervailing considerations, for assigning these activities to an upper authority or tier of government that can conduct them on a sufficiently large scale to secure the benefits of reduced costs for the group. The externality or spillover criterion becomes relevant whenever public policies or expenditures necessarily have effects that significantly affect other governments. Such effects constitute an alternative or an additional *prima facie* efficiency ground for assigning the activity in question at least in part to an upper-level authority that can encompass them. Political homogeneity refers to a similarity of preferences or tastes as expressed in shared criteria of political, social and economic choice for the provision of public goods. A high degree of homogeneity amongst defined political units should strengthen the efficiency case for the assignment of particular functions to the highest level, if efficiency justifications based on the significance of scale economies, spillovers or externalities pointed to doing so in the first place. The existence of a diversity of preferences, on the other hand, is at the core of the orthodox case for supposing that welfare will be maximized by decentralization in the provision of public goods and the conduct of public functions. The phenomenon of political homogeneity, although regularly appealed to in connection with the analysis of fiscal efficiency, is not a satisfactory criterion because of the difficulty of characterizing it in operational terms and the lack of an independent measure of its extent. In the last resort, the presence of a sufficient degree of homogeneity can be inferred only from the observed readiness of governments to integrate or transfer certain of their functions.

In its application to the functions and objectives of budgetary policy, the general inter-governmental assignment that is proposed for nation states by reference to these criteria as they find expression in their most comprehensive presentation, namely the theory of fiscal federalism (Oates, 1972, 1977), is that the resource allocation function should be shared amongst upper and lower tiers of government according to the particular 'public goods' characteristics of the services to be provided and the homogeneity or disparateness of the preferences for them, whereas both the redistribution function and the stabilization function should be carried out at the highest level.

FUNCTIONAL CRITERIA AND FISCAL INTEGRATION IN ECONOMIC GROUPINGS

There are evident limitations to the application of this analysis to the specific issue of fiscal integration in international economic groupings, in which the community's authority is identified with the highest level. Most obviously, although the most important of present-day economic communities – the European Economic Community – is more than a simple international regime, and to some observers 'incontestably represents a new level of government' (Wallace, 1983, p. 406), perhaps having some of the qualities of federation or at least of confederation, it is so far unique. The authorities of other economic groupings cannot qualify to be regarded as governments. A further limitation of assignment analysis is that it is essentially framed in wholly static terms, in the sense that the political regime and its criteria are both taken as given. Yet most present-day economic communities are basically immature and are evolving. To the extent that this is a widespread, if not indeed an essential characteristic, integration should be viewed as a process and not merely as a state of affairs. The orthodox analysis of fiscal federalism can throw little light on the dynamics of integration, yet nowhere is it more important than in relation to a consideration of community budgetary issues which not only encapsulate and reflect the whole political economy of integration, but also modify it. Nevertheless, although the criteria cited are static, elusive and only partly operational they remain within their limits analytically instructive categories. The following three sections consider in more detail their implications for fiscal integration in the specific context of economic groupings.

The Allocation Function

In the member states of most present-day economic communities, a large proportion of public expenditure is allocated to the provision of such public goods as defence and social services, notably education, health and in some cases social security. In the case of defence, both economies of scale and spillover effects are without question highly significant. So far however, without exception, the operation of political considerations has excluded the conduct of defence on an integrated basis. In the provision of social services, significant economies of scale are fewer, although modest spillover effects are not uncommon. But an overriding consideration with respect to integrated provision in this sphere of activity is that in most economic communities there is a marked lack of homogeneity of preferences, traditions and attitudes. To that extent the case for the integration of social services and policies cannot be strong.

There is also to be considered the substantial range of regulatory public functions – including some that will be called into existence by the establishment of a bloc – that concerns such matters as the implementation of technical, environmental, safety and health standards, issues of tax harmonization, the operation of the common market and customs union, state aids to industry and external trade policy issues and negotiations. For all of these categories a strong case can be made out by appeal to spillovers, scale economies, and to the need to make the market effective, for the exercise of a degree of community authority. In practice, however, few of these regulatory functions will call for any substantial public expenditures.

In short, in terms of the allocation function, the application of orthodox criteria suggests that the strictly necessary and appropriate degree of fiscal integration for those economic communities composed of market economies would appear to be modest. This indeed is what is found – even in the EC. Universally, levels of 'community' expenditure represent only a minute fraction of the expenditures of member states and a still smaller fraction of their national incomes. Such an outcome is not formally inconsistent with the rather general policy stance of fiscal federalism with respect to the provision of public goods. The indicated assignments in relation to the other budgetary functions are, however, much stronger. Are they appropriate or relevant for economic groupings?

The Redistribution Function

In unitary states, large-scale fiscal redistribution takes place from the centre to the regions primarily and automatically as a result of the operation of policies of personal taxation and public expenditure affecting individuals that are nation-wide in operation but have diverse regional impacts in the face of the varying geographical incidence of prosperity. In federations too, a substantial measure of redistribution takes place from the federal level to the states, but in this case mainly as a result of specific or general inter-governmental grants.

In its spatial aspects, fiscal redistribution serves several important and interrelated purposes:

- it contributes to a more equitable spatial distribution of the burden of cyclical fluctuations;
- it effectively compensates for the inability of states or regions to conduct their own trade and exchange rate policies for the purpose of overcoming their regional problems;
- it helps to promote more uniform and perhaps convergent economic standards and performance in the various regions;
- it helps to discourage unacceptably large inter-state or inter-regional migration flows.

Orthodox analysis points unequivocally to a fiscal structure in which the primary responsibility for the performance of the redistribution function rests with the central or highest tier of government. This assignment is rationalized chiefly in terms of the high degree of factor mobility that is taken to characterize most unions and federations. Effectively this gives rise to significant leakages and spillovers that will establish narrow practical limits to the effective jurisdiction of lower-tier governments with respect to distributional matters, and in particular to their capacity to influence the personal distribution of incomes, the economic development of their regions, or their standards of social and economic provision through tax and expenditure policies that are significantly different from those of other member states or of other regions.

In application to present-day economic groupings this particular justification for assigning the distributive function solely or primarily to the community level would carry much less weight. First, even when, as in a common market, restrictions on factor mobility are formally absent, the effective mobility of persons and, to a lesser degree, of corporations is usually much lower than is the case in economic unions as a result of linguistic and cultural factors. The effective jurisdiction of the member states is thus reinforced and is likely to be eroded only gradually with the passage of time. Another factor that reinforces their ability to influence incomes is that few economic communities have yet instituted a monetary union, so that their member states retain their nominal monetary autonomy. Consequently it is open to them to seek to influence their relative real wage costs through exchange rate changes, for the purpose of limiting the acuteness of any emergent adjustment problem. The absence of monetary union is likely in any case to pose major practical difficulties to the centralized collection of taxes. To that extent fiscal integration and monetary integration must go hand in hand.

Despite the questionable relevance for economic groupings of the principal orthodox arguments for assigning the distributive function to the top tier, distributional considerations cannot be ignored at community level, though for different if equally strong reasons. The cohesion and vigour of a community will demand that each member state has an equitable stake in its operations, and the future of some communities may stand or fall on the way in which distributional issues are resolved. The orthodox analysis, in its federalist presentation, assumes that the top tier of authority actually possesses supranational powers that enable it to tax individual citizens or enterprises directly. This is not so in present-day economic communities, where in effect community actions must be financed by submitting demands to the member states. To the extent that conventional categories of government can usefully be applied to the phenomenon of international integration and in particular to its redistributive aspects, it is thus the characteristics of a confederal rather than a federal mode that are primarily relevant. Such a mode virtually rules out the possibility of significant and deliberate redistribution other than by common consent.

In purely fiscal terms therefore, so long as this situation continues, the redistribution function in such economic communities can be exercised only through the impact of agreed expenditure policies, and ultimately through the freely agreed criteria for determining the budgetary contributions of member states to their financing. There are two well-established alternative fiscal principles in the light of which such contributions to a community budget might be determined, namely the benefit principle and the principle of ability to pay. Their implications are very different.

The benefit principle amounts to the proposition that those who reap the benefits of public expenditure should contribute correspondingly to its costs. One interpretation of this would be that each country should so far as possible get back in the form of attributable expenditure what it contributes to finance the common policies. In the context of the EC budget debate that is briefly discussed below, this is the notion of *juste retour*. It carries the implication that the budget itself should be neutral in its impact on inter-country income distribution. If it were adopted, budgetary transfers could not be used on a continuing basis to promote a convergence of living standards amongst the member states or for any long-run redistributive purposes whatsoever, although short-term spatial redistribution on a basis of long-term balance would not necessarily be ruled out.

The contributory principle that underlies most national fiscal systems is different, and rests instead on a concept of equity that has horizontal and vertical aspects. Horizontal equity is usually taken to mean that equally situated individuals should be taxed equally, while vertical equity requires that unequals should be taxed unequally. These notions have been widely interpreted to justify the use of the criterion of ability to pay as a basis for distributing tax burdens and this in turn is usually taken to imply the need for a progressive system of taxation. Applied to arrangements for international economic integration at the level of nations, the adoption of this principle would require that net budgetary contributions should broadly reflect differences in the ability to pay of different member states.

Of these two principles, the first has in its favour two important advantages: it is unambiguous and it is substantially operational. If it were to be adopted as a criterion for determining inter-state financial contributions to a community budget, it would be illogical to confine its application to the budget if there should be other important transfers directly attributable to the community's policies that arise outside the formal framework of its budget. A country might be a net contributor to a community budget but might nevertheless derive economic benefits – or incur costs – through other channels, notably through the impact of intra-community free trade on its income, employment and, so, on its public revenues. Thus, even if a primary criterion for contribution were accepted to be that of *juste retour*, it would not be possible to determine the *effective* revenue contribution of a member state without considering what its public revenues would have been in the absence of the policies reflected in the budget. Nevertheless, a concentration on the purely *formal* incidence of financial transfers or budgetary contributions is understandable because these transfers are transparent and they are for the most part capable of being attributed to member states, whereas accurate quantification and attribution of other transfers is generally difficult and sometimes impossible.

The alternative contributory principle, which emphasizes ability to pay in relation to contribution and need in relation to expenditure, would evidently be more appropriate for a community that accepts that balanced development and perhaps economic convergence should be objectives of its operations. Evidently it is the translation of this principle into operational terms that is the crux of the matter. This can be the outcome only of a political process through which acceptable guidelines to the degree and pace of its attainment can be evolved.

Macroeconomic Policy

Discussion of the conduct of macroeconomic policy in an economic community and of its implications for fiscal integration must acknowledge that, even in a national context, there is not full agreement about (1) whether in principle macroeconomic policies can have real effects on output and employment, (2) the relative efficacy of different policy instruments, or (3) the practicability of public intervention for stabilization purposes. The issues and their bearing on fiscal integration may be exposed in a highly simplified manner by contrasting different macroeconomic schools of thought and their associated policy stances.

In the mid-1970s the issue of principle could have been presented in terms of a stark contrast between the views of Keynesians and monetarists with respect to the use of monetary and fiscal policy instruments for influencing the level of aggregate demand. Today the issue is better presented in rather different terms, partly as a result of important developments in theory, but not least because of the impact of the experience of the last two decades on the way the issues have come to be viewed. Since the mid-1970s, many Keynesians and monetarists have come together on key issues that formerly divided them in respect of both theory and policy. To this eclectic approach Cobham (1984) has given the name 'the convergence school'. One of its essential features is that, although the long-run aggregate supply curve of the economy is assumed to be vertical, the short-run curve is taken to be upward-sloping, implying that in principle scope exists for influencing the real variables of employment and output in the short run. The policy recommendations of the convergence school are that monetary and fiscal policy should be used together to keep output and employment near their natural rates without causing inflation by creating excess demand.

This approach may be contrasted with what is termed the new classical macroeconomics, which has been developed by certain other monetarists. From the present standpoint it suffices to note that this school views the aggregate supply curve as being essentially vertical and that it contends that stabilization policy causes movements in prices, not output. Its policy recommendation is that stabilization policy should be confined to the use of monetary policy to prevent inflation.

These opposed perspectives on theory and stabilization policy have clear implications for the macroeconomic dimension of fiscal integration. In terms of the new classical macroeconomics, there is no justification for the pursuit of macroeconomic policy objectives through the budget, whether this be a national or a community budget. On the other hand, given that there is a role for fiscal policy as the more eclectic approach contends, a case in principle could be made out for taking any such action jointly at the community level. This will be so if the economies of the member states are structurally interdependent; the case for integration would be strengthened if there also exists *policy* interdependence. These concepts must be briefly explained.

Structural interdependence arises when certain member states are so important in the markets of the others that changes in economic events in the former significantly influence private market behaviour and so the prices, incomes and levels of economic activity of the latter, which impinge in turn on the first country. This in turn may give rise directly to a high degree of policy interdependence in the sense that the optimal course of action for one country depends decisively on the action taken by another country and vice versa. Structural and policy interdependence are a reflection of spillovers and externalities. They are likely to be present in economies that exhibit a high degree of integration in terms of trade flows. Their importance in the present context is that, where they exist, the outcome in the absence of joint action is unlikely to be efficient in the sense that policies will exist that could make all member states better off.

The issue may be illustrated by considering the example of an expansion of demand engineered in a member country (the home country) by a unilateral fiscal policy expansion. It is assumed that a flexible exchange rate regime is in force and that each member retains its monetary autonomy. If fiscal expansion raises real output and real incomes, at the initial exchange rate some part of the extra incomes would be spent on imports and thus leak. Consequently the exchange rate would have to deteriorate in order to maintain current account balance, giving rise to an initial deterioration in the terms of trade. The effect would be to erode the impact on real income of any given fiscal-induced output expansion. If the deterioration in the exchange rate generates inflation, the initial expansion in output and incomes could even be reversed. At the same time, the corresponding improvement in the terms of trade of the partner country or countries is from their point of view a positive effect and may be expected to give rise to greater output and employment. To the extent that it does, it should moderate the initial deterioration of the terms of trade of the home country.

In such circumstances, where each country can influence the other country's macroeconomic constraints, unilateral fiscal expansion may be largely ineffective and all may get stuck in a low-output equilibrium. If, however, other member countries simultaneously expand, any terms-of-trade effects could be offset or substantially moderated, and a sustained expansion might thus be feasible. In terms of the theory of fiscal integration, the policy conclusion would be that, if such gains are significant, macroeconomic policy objectives should be pursued through fiscal integration at a higher level of government that possesses a sufficiently broad jurisdiction to encompass the spillover and leakage effects and their reciprocity that essentially give rise to this problem.

There may, however, be major practical obstacles to macro-fiscal integration in an economic community. The member states may not agree on objectives – for instance with respect to the speed at which inflation shall be reduced. Or they may disagree on the impact that policy measures would have. Even if they do agree on objectives and broad policies, differences in their economic circumstances may imply very different costs and benefits for individual member states with respect to the distribution of the burdens and benefits of any fiscal action. To overcome this problem might not be out of the question, but the solution could imply a need for substantial inter-member state redistributive flows brought about through the budget.

Where circumstances do not favour fiscal integration, gains may still be pursued through a looser form of joint action, taking the form of a coordination of the magnitude and timing of the fiscal policies of member states in such a way as to take account of their impact on other members. This approach confronts other difficulties, however, not the least of which is that coordination, even if based upon rules, and still more so if it is not, would require continual negotiation and that process would take time. The time lags inherent in the decision-taking process at community level, coupled with others that are in any case inherent in the response of households and enterprises to experienced changes in policy variables, may invite scepticism about the capacity of public policy at community level to smooth out short-run fluctuations in output and employment. At the purely national level indeed, some economists have long contended that, for such reasons, stabilization policy is inherently likely to exacerbate rather than reduce fluctuations.

In any case, apart from time lags, it would be a gross oversimplification to conclude that either fiscal integration or fiscal coordination *per se* would necessarily and inevitably contribute to the overall stability of an international grouping. An unavoidable uncertainty besets both forecasts of future economic conditions and estimates of key parameters of the system. If those difficulties should result in the policies that are jointly operated being ill-chosen, synchronization may exaggerate any inherent instability.

The issues involved in international policy coordination are both analytically complex and at the same time of great potential practical significance. The growing literature and its bearing on theoretical and practical issues of policy coordination is admirably surveyed in a broad context by Cooper (1985). Empirical studies of interdependence, including the European Commission's Eurolink model are compared in Helliwell and Padmore (1985).

In considering whether coordination is worth pursuing, a crucial question is how significant its gains are likely to be. A recent empirical study (Oudiz and Sachs, 1984) confirms the presence of gains from coordinated expansion but claims that they appear to be modest, amounting to the utility equivalent of one half of one percentage point of GNP in each of the next few years for the case in which the US, West Germany and Japan are assumed to be the only countries taking the policy actions. If West German policy were matched throughout the EC, the gains to coordination should be at least twice as large. These gains might still appear to be modest, but it has to be stressed that the calculation refers to only one of several possible sources of gain from coordination.

Direct fiscal action for stabilization purposes through the budget of an economic community itself as opposed to the coordination of national fiscal policies would in any case pose three important related problems not mentioned up to this point, namely: (1) the financing and management of any ensuing debt; (2) the scale of the budgetary operations that would be required to achieve an adequate stabilization impact; and (3) the specific expenditure and revenue implications of the operations. To conclude this discussion, these three issues will be briefly commented on.

As to debt management, to the extent that the operation of a community fiscal stabilization policy would from time to time require the financing of deficits it would call for the adoption of a formula for distributing the burden of the resulting community debt amongst the member states. Moreover, if monetary integration is lacking and monetary policy rests wholly with the national authorities, it would not be possible for community-level fiscal stabilization measures to be financed through monetary expansion brought about by the community authority itself. In principle, a community could be authorized to finance stabilization initiatives by means of deficits financed by the issue of its own bonds on the separate national capital markets of the member states. Such a power could be an important instrument for bringing about an integration of the group's capital markets. But since it would necessarily interfere with national control over monetary conditions, it is unlikely to be feasible except within narrowly prescribed limits, unless monetary integration were itself practicable. Without monetary integration, a community's borrowing capability must ultimately depend on the goodwill and the policies of the national monetary authorities. The conclusion must be that the debt management policy needed to operate a community-level fiscal stabilization policy could only be conducted either in conjunction with arrangements for effective cooperation with the member states or on the basis of monetary integration.

As to the question of the critical scale required for effectual macroeconomic intervention at community level, the typically small size of a community budget in an immature economic community implies that, if it were to have the capacity for exercising a significant stabilization effect on the community's economy, it would be necessary for the balance of the budget to swing by enormous fractions. For the EC itself even, it has been suggested (Commission, 1977a) that a swing of as much as 50 per cent would be required. It may thus be necessary for certain allocative functions to be assigned to the community level specifically in order to give it enough scope for performing a stabilization function.

In short, any *prima facie* justification based on considerations of spillover and interdependence for the assignment of a stabilization role to the community, and for the development of a corresponding degree of fiscal integration in highly trade-integrated groups, has clearly to be set against other important considerations. The principal obstacle to fiscal integration for this purpose is that countries differ in their objectives and needs, so that there may be conflicting targets. Even if this consideration is not significant, the scope for and the pace of any such integration and intervention by the community will be constrained both by the progress that can be made towards the coordination and integration of monetary policies and by the scope for the adoption of community-level policies that could serve as the basis of a substantial and easily rephasable programme of community revenue and expenditure with potentiality for a strongly redistributive effect. In the face of such obstacles, the only practicable course may be to seek an improved coordination of national fiscal policies. However, the process of achieving coordination by perhaps protracted intra-community negotiation is likely to mean that some of the practical difficulties in the way of timely intervention may be even more intractable at the community level than they are at the national level.

In the light of this analytical discussion of issues of fiscal integration we turn next to an outline of the EC budget and to a brief review of how some of the issues that have been identified in this section have made themselves felt since 1970.

BUDGETARY ISSUES IN THE EUROPEAN COMMUNITY

The budget of the European Community differs in several key respects from the national budgets of its member states:

- its size is minuscule in relation to the Community's economy;
- under the Treaty of Rome, revenue and expenditure must be in balance;
- the budget does not perform a significant redistributive function, although *de facto* it has redistributed resources in a regressive way;
- the budget has no stabilization role.

At the present stage of the EC's development its budget is to be viewed simply as the instrument for financing a limited range of policies of very varying importance that the EC has agreed to establish, notably the common agricultural policy (CAP), regional, social and overseas aid policies, and a few lesser activities in the fields of industry, technology and research.

The Budgetary Process

The process of determining the Community's budget is lengthy and complex. The main stages are as follows:

1. Presentation of the Preliminary Draft Budget by the European Commission (June).
2. Amendment and adoption of Draft Budget by the Council of Ministers (July or September).
3. First reading by the European Parliament (October or November).
4. Second examination by the Council of Ministers (November).
5. Second reading by the European Parliament (December).

The preliminary draft budget, which is prepared by the Commission (taking account of guidelines laid down by the Council at its initial budget discussion in April), can be amended by both the Council and the Parliament. In considering the power to amend, two types of Community expenditure must be distinguished. 'Compulsory' expenditure is that which is required to meet the EC's legal obligations, such as support prices for farmers and finance committed to developing countries under international agreements.

'Non-compulsory' expenditure is broadly all other expenditure undertaken with the aim of fostering the process of European integration. In its first reading of the budget, Parliament can propose 'modifications' to obligatory expenditure; these can be overturned by the Council (which takes its decisions by qualified majority vote) on its second examination. Parliament can also propose 'amendments' to the items of non-compulsory expenditure, subject to certain ceilings, and even if these amendments are rejected by the Council they can be reinstated by Parliament at its second reading when it votes on the budget as a whole and may reject it (as it did in December 1979 and in December 1984). In the event of rejection, the financing of the Community can proceed only month by month on the basis of the last agreed budget. To facilitate the budgetary process, a procedure for dialogue between the Commission, the Council and the Parliament has been adopted that seeks to reconcile conflicting views before formal positions are adopted at each stage of the budget process.

Since 1970 the European Parliament's budgetary powers and its influence over the budgetary process have been considerably strengthened, first as a result of the Amending Treaty of 1970, which provided that the EC's operations should be financed by what are termed its 'own resources', and second by the 1975 Treaty, which strengthened the Parliament's powers of amendment and modification and gave it the sanction of rejecting the budget as a whole. This change in the balance of decision-making on budgetary questions in favour of the European Parliament, which may be seen as a step towards the establishment of joint financial responsibility between it and the Council, was accepted even by those member states that have consistently expressed reservations about any extension of Parliament's powers. Once the decision had been taken to establish the system of 'own resources' for the budget, it proved impossible to resist the logic of allowing a degree of Parliamentary influence over it, since otherwise there would have been no democratic check on Community taxation and expenditures.

The consequent changes have, without doubt, introduced important new factors into the EC's budgetary process but ultimately it continues to turn on negotiations carried on among the governments of member states at the level of the Council of Ministers or the European Council. Parliament's role, though undoubtedly strengthened, remains a modest one. The decisions of the 1985 Intergovernmental Conference on the Treaty and the resulting Single European Act did nothing to meet Parliament's demands for further budgetary powers (Lodge, 1986).

The Financing and Trend of the General Budget

For 1985, the budget adopted by the EC amounted to about 28,000 million ECU (European Currency Unit), a sum equivalent to 0.9 per cent of the combined gross national products of member states and 2.8 per cent of combined national budgetary expenditures. In 1973 the corresponding ratios were 0.5 per cent and 2.0 per cent. Over the decade there was thus a relative expansion in the size of the EC's budget and, in real terms, its value approximately doubled, reflecting in part a development of new policies.

The EC's revenue is derived from what are known as its 'own resources', which are tax revenues that in legal terms belong to the EC in its own right, although they are largely collected by the member states. Member states retain the right to set an effective ceiling to this source of income by jointly fixing the EC's maximum share of its most important component, namely value added taxation (VAT), and by agreeing periodically to any increases that are sought.

The EC's revenues consist of: customs duties on products imported from the rest of the world; revenues from agricultural levies that are charged at the external frontiers of the Community to bring the prices of certain imported foodstuffs up to the EC levels as determined by the CAP; the proceeds of levies on sugar and iso-glucose, established to limit surplus production by obliging producers to pay part of the cost of excess quantities; a proportion of the proceeds of national VAT. Since systems and rates of VAT differ amongst member states, this precept is applied to a notional common base (Commission, 1977c) so that Community receipts are not affected by the lack of harmonization. In 1970 when the own resource system was agreed, it was decided that the Community share should be limited to a 1 per cent VAT rate unless a higher figure was approved by all national parliaments. Table 7.1 indicates the contributions of these different sources of revenue in 1986, from which date the maximum rate of mobilization of VAT was 1.4 per cent.

Over the period 1973–83, total Community expenditure increased more than fivefold. Since prices increased by approximately 2.5 times, the real value of the EC budget over this period approximately doubled. Table 7.2 summarizes the main categories of expenditure for 1973, 1983 and 1986. Apart from administration and the miscellaneous category, which includes not only costs of revenue collection but, from 1986, the cost of the refunds (initially 87 per cent) to Portugal and Spain of their VAT contributions, the bulk of expenditure is for economic and social purposes within the

Table 7.1 European Community budget; 1986 revenue

Source	Million ECU	%
Customs duties	9,700	29.3
Agricultural levies	1,585	4.8
Sugar and isoglucose levies	1,114	3.4
VAT	20,468	61.9
Others	190	0.6
	33,057	100

Source: Budget of the European Communities

member states. This is referred to as the allocated budget – that is, it is attributed to the member states. Except for expenditure on agricultural guarantees, allocated expenditure is mainly of a matching nature, that is, the EC finances a proportion of the costs of certain projects submitted to it by member states or by public or private bodies. The remainder of the budget consists of expenditure outside the EC on overseas aid. This is termed the unallocated budget. The main categories of expenditure are as follows:

- *Agriculture and fisheries* account for 67.2 per cent of total spending for 1986. The support of farm prices alone took 63.6 per cent. The remainder of agricultural expenditure supports the modernization of farming and fisheries. Agricultural

Table 7.2 European Community budget: expenditure

Chapter	Million ECU			% share		
	1973[a]	1983[a]	1986[b]	1973	1983	1986
Agriculture and fisheries	3,627	16,475	22,009	80.6	66.4	67.2
Regional policy	—	2,381	2,456	—	9.6	7.4
Social policy	249	1,419	2,153	5.5	5.7	6.5
Research, energy, industry and transport	70	1,383	762	1.6	5.6	2.3
Cooperation and development	61	981	1,172	1.4	4.0	3.6
Miscellaneous	250	1,050	3,159	5.5	4.2	9.6
Administration	248	1,119	1,049	5.5	4.5	3.2

[a] Actual amounts
[b] Budgeted amounts

Source: Budget of the European Communities.

expenditure first entered the EC's budget in 1965 when the common agricultural policy started to come into effect. Its share rose to more than 80 per cent in 1973 but was subsequently substantially reduced in part as a result of the creation of new policies – such as regional policy – in other sectors and in part by economy measures in agriculture. In the last few years the share of agriculture has again been on the increase as a result of world price movements and the fall of the dollar.

- *Regional policy* dates from the first enlargement of the EC in 1973. Its principal financial instrument is the European Regional Development Fund, which was set up in 1975 to assist poor regions and areas hard hit by the recession. The Regional Fund co-finances infrastructural development and new projects in the industry and service sectors. In 1986 regional policy absorbed 7.4 per cent of the budget.
- *Social policy* absorbs 6.5 per cent of the budget. Of this, nine-tenths is spent through the European Social Fund, which co-finances training and retraining schemes and job creation projects. Finance is also provided for education, culture, the environment and consumer protection.
- *Energy, research, industry and transport* absorbs 2.3 per cent of the budget. Member states have recently decided to expand Community research efforts and to launch new energy, industrial and transport projects.
- *Overseas cooperation and development* took 3.6 per cent of the budget in 1986. The expenditure goes mainly on food aid and on other assistance to Mediterranean, Asian and Latin American countries.

It should be noted that the general budget of the EC does not provide a complete picture of the financial operations of the Community since substantial expenditures are undertaken by Community institutions on the basis of finance that falls outside the general budget. Thus, through the European Development Fund, which is partly financed by separate national contributions, aid is provided to the amount currently of some 7,500 million ECU over five years to those African, Caribbean and Pacific countries that have signed the Lomé conventions, in addition to European Investment Bank (EIB) loans. The EIB raises finance on the capital markets to support a range of expenditures in Europe in the field of industry, energy and infrastructure, and priority investment in the regions, as well as development projects in Third World countries. The Commission itself borrows funds for the purpose of financing investment, for instance in nuclear power. In 1983, loans through these various channels amounted to more than 7,000 million ECU, equivalent to some 30 per cent of the ordinary Community budget. Finally, the European Coal and Steel Community has a substantial separate budget of its own.

The Emergence of Distributional Issues

Since 1970 several acute budgetary issues have preoccupied the EC and its member states. Their resolution has been a necessary condition for enabling the package of policies and rules agreed under the treaties and in the period up to 1973 (the then *acquis communautaire*) to continue to function after enlargement, although some of the solutions advocated have looked towards new directions, and the fact of enlargement itself has inevitably affected the Community's character and its preoccupations. Apart from the question of budgetary control and the budgetary powers of different Community institutions, four interrelated issues have demanded attention, namely: (1) the need to provide additional finance for new policies deemed necessary for the functioning and progress of the Community; (2) the need to make specific budgetary provisions for the accession of new members (the United Kingdom, Ireland and Denmark in 1973, Greece in 1981 and Portugal and Spain in 1986); (3) the high and disproportionate share of the budget taken by the compulsory expenditure required to support the CAP, and (4) the alleged distributional inequity produced by the budget – which is closely related to the CAP expenditure distribution.

The distributional dimension, which is present in every one of these issues, has always been latent in the operations of the EC, but it was thrown into relief and became an increasingly acute issue during the period 1970–85. This has come about largely as a result of four factors: the period of financial stringency for the Community – which is not yet over – that was ushered in at the beginning of the 1970s by the world economic crisis; the greater economic heterogeneity of the Community that has resulted from its successive enlargements and in particular from the accession of Ireland and the Mediterranean countries; the adoption of the 'own resources' decision, which bore more heavily on some states than others in the financing of the agreed EC policies; and the increasingly important distributive impact of expenditure under the CAP.

The original treaty establishing the EEC did not include any specific provisions for dealing with distributional issues. Although it does refer to matters that have important distributional

dimensions, including the need to promote harmonious development, to reduce the differences between regions and to promote
balanced expansion – in a word, to what has later been termed
'convergence' – these allusions (as Robert Marjolin has remarked
of many similar Community declarations) may be said to have
represented an act of piety rather than a commitment to specific
action. Evidently, when agreeing to establish the EEC, the original
Six did not neglect the distributive implications of integration, but
their separate interests were clearly thought of as being safeguarded
through the overall impact of the package of common policies that
had been agreed upon. Moreover in the first decade, when Community priorities were directed towards consolidating the internal
market and the development of certain key sectoral policies (initially for coal and steel and later for agriculture), distributional
consequences were relatively unimportant and could largely be left
to take care of themselves. The possibility that significant distributional difficulties might later emerge was not ignored, but the
dominant Community view has emphasized the paramountcy of
policies rather than of fiscal adjustments as a means to resolve any
arising problems.

The negotiations on the first enlargement of the Community in
1973 brought the distributional issue explicitly to prominence.
Britain in particular felt unable to accept the financial implications
of the existing *acquis*. The force of some of her reservations was
accepted by her prospective partners and it was proposed to deal
with them by the establishment of a range of new EC policies, from
which Britain was to derive substantial benefit, and which could
also have contributed to the further progress of the EC. In the
event, virtually the only major policy innovation to follow enlargement was the establishment of a Community regional policy under-
pinned by a modest European Regional Development Fund. The
subsequent period of financial stringency made it virtually impossible for further new policies to be adopted because to do so would
have required not merely a changed emphasis in the allocation of
additional funds, but an absolute reduction of the already existing
benefits of some members in order to improve the position of
others. The enlarged Community then found itself with a set of
budgetary arrangements unaltered in substance by accession, and
in particular with spending policies still largely based on pre-
enlargement principles that generated a pattern of distributional
impacts on countries, regions and sectors that derived from decisions made in fundamentally different circumstances.

Just how unsatisfactory that distributional pattern was to become
was not at first apparent. Its emergence and some of the specific

reasons for it can be illustrated by examining the distributional impact of the revenue and expenditure policies of the EC on individual member states in terms of the concept of net budgetary contributions.

The Distributional Impact of EC Revenue and Expenditure Policies between Member States (1978–84)

What is termed the net contribution of each member state to, or its net receipts from, the budget refers to the difference between its calculated gross contributions to and its gross receipts from the allocated budget. This relates to the part of EC expenditure (more than 90 per cent of the total) that can be attributed to member states, the rest consisting of expenditure outside the Community on overseas aid. By definition, net contributions and receipts sum to zero, the net receipts of any member state or states being exactly equivalent to the net contribution of the others. The interest of these figures is that, with certain qualifications, they measure the net transfer of resources that takes place through the EC budget from the taxpayers and consumers of the net contributory countries to the beneficiaries of EC policies in the net recipient countries.

Calculations of total and per capita net contributions for all member states have been published by the Commission for the period 1978–82 in connection with budgetary reform and the attempts to resolve the issue of the UK's budget contribution. These calculations are summarized in Table 7.3, to which have been added unpublished estimates for later years and figures for nominal and real relative per capita incomes in the member countries. This table illustrates a consistent pattern. Over the period, two member states – West Germany and the UK – are substantial net contributors, while the rest are net recipients (except that France made a net contribution in 1978 and in 1979). This pattern mainly reflects the budgetary impact of the CAP, which accounted for some three-quarters of the allocated budget in the period. For temperate products, the larger a member state's surplus of production over consumption, the larger its gross receipts from the budget will tend to be. The regime for Mediterranean products also gives substantial receipts to member states that are large producers.

Although the relative gross contributions of member states to financing the EC's expenditures broadly reflect the relative levels of GNP, the relation is far from exact. The UK's share, for instance, has tended to exceed significantly its share of Community GNP, whereas that of France has been disproportionately low. There are two main reasons for Britain's relatively high share in relation to its

Table 7.3 European Community: net contribution to (−) and receipts from (+) the allocated budget by member states (ECU)

	1978		1979		1980		1981		1982		1983		1984		Population 1984 '000	Relative national income per capita 1984	
	m.	per capita	m.	per capita	m.	per capita	m.	per capita	m.	per capita	m.	per capita	m.	per capita		Nominal	Real
Before UK compensation																	
Belgium	+337	+33	+610	+60	+237	+24	+276	+28	+253	+26	+233	+24	+343	+35	9,855	96	105
Luxemburg					+206	+515	+239	+597	+256	+640	+263	+657	+282	+705	366	115	124
Denmark	+381	+75	+380	+74	+327	+64	+279	+55	+253	+50	+319	+63	+497	+98	5,112	134	116
France	−371	−7	−78	−2	+431	+8	+576	+11	−19	−0.4	+68	+1	−367	−7	54,947	111	109
Germany	−597	−10	−1430	−23	−1526	−25	−1684	−27	−2086	−34	−2439	−40	−2957	−48	61,175	125	115
Greece	—	—	—	—	—	—	+173	+18	+685	+70	+1015	+104	+988	+100	9,910	42	54
Ireland	+326	+98	+545	+162	+650	+191	+582	+169	+732	+209	+757	+216	+926	+264	3,535	62	67
Italy	−334	−6	+534	+9	+737	+13	+788	+14	+1616	+29	+1161	+20	+1691	+30	57,002	76	87
Netherlands	+41	+3	+288	+21	+454	+32	+239	+17	+304	+21	+411	+29	+536	+37	14,442	106	101
UK	−228	−4	−849	−15	−1512	−27	−1419	−25	−2036	−36	−1790	−32	−1938	−34	56,488	94	96
After UK compensation[a]																	
Belgium	..		..		+174	+18	+206	+21	+196	+20	+191	+19	+294	+30			
Luxemburg	..		..		+203	+507	+235	+588	+253	+632	+261	+652	+278	+695			
Denmark	..		..		+294	+57	+242	+47	+262	+51	+295	+58	+468	+92			
France	..		..		+81	+2	+139	+3	−397	−7	−206	−4	−705	−13			
Germany	..		..		−1957	−32	−2185	−36	−2317	−38	−2574	−42	−3201	−52			
Greece	..		—		—		+161	+17	+660	+67	+996	+102	+965	+98			
Ireland	..		..		+639	+188	+568	+165	+717	+205	+747	+213	+913	+261			
Italy	..		..		+527	+9	+549	+10	+1391	+25	+977	+17	+1468	+26			
Netherlands	..		..		+376	+27	+94	+7	+218	+15	+351	+24	+462	+32			
UK	..		..		−337	−6	−9	−0.2	−985	−18	−1040	−18	−938	−17			

.. not available

[a] and German compensation post-Fontainebleau

Source: European Commission; Eurostat.

GNP. First, its import ratio from countries outside the Community is high compared to that of other EC countries in proportion to its GNP, so that it generates a relatively high share of the customs duties that are automatically and wholly transferred to the EC. Secondly, the UK is also taxed relatively heavily in respect of its VAT contribution having regard to its relative GNP because imports are included in the tax base whereas investment and exports are excluded. Consequently, member states like Britain with a low investment ratio will have a higher VAT tax base in relation to their GNP share than their partners who enjoy the opposite position. In the 1970s, Britain's balance of trade deficit reinforced that tendency.

There are a number of important qualifications – mainly statistical – that must be borne in mind in any use of these estimates as a measure of the net transfer of resources through the budget. One relates to what has been termed the 'Rotterdam–Antwerp effect'. The calculation of net contributions assumes that customs duties and agricultural levies collected in a member state are a charge on the taxpayers or consumers of that state. This obviously requires qualification where one member state's imports enter the Community through the ports of another, which itself collects the levies and is thus credited with the proceeds as part of its gross contribution. This factor is probably only significant in the cases of West Germany (whose contribution is as a result understated) and Belgium and the Netherlands (whose contributions are overstated). Other qualifications, of varying significance, are discussed in Ørstrøm-Møller (1982) and Denton (1984).

In any case, it should be emphasized that the net contributions do not represent the full redistributive effects of the EC's policies, but only those aspects that operate through the budget. In addition, certain non-budgetary transfers between countries are automatically produced as an integral consequence of the impact of the CAP and the CET on the prices received by exporters in intra-Community trade. Their effect, of significance only for agricultural products, is to transfer resources from net importing countries to net exporters through the higher prices that are paid directly by consumers to producers. This effect may reinforce or partly offset the results shown in the table.

The Fontainebleau Agreement of 1984

The most recent period of controversy in the EC's budgetary history has centred primarily on two of the issues distinguished above. First, as EC expenditure has risen (mainly under the burden of higher agricultural price support spending), it has approached and surpassed the limit of available resources under the 1970 ceiling. In 1983 the Community levied a VAT rate of 0.997 per cent on the common base, which provided 55 per cent of a total revenue of 24.8 billion ECU. By 1984 resources were inadequate even to meet existing commitments and fell far short of the amount necessary to fund the extension of the EC's activities envisaged by the Commission. Secondly, the British Conservative government that was elected in 1979 determined to change the regressive redistributive effects of budgetary contributions and the existing balance of Community policies. It has already been noted that recent patterns of net contributions showed no close relationship to relative prosperity. Britain has consistently been the second largest net contributor (after West Germany) although it has only the third largest GNP in absolute terms and is sixth out of ten in terms of nominal per capita income. Between 1980 and 1983 the UK negotiated what were effectively refunds from the EC which amounted to £2.6 billion, and resulted in its receiving back 75 per cent of its gross financial contribution to the budget. However, these refunds were agreed only after long and often acrimonious yearly negotiations that ultimately threatened to absorb the bulk of the energies of the EC institutions, if not to paralyse their operation. The prospective difficulties of the existing arrangements for Greece and for Portugal and Spain, coupled with growing German dissatisfaction about the size of its own financial contribution, made the issue and its solution of much wider interest.

These two budgetary issues thus became the major preoccupation of the European Council meetings in 1983 and 1984. After its initial failure to resolve any of the issues in Athens in December 1983, the European Council at Brussels in March 1984 *inter alia* agreed in principle to limit the growth of net expenditure on agricultural price support spending to less than the rate of growth of the own resources base. In the long term this should reduce the share of agriculture in total spending. So far, however, it has not done so, largely because of the fall of the dollar, which has raised the cost of the CAP. Also, there is still no effective agreement on how to impose the necessary 'budgetary discipline'.

On the side of budgetary contributions, the important decisions were not taken until the Fontainebleau European Council meeting in June 1984. It was then agreed in principle to redress the perceived imbalance in the UK's contributions by a lump sum payment of 1 billion ECU for 1984, and thereafter by the payment of 66 per cent of the difference between the UK payments from VAT and its receipts from the EC budget. The refund is made by lowering the

UK's contributions rather than by the Community's undertaking additional expenditure in the UK. The VAT contributions of other members will be raised but, in recognition of its disproportionately heavy contribution, West Germany will have to shoulder only part of its share of the extra contribution that would normally be required of it. It was also agreed to increase the maximum rate of mobilization of VAT to 1.4 per cent from 1 January 1986. These two decisions which run for concurrent periods, were formally agreed by the Council of Ministers in May 1985. The decision on increasing own resources was subject to ratification by national parliaments, which eventually took place.

The Fontainebleau Agreement represented an outcome for the United Kingdom that promised to be not unreasonable, irrespective of the precise character and level of the EC's prospective expenditure policies (Denton, 1984), but by the same token it diminishes its concern with the development and reform of those policies. For the Community at large it appeared to offer the prospect of a few years' respite from budgetary disputes. By 1986, however, that prospect had receded, and the results of the Community's failure to address basic issues and to grasp the nettle of reform, particularly of the CAP, were all too visible. The additional resources from the newly raised VAT ceiling had been completely used up by the increased costs of the CAP, by the abatement of the UK's contribution, by the degressive refunds to Spain and Portugal that are required under the Treaty of Accession to enable them broadly to enjoy budgetary neutrality in terms of their net contributions during the transitional period, and by the costs of implementing earlier commitments to expenditures in other parts of the budget. As the EC tackles the problem of how to finance the 1987 and 1988 budgets, disputes among the members promise to become at least as difficult as they were earlier in the 1980s.

Budgetary Development in the EC in the Longer Term

The EC budget at present plays a negligible role in the allocation sphere except for its important impact on the agricultural sector; likewise its distributional impact has been insignificant (though, if anything, regressive); while any stabilization role has been totally absent. Nevertheless, the possibility of assigning a more important role to the budget in the longer term in each of these spheres has been considered from time to time. The impetus to do so was provided initially by aspirations on the part of some of the Community's leaders to move towards closer economic integration and to a monetary union, and their simultaneously held belief that the establishment of an enlarged role for the budget would be crucial to this process. That belief seems to be well founded.

Closer economic integration would almost certainly intensify and accelerate economic change in ways that cannot be fully predicted. Therefore, as Brown put it (1985, p. 309): 'A built-in system of net transfers from whoever is doing well at the moment to whoever is doing badly is an insurance against economic misfortune, which may well be regarded as essential to entering on a more dangerous (even if, it is hoped, generally a more rapidly progressive) way of economic life.' This is the primary relevance of the scale and pattern of the budget to closer integration. Monetary integration would further enhance the need by reducing the member state's own ability to deal with its adjustment problems.

The report of the MacDougall Study Group to the Commission (1977a) dealt exhaustively with the issues in this context, and attempted some quantification of what might be involved. Particular attention was given to two budgetary scenarios. First the development of a budget that would be sufficient to meet the specific needs of economic and monetary union with particular reference to the perceived need to redistribute income on a continuing basis and to cushion short-term and cyclical fluctuations. In this context the report noted that, in existing federations such as the USA and West Germany, federal public expenditure was around 20–25 per cent of GNP. The group itself however envisaged instead a rather novel high-powered budget model that could fulfil the continuing redistributive and macroeconomic functions that would be needed, but that would require only a minimum level of Community public expenditure. This, it was thought, could be engineered if the budget operated largely through net resource transfers or subsidies with a high leverage effect. Effectively the envisaged extension of EC functions would involve not giving rather more to the poor than to the rich, but giving to the poor only. Given a suitably progressive tax base in place of, or to supplement, VAT, it was thought that a Community budget of 5–7 per cent of GDP might suffice, excluding any transfer of defence. The report suggested that such a budget could provide both the degree of equalization found in the fully integrated economies examined (where an equalization of up to 40 per cent of regional income differentials was produced) and the cyclical or geographical stabilization effects that would also be required. Transfers of 2 per cent of Community GDP could not only equalize inter-member state differentials to the extent of 40 per cent but could also have financed a large part of the payments deficits of the beneficiary states in the years in question.

The group recognized that any development along such lines was far off, given the reluctance of member states at the time to admit any significant increase in public expenditure. They therefore concentrated their attention on the implications of a much more modest total EC budget – rising to about 2–2½ per cent of the combined GDP of the EC – which even so would have involved an approximate trebling of its size. This was to be achieved by a transfer to the EC budget of most of national external aid, a partial takeover of unemployment benefits by the establishment of a Community Unemployment Fund and of vocational training, and the provision of various forms of grants specifically directed towards its weaker states – for instance, budget equalization and cyclical grants (Commission, 1977a, vol 1, p. 15). The net cost of the proposals was put at about 1 per cent of GDP and it was envisaged that they would be financed by an increase in VAT, but on a formula that would involve a progressive tax base.

These more modest 'pre-federal' proposals would have resulted in an equalization of only about 10 per cent of the then existing per capita income differentials in the EC, which would amount to about one-quarter of the equalization that had been observed to take place in the fully integrated economies examined. The group, with some exceptions, thought that this degree of equalization would suffice to underpin a move to monetary union – though not all members shared the view that redistribution was an indispensable corollary of monetary union. In any event, it was not felt that a budget of the order considered either could or should be used for helping to stabilize short-term fluctuations, on the ground that the budget and its balance would have to swing by enormous percentage fractions to have any perceptible effect.

The specific budgetary 'proposals' of the MacDougall Group, as opposed to its analysis of the issues, are today of historical interest only. It is indeed ironic that the group should have been appointed to consider such issues at a time when the climate of opinion was moving so decisively in favour of retrenchment rather than expansion. But in any case, the subsequent enlargement of the EC by the entry of Greece, Portugal and Spain will have greatly increased the scale of fiscal effort that would be required to bring about a significant measure of equalization.

Nevertheless the concern of the Community with convergence has undoubtedly persisted and it has perhaps even sharpened with the prospect of blocking minorities. Convergence has been embodied as an integral objective of the Treaty as amended by the Single European Act (SEA). In that context, however, it is specifically related to the requirements of the programme for the completion of the internal market rather than to those of a monetary union.

Several articles of the SEA deal with convergence and with the reform of the structural funds with this end in mind. How the programme for the completion of the internal market and the provisions of the SEA will affect the future development of the EC budget remains to be seen. A number of radical proposals are made in the report of a study group established by the Commission to consider these issues (Padoa-Schioppa, 1987). What does seem unavoidable is that for some time to come, unless there is a marked change in the climate of opinion, in its budgetary dimension convergence will have to be pursued primarily by restructuring the budget rather than by any substantial expansion of existing expenditures or the development of new policies.

CHAPTER 8

Fiscal Harmonization

International economic integration embraces a spectrum of arrangements ranging from free trade areas to economic unions. For a full economic union to be feasible, member countries must share similar policy objectives in major fields and similar preferences for public goods and patterns of income distribution. In such circumstances a high degree of fiscal integration, involving uniform fiscal systems and policies, will be appropriate. The theory of fiscal harmonization takes as its starting point forms of integration short of economic union in which diverse public policy objectives exist in the member states, and it evaluates the significance of differences in jurisdictional principles, and in types and rates of taxation, in the light of both union and member-country objectives. The implications of different ways of coordinating fiscal systems for the attainment of these objectives are also considered.

The analysis may be conducted for any form of integration, but a basic distinction must be made between customs unions, where products alone are free to move without restriction, and common markets, where factors are also free to move. For each form of integration, harmonization issues may be analysed for different monetary arrangements, the principal alternatives being: perfectly flexible exchange rates; fixed exchange rates; and monetary union.

Tax harmonization issues must be analysed with the usual range of economic criteria in mind, namely, resource allocation, adjustment and stabilization, growth and distributional considerations. One aspect of the latter, in the shape of the inter-country revenue implications of alternative tax harmonization arrangements, may be particularly important and constitute a significant source of gain or loss that needs to be separately considered. In the case of advanced countries, where tariffs are typically a relatively small source of revenues, a customs union itself may often be evaluated without specifically considering issues of tariff revenue allocation (it is implicitly assumed that revenues are allocated on the basis of consumption). Such a procedure will be inappropriate for the analysis of harmonization issues in relation to internal taxes, if they constitute major sources of revenue. In such cases, tax harmonization analysis normally demands some consideration of the inter-country revenue implications of alternative harmonization arrangements.

The resource allocation criterion has nevertheless dominated tax harmonization analysis, reflecting the emphasis of orthodox integration analysis upon improving the allocation of resources. Tax harmonization analysis has two principal foci, corresponding to the main types of internal taxes. For indirect taxes the problem is to determine the efficiency impact of tax differences on commodity trade. In the case of direct taxes the efficiency considerations arise principally in connection with the impact of tax differences upon factor movements, particularly movements of capital. Some attention has been given to the implications of tax harmonization for the attainment of other policy objectives, in particular that of economic stabilization.

This chapter commences by analysing the implications for tax systems if tax-induced distortions are to be avoided with respect to the movement of goods and factors. This is the 'neutrality' criterion, and its implications are taken up for indirect and direct taxation in turn. There follows a brief review of the implications of some other goals and criteria for tax harmonization issues. In the light of this discussion the final section briefly comments on progress towards tax harmonization in the European Community. Throughout the chapter the approach is to inquire into the implications of given union or national policy goals for the adjustment of national tax systems. However, the policies adopted in a union not only reflect preferences but may also influence and help to mould them. If the question is posed of what kinds of changes in internal revenue systems will help to stimulate the formation of a customs union, or a progression from a customs union to a more complete form of economic integration, a uniformity of internal revenue systems may be helpful, independently of its justification in terms of allocation or other orthodox effects. This is a consideration to which much weight has been attached by advocates of fiscal harmonization in the EC.

THE HARMONIZATION OF INDIRECT TAXES: THE ALLOCATION ISSUE

Even when a customs union has eliminated the impact of all external duties within the union, a diversity of internal indirect taxation systems may influence intra-union trade flows. Such influences may become more significant, and are certainly likely to be more evident, when tariffs no longer exist. The main issues that arise in connection with the harmonization of indirect taxes are:

(1) Does the use of different forms of indirect taxation in the various member countries produce a tax-induced misallocation of resources?
(2) Does the choice of jurisdictional principle affect the allocational effects of indirect taxes?
(3) Do differences among member countries in their relative reliance on direct as compared with indirect taxes give rise to distortions?
(4) If tax-induced distortions are to be avoided, is it necessary for country rates of indirect taxation to be equalized?

The theory of fiscal harmonization is largely concerned with the neutrality criterion applied to goods and factors moving within the union. The question of possible union tax-induced distortions on flows with the outside world – that is, world efficiency considerations – may also be relevant. Here the considerations are akin to those discussed in the orthodox theory of trade diversion and trade creation. The theory of tax harmonization is complex. To simplify the discussion it will be assumed that, apart from traditional excise taxes on such commodities as alcohol and tobacco, indirect taxation is levied by means of a value added tax (VAT). The first of the four issues mentioned above will therefore be largely neglected.

We may begin the discussion with a consideration of the second issue. This is posed by the fact that, for indirect taxes, a choice exists between two alternative jurisdictional principles, which correspond to the imposition of the tax on a production or a consumption basis. Under the origin principle, the tax is imposed on the domestic production of goods, whether they are exported or not, but not on imports. Under the destination principle, the same tax is imposed on imported goods as on domestically produced goods destined for consumption by domestic consumers, but domestically produced goods destined for consumption by foreigners are not subject to the tax. Are there any theoretical reasons, stemming from resource allocation considerations, why one principle should be preferred to the other when indirect taxes are applied to internationally traded commodities?

The issues may be illuminated with the help of a simple comparative cost model, following the approach of the Tinbergen Committee (European Coal and Steel Community, 1953). No attempt will be made to explore the complicated issues that arise when the assumptions of the basic comparative-cost model are relaxed. For simplicity, a two-country framework is adopted. The analysis assumes that the initial rate of exchange is the equilibrium rate, that trade is in products only and that exchange rates are perfectly flexible. The model assumes two countries, H and P, that produce two commodities, namely, clothes and motor vehicles. Country H has a comparative advantage in clothes and country P in vehicles, but neither country specializes completely because of increasing cost conditions. In the initial situation there are no tariffs or internal indirect taxes affecting trade between the two countries. Country H will export clothes and country P vehicles. Internal indirect taxes are now introduced, and two principal cases are considered: in the first case each country imposes a VAT at a uniform rate on every product and applies the same principle to each product; in the second case a differentiated tax is assumed to be applied in at least one of the countries. It is further assumed that the proceeds of the tax are used to reduce the proceeds from a general income tax from which public revenues are derived, leaving aggregate public revenues and expenditures unchanged.

Uniform Indirect Taxes: Different Levels

Assume that country H imposes a perfectly general VAT at a rate of 20 per cent, whereas country P imposes a similar tax at a lower rate of 10 per cent. How will the imposition of these taxes affect equilibrium?

If the tax is imposed on the destination principle and factor prices are given, then, since all exports will be exempted from the tax, the relative costs of clothes and vehicles produced for export will not be affected by the tax. Internally, both domestic production and imports will be subject to taxation at the domestic rate, leaving their relative prices unchanged. Comparative costs will therefore be unaffected. No trade effects will result, and there will be no effect on exchange rates.

If the tax is imposed on the origin principle and factor prices are given, all exports will have to pay the tax; but as this is levied on both products, the relative costs of clothes and vehicles will be unchanged. Comparative costs will again be unaffected. At the initial rate of exchange there will, however, be an increase in the price of country H's exports relative to foreign goods, which will be unfavourable to its exports, and a reduction in the price of country H's imports relative to domestic goods, which will be favourable to its imports. These effects will be automatically offset by a tendency for country H's exchange rate to depreciate relative to that of country P.

If the tax is imposed on the destination principle and factor prices are flexible, a fall in factor prices will accompany the increase in indirect taxation and comparative costs will again be unaffected; but for country H, at the initial rate of exchange, the price of exports relative to foreign goods will fall, and the price of imports relative to domestic goods will increase. This will give rise to a tendency for the exchange rate of country H to appreciate relative to that of country P, maintaining trade in balance.

If the tax is imposed on the origin principle and factor prices fall with the increase in taxation, leaving prices unchanged in each country, there will be no trade effects and no exchange rate change.

In general, the direction and extent of the price adjustment that comes about will depend on the nature of monetary policy and on the degree of price flexibility in factor and product markets. If factor prices are rigid downwards, however, the price effects that accompany increases in both origin and destination taxes will be likely to be upwards.

Several important conclusions may be drawn from this analysis. First, given flexible exchange rates and a perfectly general indirect tax, the choice between the origin and destination principles has no effect on the composition and level of trade, irrespective of the direction of price change. Secondly, the existence of different levels of the uniform general indirect tax in the countries in question will not affect the composition or level of trade either. Thirdly, a decision of a country to change from one principle to another should have no effect on trade. It can readily be shown that these conclusions hold for more than two countries. They also hold if the members of a customs union use the origin system among themselves and the destination principle for trade with countries outside the customs union – the so-called restricted origin system (Johnson and Krauss, 1970; Meade, 1974).

There may, however, be important fiscal differences between the two systems. Since the location of the tax imposition determines to which government the revenue accrues, taxes imposed on the origin and destination principle may differ with respect to their revenue impact. This could present a particular problem if the restricted origin system were employed while at the same time internal fiscal frontiers were abolished in the customs union, since trade deflection could occur, resulting in losses of revenue for the high-tax country. One way of overcoming the problem would be to institute a common external tax rate that was applicable to all compensatory import taxes and export refunds (Shibata, 1967; Johnson and Krauss, 1970).

In short then, with flexible exchange rates, perfectly general indirect taxes imposed on the same principle on all commodities in any country at a uniform rate will not prevent the basic resource allocation objectives of a customs union from being achieved. The maximization of production in member countries and the optimum distribution of the commodities produced among its members will both be achieved.

There are, however, several considerations that may qualify the significance of this conclusion in the context of integration. To apply perfectly general indirect taxes accurately may be extremely difficult. For instance, in practice, trade in services is often important, but it may partially escape destination-principle adjustments. In addition, if the initial position is not one of equilibrium, it is not clear that the equivalence of the two taxes will hold (Shoup, 1953). Moreover, the conclusion relates to long-term static equilibrium and ignores adjustment problems. In the short run, even under a flexible exchange rate regime, exchange rates or factor prices may be fixed. Consequently, the choice of one jurisdictional principle rather than another may have temporary implications for a country's international competitive position and its balance of payments, for the tendencies noted above will not be immediately offset. But above all, the equivalence theorem depends crucially on exchange rate flexibility. In a common market, exchange rate stability is likely to be an important goal and, in a monetary union, exchange rates amongst the member states will be immutably fixed. In these circumstances, the choice of jurisdictional principle may have important longer-term implications for trade and resource allocation in the union.

Differentiated Indirect Taxes

Let us now remove the assumption that the indirect tax is levied at a uniform rate on all commodities. It will then no longer be possible to achieve full optimization. In general, when any member of a customs union applies indirect taxes the rates of which are differentiated according to product, a choice must be made between the objectives of optimizing production and optimizing trade. The destination principle is compatible with the maximization of production but not with the optimization of trade, while the origin principle is compatible with the optimization of trade but not with the maximization of production.

Assume that country H levies a 20 per cent VAT on vehicles only, whereas country P imposes a uniform tax of 10 per cent. If in this situation both countries apply the destination principle, the relative prices net of tax of producers supplying country H's market will be unaffected, and country H's exporters will be free from tax under the destination principle. Similar considerations will apply to country P. Thus, the comparative costs of producers in countries H and P will be unaffected by the tax, and production will continue to be maximized. On the other hand, relative consumers' prices will be distorted because vehicles will be more expensive relative to clothes in country H than they will be in country P. As a result, consumers in country H will buy more clothes and fewer vehicles than they would do otherwise, and the opposite tendency will prevail in country P. Consumers in both countries would gain from a transfer of vehicles from country P to country H and of clothes from country H to country P. In other words, trade between the two countries will not be optimized.

Alternatively, assume that both countries apply the origin system. Relative consumer prices will then be the same in both countries, and therefore trade will be optimized. However, the tax will interfere with the maximization of production, because producers' prices net of tax will be reduced in a non-proportionate way. Producers in country H will therefore be encouraged to produce clothes rather than to manufacture vehicles, and the opposite tendency will prevail in country P.

Let us now digress briefly to consider the implications of the application of different jurisdictional principles to different commodities within the same country. This possibility was considered at length by the Tinbergen Committee. The issue is significant only if the rates of tax differ in the member countries of the union. If they do not, it will be immaterial whether the same principle applies to all commodities in each country or not.

Assume that, in the example initially discussed, country H applies the origin system to the trade in clothes and the destination system to the trade in vehicles. It will be recalled that country H is assumed to possess a comparative cost advantage in the production of clothes. The levy of a 20 per cent tax on all clothes produced, whether for home consumption or for export, and the imposition of a compensating duty on purchases of vehicles from country P, will clearly distort the comparative cost position in country H and may even result in country H exporting vehicles and importing clothes. If, instead, both countries levy a tax at a uniform rate of 10 per cent on all products, it will be possible for them to adopt the destination principle for vehicles and the origin scheme for clothes without giving rise to distortions. In such a case, whatever the principle employed, each commodity will be subject to a tax of 10 per cent, and hence relative producers' and consumers' prices will be unaffected. Important fiscal consequences may, however, follow from the choice adopted. For instance, assume that country H has an export surplus in clothes and that the two countries have agreed to adopt the origin principle for this commodity. Country P, on the other hand, is assumed to have an export surplus in vehicles, for which the destination principle is adopted. It can be seen that the fiscal revenues of country H will be greater, and those of country P less, than they would be if either the origin or the destination principle were applied to the whole of their trade, assuming that overall trade was in balance.

In conclusion, if the rates of tax are not identical for all commodities in any one country, a distortion will arise, no matter whether the origin or the destination system is chosen. The question then arises whether it is more important to maximize production or to optimize trade. If the destination principle is adopted (involving explicit border tax adjustments between member countries), the location of production in the low-cost country will not be interfered with. At the same time consumption losses may arise. These losses will be domestic in nature, however, and would arise even in a closed economy. Although that is no ground for disregarding them, it has been argued (Musgrave, 1969) that there are two reasons for suggesting that fiscal harmonization in a union should be concerned primarily with production efficiency. In the first place, potential production losses are likely to outweigh the consumption burden (Johnson, 1960). Secondly, consumption burdens resulting from discriminatory destination taxes are largely borne by the country that imposes them, whereas production inefficiencies are shared outside the taxing country.

Trade Creation and Trade Diversion

It is possible to relate discussions of fiscal harmonization to trade with third countries, and so with certain qualifications (Dosser, 1967; Musgrave, 1967), to the concepts of trade creation and trade diversion. The subject will not be pursued here, for several reasons. It is implicit in the foregoing discussion of indirect taxation that, if the pre-tax situation (or the pre-union situation) is one of destination taxation, the initial situation must be world-efficient in production terms. A tax union starting from this initial position can never be trade creating in the absence of other distortions. This is important to bear in mind, because international trade is in effect generally conducted on a destination basis, any origin taxes being subject to border tax adjustments as permitted by the General Agreement on Tariffs and Trade (GATT). This is also the current situation for intra-EC trade. Equalization of destination rates would leave the world production situation unaffected. The adoption of equalized origin rates in the union and the destination principle for trade with countries outside the union would also leave production unaffected. It is, of course, possible to conceive of situations in which fiscal harmonization involving rate unification could give rise to trade creation and trade diversion and other effects foreign to conventional customs union theory – for instance, if the universal origin system were adopted towards all countries (Musgrave, 1967; Georgakopoulos, 1974). These cases are of little practical significance, and will be disregarded here.

THE HARMONIZATION OF DIRECT TAXES: THE ALLOCATION ISSUE

Harmonization issues will next be considered in relation to direct taxes. To the extent that direct taxes exert their influence on incomes rather than on the absolute and relative prices of goods and services (except for the possible forward shifting of the corporation income tax), the main issues that arise in connection with the harmonization of direct taxes are different from those that arise in connection with indirect taxes. The principal efficiency issue concerns the impact of differences in net tax burdens between countries on the international migration of factors and the implications of this for resource allocation and the fiscal autonomy of members. Other important issues have to do with: (1) the problem of double taxation arising from the overlapping of tax jurisdictions on a single economic activity, which raises issues of inter-individual equity; and (2) the problem of the international distribution of tax revenues, which raises questions of equity between member states. The following discussion concentrates on the first issue.

As in the case of indirect taxes, two alternative jurisdictional principles are mainly used for direct or income taxes. The first is the residence principle, under which taxation is applied to the total income of each resident regardless of the place where the income is earned. The second principle is the source principle, under which tax is applied to all income earned within the taxing jurisdiction whether by residents or non-residents. If there is no foreign investment and no factor mobility, the two principles will be identical.

These principles are normally modified by jurisdictional tax adjustments that attempt to accommodate foreign investment and factor mobility. The adjustments are motivated partly by equity considerations and partly by revenue considerations. Within a common market the issue of efficiency may also be important. On the *tax credit* approach, taxes imposed abroad are fully credited by the country of residence against its own tax assessment. This effectively treats taxpayers in the country of residence equally, irrespective of whether their income arises from domestic or foreign sources. A country employing this rule has to adjust to income taxes paid abroad, reducing the domestic tax taken fully by the amount of the foreign tax where that is less than the domestic tax and, in principle, providing a refund if the foreign tax is more than the domestic tax. A second approach permits only a deduction of foreign income taxes for the purpose of arriving at net income for tax purposes. On this approach, taxpayers with equal incomes pay different amounts of tax, depending on the proportions in which their incomes are derived from domestic or foreign sources. Each country is then able to collect whatever income tax it chooses, without any adjustment to income tax paid by its residents to other tax jurisdictions.

What are the allocational implications of direct tax differentials and alternative jurisdictional principles within a union? This will depend primarily on the degree of factor mobility between the countries and on the actual incidence of the tax. If factors of production are immobile, as they are assumed to be in a simple customs union, and direct taxes are not shifted, they will play only a minor allocative role. If international factor mobility is assumed, as would be appropriate to the consideration of a common market, direct taxes may acquire considerable allocative significance if the rates vary between countries. Direct tax differentials can affect the international migration of capital or labour, depending on whether the tax falls on profits and other capital income or on wages and salaries. In this chapter, attention is concentrated on profits and capital taxation, since capital is the most mobile of factors and the principal problems are consequently likely to arise in this area. If the direct tax on profits is shifted to leave factor returns in the short run unaffected, profits tax differentials among the members of a common market may also make themselves felt in trade distortions among the member countries.

Consider the case of two countries, H and P, which adopt profits taxes, that of country H being higher than that of country P. Assume, first, that the profits tax is not shifted. In this case capital incomes in each country will be reduced by the taxes, and capital will flow from the high-tax to the low-tax country. The tax-induced distortion that exists in the union capital market may even induce capital to flow into areas where its real rate of return is lower.

Capital market distortions in this case can be removed in one of two ways: by equalizing the profits tax in each country where taxation is by source of income; or by providing a full foreign-tax credit. The adoption of either of these harmonization arrangements would not interfere with the investor's choice among countries; that is, the tax would be neutral with respect to capital export.

Such an arrangement is in one sense not wholly neutral, however, because it does not provide for equal treatment among union investors competing in any one union country. Investors who are resident in country H but who invest in country P may be subject to a higher tax for any given income than their competitors who are nationals of country P. This may reduce the ability of country H's investors to compete, either by reducing their available reinvestment funds or by making it more difficult for them to attract outside capital. On such grounds it may be argued that neutrality requires equal taxation for all union investors in country P. This may be termed 'neutrality of capital import', as distinct from 'neutrality of capital export', which is secured by crediting.

Import and export neutrality with respect to capital cannot both be achieved, except by the adoption of uniform tax rates in all countries. Otherwise, one or other type of neutrality must be sacrificed. Musgrave (1969) has argued that the two requirements are not of equal importance and that, from the point of view of efficient resource allocation under competitive conditions, it is export neutrality that should be aimed at.

In conclusion, the case is considered in which, as before, the two countries H and P adopt different rates of profits tax, but now the profits tax is assumed to be shifted forwards through a rise in the price of products. Assume specifically that country H, the capital exporter, can shift the profits tax only to the extent of country P's lower tax, because foreign capital is a relatively small part of total capital in country P. In this case, tax-induced distortions of both commodity and capital flows will arise in the absence of harmonization measures, and neutrality would call for the equalization of profits tax rates coupled with an export-rebate import-compensating tax. Depending on the precise nature of the tax-shifting assumptions made, a wide variety of different adjustments would be called for to produce neutrality (Musgrave, 1967).

OTHER CRITERIA FOR TAX HARMONIZATION

In evaluating the rationale for tax harmonization in economic groupings, considerations other than resource allocation may have to be taken into account, although some are relevant only for forms of international integration that go beyond free trade areas and customs unions. This section briefly reviews some of these other considerations and summarily indicates their interrelationships with the resource-use considerations discussed so far.

Administrative Considerations

From an administrative point of view the origin principle was for many years perceived to have one major advantage over the destination principle, in that its adoption would make it possible to dispense with fiscal frontiers within a union. Rebates and compensating taxes would not be required at intra-union frontiers, and goods may therefore pass without control, except for what may be required for other purposes (for instance; health or drug control). The resulting savings in administrative costs both for the state and for private enterprises could be considerable. Moreover, the retention of internal fiscal barriers typically constitutes a substantial physical and psychological obstacle to intra-union trade. In Europe the procedures used and the formalities required in connection with VAT and excises at intra-Community frontiers are notoriously complicated, cumbersome and costly. Their cost has been put at 5–7 per cent of the value of intra-EC trade (Cnossen and Shoup, 1986). In 1984, indeed, anger over these problems boiled over and led to a dramatic protest by the drivers of heavy goods vehicles in France that completely blocked a major European arterial route – the Mont Blanc tunnel – for several days. Finally, the retention of fiscal controls at frontiers also makes it technically feasible to resort to non-tariff barriers in case of economic difficulty, and the mere possibility of this may be an important psychological obstacle to the full integration of markets. Without doubt, if, as in the EC, it is desired that a common market should have characteristics that are similar to those of an internal market, and if internal indirect taxes imposed on the destination principle can be collected only at the borders, the origin principle would have important advantages from this standpoint.

The principal difficulty with origin taxes, as noted already, is that if they are imposed on a significantly differentiated basis they will give rise to inter-member production distortions. From this point of view an origin tax is acceptable only if it is imposed at a fairly uniform rate within each country, although it is not necessary for it to be imposed at the same initial rate in all member countries. If exchange rates are fixed, however, then, although initial tax differences reflected in the initial equilibrium exchange-rate may continue, changes in origin tax rates may not be compatible with continued equilibrium in the absence of offsetting changes in factor and product prices.

Fortunately computerization means that there is no longer any reason why border tax adjustments have to be made at the border, and the proposed arrangements for the EC outlined below, while maintaining the integrity of the destination principle, could avoid most of the difficulties referred to in this section.

The Problem of Special Excises

It has been shown that, even if border tax adjustments are employed, differentiated indirect taxes will give rise to distortions. This may suggest that differentiated taxes (or subsidies) should be ruled out on allocative grounds, unless they are necessary to offset some other imperfection in the market mechanism. However, differences in fiscal structures also reflect differences in social philosophy and public goals, and many instances of differentiation will be specifically designed to influence patterns of production and consumption with these goals in mind. The theory of fiscal harmonization assumes that countries should be permitted to retain differences in their fiscal systems that reflect important differences in social philosophy. In the case of the EC, the need to do so has been repeatedly emphasized and is accepted.

It is sometimes difficult in practice to separate special treatment aimed at the provision of illegitimate protection from justifiable interferences based on compensation for externalities or on the weight attached to social values. An arresting question posed by Meade makes the point colourfully:

> In the United Kingdom the consumption of wine is heavily taxed and that of milk subsidised. Is this an inadmissible interference with the optimisation of a home industry, since milk is home-produced and wine imported? Or is it a legitimate case of social economies and diseconomies to encourage the feeding of milk to British babies at the expense of the drunkenness of British fathers? (1953, p. 24)

If substantial differences in social values exist in a union and are permitted to influence fiscal systems, it is difficult to see how the retention of a system of special excises with border tax adjustments could be avoided even if there were substantial progress in general indirect tax harmonization. Moreoever, if substantial excise rate differences should be in prospect, any attempt to shift the required adjustments away from the border in the way described in the following section would almost certainly call for the development of both a system of in-bond transportation and a connected system of bonded warehouses.

Adjustment and Stabilization

There may be a conflict between the desirability of uniformity of structure and rates on allocational and perhaps administrative grounds and the merits of retaining flexibility in the interests of facilitating national structural adjustment and stabilization policies. Any such conflict will be more pronounced in a situation of monetary union where the national use of monetary and credit policy for facilitating domestic adjustments is excluded, and it is likely to be more important for some taxes than for others.

On allocational grounds, rate variations for the purpose of facilitating adjustments should be confined to those that will least affect the flows of factors and commodities, or that can be offset by neutralizing arrangements in the form of border tax adjustments. This suggests that variations in corporation tax rates should not be employed for stabilization purposes because small differences are likely to affect net profit margins significantly and to have long-term distorting effects in the case of capital, which is a highly mobile factor. On the other hand, in so far as labour is not highly mobile, variations in personal income tax rates for stabilization purposes need not be severely detrimental to efficiency considerations.

As to rate variations in indirect taxation, the implications may be considered for two alternative situations; namely, fixed exchange rates and monetary union. It will be assumed that indirect taxation takes the form of a uniform VAT. Suppose that an external imbalance arises under a fixed exchange rate regime, rendering some long-run adjustments necessary. If the VAT were levied on the destination principle (that is, with border tax adjustments), variations in its rate would be neutral with respect to trade and would therefore have no effect on the balance of payments, assuming that such variations were accompanied by product price changes rather than by factor price changes.

If instead, the VAT were levied on the origin principle, without border tax adjustments among the members of the union, then, for a situation in which it was again assumed that variations in VAT were accompanied by product price changes rather than factor price changes, the outcome would be different. In this case a reduction in

VAT would increase the cost of country H's imports from its partners relative to that of domestic goods and reduce the cost of its exports by comparison with those of country P. The effect of the change would be akin to a depreciation of the currency of country H, and there would be a tendency for the external imbalance to be corrected in the case of a common market with fixed rates of exchange. If the situation were one of monetary union and the problem were that of a structural imbalance between countries H and P, with surplus labour and capital in country H, a downward variation of VAT in country H would also result in a tendency for the imbalance to be corrected. If the problem in country H were a cyclical or conjunctural one, again a downward variation in VAT should contribute to the restoration of equilibrium.

The above point may be put in a slightly different way. The merit of the destination system is that, given the above-mentioned shifting assumptions, it enables countries to pursue their own indirect tax policies without regard to balance of payments considerations. This is not possible if the origin system is employed.

In short, from the standpoint of stabilization and adjustment objectives in a common market, there would be an argument for adopting the origin system of indirect taxation for intra-union trade (so dispensing with border tax adjustments among members), while retaining the destination system for external trade. This is the so-called restricted origin principle, which was recommended in the Neumark Report (Commission of the EEC, 1963). In a common market with a monetary union but an undeveloped fiscal policy the argument for such a course might be even stronger. But any advantages secured in terms of stabilization or adjustment would be obtained at the cost of sacrificing some of the resource allocation advantages of a distortion-free system. Administrative considerations may also favour the use of the destination system.

TAX HARMONIZATION IN THE EC

At the time of the establishment of the EC the member countries exhibited substantial differences of structure and rates with respect to the five main types of tax – namely, sales tax, excises, corporation taxation, personal taxation and social security levies. In the field of indirect taxation the general sales tax took the form of a VAT in France, a cumulative or cascade sales tax in West Germany and a single-stage tax in Italy. Excises were even more varied and included fiscal charges of all kinds and state monopolies of manufacture and sale. In the field of direct taxation a similar diversity existed in corporation and personal taxation. The three standard forms of corporation taxation were found: the so-called separate or classical system; the split rate system; and the tax credit system. One country (Italy) had no corporation tax in the modern sense. Personal income taxes were also extremely diverse in their bases, rates, allowances and degree of progressivity. In the field of social security finance there were large differences in coverage and methods of finance. Over and above formal statutory differences there were differences in the method and efficacy of enforcement, which were reflected in the differences between countries in the percentage of the due tax that was actually collected.

Of the five types of tax distinguished above, fiscal harmonization is so far sought by the EC only for sales tax, excises and corporation tax, all of which are significant for the operation and efficacy of the common market. There are no plans for the harmonization of personal income taxes, which are regarded as falling exclusively within the domain of national economic policy. The harmonization of indirect taxation was explicitly demanded by Article 99 of the Treaty of Rome, and the harmonization of corporation tax was implicitly required by Article 100. The treaty itself, however, provided little specific guidance to policy formulation in those areas, and the details of tax harmonization in these areas have had to be worked out subsequently with the help of a number of important reports produced for the Community by independent experts. Of these, the Tinbergen Report (European Coal and Steel Community, 1953), Neumark Report (Commission of the EEC, 1963) and van den Tempel report (1969) are the most notable. Much light has been thrown on the issues of fiscal harmonization also by the important studies initiated by Carl Shoup of Columbia University (Shoup, 1967).

To date, progress has been slow. Effectively every decision relating to taxation has required the unanimous agreement of the Council of Ministers. The principal achievement in tax harmonization has been the adoption of a unified form of general sales taxation in the EC. Following the Neumark Report (Commission of the EEC, 1963), which recommended that the VAT should be adopted as the EC's sales tax, directives were eventually adopted establishing a common structure for VAT in all member states. Other important recommendations of the Neumark Report envisaged rate harmonization and an eventual shift to the restricted origin principle.

In relation to excise duties and other special forms of indirect taxation, little progress has been made towards harmonization. Although an attempt was made in 1972 to harmonize the structure of the traditional excises on beer, wine and spirits, tobacco and mineral oils, common rules have so far been adopted only for cigarettes.

Directives on the harmonization of provisions relating to capital duty (indirect taxes on the raising of capital) have also been adopted. A directive on the harmonization of indirect taxes on transactions in securities has also been laid before the Council. The aim of this proposal is to eliminate certain tax obstacles to the free movement of capital, which is part of the changes directed towards establishing a European capital market. The Commission's long-term object is to abolish such taxes.

With respect to corporation tax, the van den Tempel report (1969) recommended that the separate system (the so-called 'classical' system) should be adopted as the EC's harmonized tax. With the three different systems in use at that time there were strong grounds for believing that capital movements in the Community were likely to be seriously distorted. Harmonization proposals were not made until 1975 when the Commission submitted to the Council of Ministers a proposal for a directive on the harmonization of systems of corporation taxation that aimed at tax neutrality (Commission, 1975). The Commission's proposals departed from van den Tempel's recommendations by suggesting a common imputation (tax credit) system, which would have partly relieved the double taxation of dividends and would have involved also some narrowing of differences both in the rates of tax on profits (the band suggested was 45–55 per cent) and in those of the tax credit. These proposals have not so far been adopted.

Significant advances in the field of fiscal harmonization in the EC at last seem to be in prospect as a result of commitment by the European Council to the principle that internal economic frontiers are to be removed by 1992. The White Paper subsequently produced by the Commission and presented to the Council (Commission, 1985) lays down a programme for the removal of physical, technical and fiscal barriers to a single internal integrated market free of restrictions on the movement of goods. In the crucially important area of fiscal barriers, the Fourteenth VAT directive of 1982, not yet adopted by Council, pointed the way to improvement by making provision for a shifting of the point of tax payment away from frontiers to internal tax offices, as in fact is already done by Belgium, Luxemburg and Netherlands for trade amongst themselves. The adoption of this practice throughout the EC would be an important contribution to the reduction of frontier obstacles, but documentation would still have to be provided at the frontier. To allow fiscal frontiers to be abolished completely, the Commission in

its White Paper wishes to go further and it proposed a new procedure by which sales and purchases across borders between regis-
tered traders would be treated exactly as similar sales and purchases
within the borders of member states. The sale would be taxable in
the hands of the vendor, who would charge the buyer VAT at his
relevant national rate. The VAT so charged would be deductible by
the foreign purchaser, irrespective of the member state in which it
had been initially charged. This would be coupled with the establishment of a Community Clearing House System to ensure that the
VAT collected in the exporting member state and subsequently
deducted as an input tax by the purchaser in the importing member
state was reimbursed by the exporting state to the importing state.
Each country would still receive VAT on consumption within its
borders at its own rates and the destination principle thus remains
unaffected. For excisable products a system of bonded warehouses
would be required in addition.

It seems clear that the system outlined could only work without
fraud and evasion if tax rates and coverage were not significantly
different as between the member countries; the proposal therefore
has major implications for tax harmonization. The Commission
takes the view that differences of up to 5 per cent at frontiers could
be accommodated, which would suggest a margin of $\pm$ $2\frac{1}{2}$ per cent
on either side of specified norms or target rates.

A 'standstill' is to be proposed by the Commission to ensure that
existing indirect tax differences are not widened. This was to be
followed in 1986 by the presentation of target rates or norms with
proposed ranges of variation. Member states are then to be given
the option of moving their taxes towards the band at once or in a
series of shifts. In the light of recent Community history the fiscal
proposals can only be described as breathtakingly ambitious, necessary as they undoubtedly are for dealing with the problem.

The preceding outline of the tax harmonization policies of the EC
makes it clear that they have been undertaken primarily from the
standpoint of resource allocation considerations. The aim has been
both to unify structures and to equalize rates in the first place in
order to prevent trade distortions. Rate equalization (and initially
the adoption of the restricted origin principle) has also been sought
for administrative and other reasons, in order to permit the abolition of fiscal frontiers within the EC. Similarly, a unification of the
structure of the corporation tax and a harmonization of rates have
been sought in order to avoid distortions in the capital markets.

The equalization or unification approach emphasized by the
Commission may be criticized on two grounds. First, unlike the
position for the tariff, the equalization of domestic indirect taxes

among member countries cannot be undertaken at zero but requires a positive rate. It is possible that a nominal equalization of rates will not equalize the *effective* rates of taxation facing enterprises, because of different tax-shifting possibilities in different sectors and markets. Consequently, even when equalized, indirect taxation need not necessarily be neutral or distortion free (Dosser, 1967).

Secondly, the equalization approach gives no weight to adjustment or regional policy objectives. If the levels of major revenue-producing taxes are harmonized, their use to promote such objectives will necessarily be largely ruled out, even though tax differentials might be particularly appropriate for the purpose. For instance, from the standpoint of the maintenance of external equilibrium among the members of a common market, it might be advantageous, if the restricted origin principle were in force, for a country to be able to raise its VAT rate above the uniform rate or band if it experiences a balance of payments surplus, and vice versa for a deficit, thus reducing or eliminating the need for exchange rate changes. In the case of a monetary union, such flexibility could be even more important since variations in VAT (with origin taxation) would be one of the few remaining national measures open to a country for alleviating adjustment problems.

A full harmonization of VAT and corporation tax rates in the EC is unlikely to be acceptable unless and until the fiscal role of the Community itself becomes much greater than it is today. This would almost certainly imply an EC budget that was: (1) substantially larger in relation to national budgets than is now the case; (2) perhaps endowed with the capacity of levying its own supplementary VAT; and (3) able to utilize its revenue in part for transfers among member states. These considerations underline once again the close links between proposals for monetary integration, fiscal harmonization and regional policy.

CONCLUSION

This brief survey of the issues and problems involved in fiscal harmonization in economic groupings indicates the complexity of the problems. In order to reduce the analysis to manageable dimensions the approach commonly followed is to consider a single tax in isolation from other taxes, expenditure patterns and other areas of government policy, such as exchange rate and monetary policy, and on the basis of alternative assumptions about incidence to deduce a suitable pattern or system of tax harmonization to promote neutrality or whatever other objective may be relevant. Despite its highly restrictive nature, even this approach is not free from analytical difficulties. In the first place, the criteria for tax harmonization are several, and their requirements may conflict. Secondly, the impact of taxes is likely to be affected by other variables that are subject to government control, including monetary conditions and public expenditure patterns. In particular, different monetary conditions in the member countries of a common market may produce differing tax-shifting patterns. Where a common monetary system does not exist, to elaborate an appropriate regime for effective fiscal harmonization thus becomes a complex, if not an impossible, task. The analysis becomes still more complex if the simplifying assumptions of the orthodox comparative-cost model are relaxed.

CHAPTER 9

Monetary Integration

Monetary integration has two essential characteristics: (1) exchange rates in the integrated area must bear a permanently fixed relationship to each other, although they may jointly vary with respect to other currencies; and (2) there must be full convertibility in the sense that there are no exchange controls on either current or capital transactions within the area (convertibility for trade-related transactions is indispensable for the effective functioning of a customs union; convertibility for capital transactions is a principal ingredient of capital market integration, which is itself an essential characteristic of a common market). If these two characteristics are to be adequately guaranteed and to be truly immutable, two other requirements would also be essential.

First, since immutability of fixed exchange rates would depend on mutually consistent monetary policies within the area, the use of the standard instruments of monetary policy must be assigned to the community and exercised solely by its monetary authority, leaving no autonomy for member states in this field. *Inter alia* this would imply that, beyond any agreed amount of credit to which a member might be given access, any member state's budget deficit would have to be financed in the capital market.

Second, since any change in the rate of exchange between an external currency and those of the area must be uniform, responsibility for exchange rate policy with other currencies and for the balance of payments of the entire community with the rest of the world must also be assigned to the community and its monetary authority must control the pool of exchange reserves. Under such a system it may not be possible for a member state to calculate its balance of payments with its partners and with the rest of the world.

When all of these requirements are met, the resulting arrangement can be described as one of complete monetary integration, or of monetary union. Effectively there would then be a single currency, although several nominally differentiated currencies might continue to coexist, as is the case in Belgium and Luxemburg.

It would be possible for the member states of a customs union or a common market to seek to establish the two essential characteristics of monetary integration merely by agreeing amongst themselves to fix their exchange rates permanently and to maintain full convertibility and to back this agreement up with promises of economic policy coordination, but without integrating their monetary policies or establishing a common pool of foreign exchange reserves and a single central bank. Such an arrangement may well help to make market integration more effective, but it could not guarantee the immutability of the relationships among currencies that is essential to the concept of complete monetary integration or monetary union. The term pseudo union (Corden, 1972a) is often applied to this degree of monetary integration.

Monetary union involves an additional limitation of national autonomy in economic policy beyond that required by the membership of a customs union, where only tariffs and other measures of equivalent effect are ruled out as policy instruments for regulating intra-union economic relations. Countries that integrate their product markets but do not choose to establish a monetary union as well will usually find it desirable in any case to coordinate or harmonize their monetary policies to some extent in order that payments difficulties or exchange rate volatility should not frustrate the working of the market. For this purpose, the policy constraints of a *pseudo union* might be accepted. Complete monetary integration would, however, entail a definitive loss of control over a supposedly important instrument of policy that is particularly associated with the emotive concept of national sovereignty. This requires justification. What are the relevant considerations?

A widely followed approach to the question of whether a country should establish a common currency with other countries or should instead maintain its separate currency has proceeded by trying to single out a crucial economic characteristic as the criterion for determining the appropriate domain of a currency area. The leading contributors to this debate have emphasized different attributes, but have usually judged optimality with reference to the costs of balance of payments adjustments under alternative regimes.

The initial contributor to this debate was Mundell (1961) who identified factor mobility as the strategic attribute of an optimum currency area, the argument being that, when factors move freely within the area, adjustments to real disturbances can take place without the need for large and damaging price and income changes in its constituent members. McKinnon (1963) emphasized instead the importance of a high degree of openness of the individual economies, which is crucial for determining the extent to which, in any case, the prices of domestic outputs must remain in line with foreign prices. In a later contribution, Kenen (1969) has stressed the primacy of a high degree of diversification, on the ground that the higher the degree of diversification, the more likely it will be that real disturbances will average out. MacDougall (1975) and Allen (1982, 1983) have both emphasized the crucial significance of a high degree of fiscal integration to maximize the feasibility and effectiveness of intra-union measures such as fiscal transfers for facilitating the process of adjustment and stabilization.

The traditional optimum currency area approach provides a number of insights into the issues of monetary union, but is open to several crucial objections. In the first place, the relevant characteristics are difficult to measure unambiguously. Secondly, it is evident that no single country is likely to possess all of the attributes required to make it an ideal member of a monetary union, yet the criteria proposed cannot formally be weighed against each other. Vaubel (1978) was thus led to propose a measurable attribute, namely the smallness of countries' revealed need for real exchange rate variability as the crucial characteristic, which he claimed to comprise the relevant implications of all other criteria. If it is viewed as a criterion for guiding future policy choices, however, past experience in this respect is clearly an insufficient basis in itself, since it can provide no assurance that a need for significant real exchange rate variability may not arise in the future.

Present-day appraisals of monetary integration predominantly follow a broader approach. Instead of appealing to any single criterion or goal, emphasis is placed on the range of costs and benefits that may be anticipated from monetary integration and attempts are made pragmatically to weigh them and their significance for the attainment of the bundle of objectives of the individual member states and of the group as a whole, and to emphasize the trade-offs amongst the objectives that are involved. In this respect, the analysis of monetary integration has evolved in a similar manner to that of other branches of the theory of international economic integration. This chapter selectively considers some of the leading aspects of the recent debate and outlines the EC context.

THE RATIONALE FOR MONETARY INTEGRATION

The fundamental case for superimposing monetary integration upon product and factor market integration is that it will make the integration of these markets more effective, with beneficial effects on economic efficiency and growth. The argument has been particularly well put by Scitovsky (1958). If the creation of a customs union or common market is to have its full beneficial effects on output, it must modify the nature, scale and geographical distribution of economic activity. In market economies this will result primarily from the influence exercised by the existence of the union on the investment decisions of private enterprises. Since business investment decisions are long run in nature, this influence will not make itself fully felt unless entrepreneurs can assume with confidence that the free market will be maintained and that intra-union economic relations will not be disrupted by trade restrictions, exchange controls or exchange rate adjustments that may have similar effects on trade as tariffs. The complete fulfilment of these conditions would effectively demand the establishment of a common currency. This basic argument for monetary union rests on the desirability of exchange rate certainty.

Secondary benefits may also arise from the establishment of a common currency. When a common currency is established and a common pool of foreign exchange is created, economies in the use of foreign exchange reserves should be possible for two reasons: (1) if members are structurally diverse, any payments imbalances may be offsetting, and a pooling of reserves should enable the minimum level to be reduced; and (2) foreign exchange will no longer be needed to finance intra-union trade. Reduced costs of financial management may also be possible since a common currency should make it possible to spread the overhead costs of financial transactions more widely. In addition some part of the activities of institutions dealing in foreign exchange could be dispensed with, thus generating further resource use savings.

If capital markets are also integrated, as would be the case in a situation of full monetary integration, other allocational and resource-saving benefits may be anticipated. First, the removal of controls over foreign direct investment should reinforce the allocational benefits from more rational investment decisions. Second, the increase in the effective size of the market may enable operational economies of scale to be exploited so that the resources employed in the processes of financial intermediation and in transforming savings into investment are reduced. Third, financial market integration may improve the allocational efficiency of the financing process itself to the extent that it provides both borrowers and lenders with a broader spectrum of financial instruments, so enabling more efficient choices to be made in terms of duration and risk. Discontinuities in the range of available finance may also be reduced, so facilitating the financing of operations of optimal scale by enterprises. Resource allocation gains may be obtained from increased intra-union trade in securities as a result of a tendency for returns to different kinds of capital to come closer together in the member countries.

It should be observed that the creation of an effective union-wide market for assets that could be expected to have such effects would involve more than the removal of controls over private capital inflows and outflows of different types. It would also require the concerted adoption of positive measures to harmonize national financial regulations and the structures of financial and capital market institutions of member countries, as the Segré Report long ago emphasized in the case of the EEC (Commission of the EEC, 1966). Such measures should result in a high degree of substitutability between financial assets and securities of a particular type in the markets of the member states. In the limiting case of perfect integration the markets would function as a single market, so that a simultaneous sale in one market and purchase in another would leave the price of the asset in question unchanged.

The magnitude of gains from these various sources is virtually impossible to quantify accurately, but even modest gains would be worth seeking if monetary integration were to involve no offsetting costs with respect to other goals of policy. Are there such costs to be set against the resource allocation and cost-reducing benefits to be expected from monetary integration? If so, what are they and what are the factors that influence their magnitude? More generally, what are the conditions that have to be satisfied if monetary integration is to be feasible, to endure, and to be successful?

THE COSTS OF MONETARY INTEGRATION

Even if monetary integration is capable, as many believe, of generating significant resource allocation gains, they may not be distributed acceptably amongst the member states. In that perspective, one particular cost, bound up with structural effects, calls for mention. Balanced growth is often a declared policy objective of economic groupings. In this respect, the implications of monetary and capital market integration are ambiguous. Although monetary integration might encourage a greater convergence of factor rewards, its impact on capital flows might equally operate to enhance regional imbalances within the area, as already noted in Chapter 6. Discussion of the costs of monetary integration has not in fact centred on such issues, but principally on the macroeconomic implications of the constraints that such a regime would place on the conduct of the monetary, the fiscal and, in particular, the exchange rate policies of the participants. The crucial issue is the extent to which an acceptance of these constraints would significantly impair the effective pursuit of national macroeconomic policy objectives, in respect of economic stability, growth and external balance. This is a complex and controversial matter. Macroeconomic theory – and particularly open-economy macroeconomics – is in an unsettled state. There are many unresolved issues and considerable disagreement amongst economists about the way in which economies behave and should be modelled. Although there are some signs of convergence, a satisfactory synthesis and consolidation of a mainstream view that would be generally accepted cannot yet be offered.

It can be said, however, that contemporary analyses predominantly view exchange rate determination as a function of financial asset market variables in the short run and of current account variables in the long run. In this framework, considerations of competitiveness that alone are relevant when capital is immobile or exogenous retain their fundamental relevance by determining the long-run real exchange rate of one currency for another (indicating the price of tradable goods relative to home goods). Capital flows themselves are viewed as being determined not merely by nominal differences in yield but also by expectations about the exchange rate. Changes in expectations, perhaps related to changes in monetary policy, can in these interactive analyses be an independent cause of exchange rate changes. Typically they predict an over-shooting of the exchange rate adjustments that come about in response to a change in monetary policy when considered in relation to fundamental long-run requirements. Competitiveness and aggregate output may thus be adversely affected. The range of specific models in this vein is immense (Krueger, 1983). Differences in their conclusions hinge critically on the assumptions that are made about expectations and wage–price flexibility. In particular, hypotheses relating to the formation of expectations crucially affect the relative time paths of adjustment towards the long-run real level or current account-determined path.

A realistic analysis of the central issues of monetary integration must obviously take capital mobility into account as well as current account variables. A high degree of capital mobility is not only a dominant feature of the world economy of the late twentieth century but it is an essential feature of a common market even in the absence of monetary integration. Where capital mobility is present, foreign exchange transactions do not originate solely in current trade flows. External equilibrium does not require that trade should be balanced; the concept of external balance is no longer clear cut. The fundamental issues may nevertheless be grasped with the aid of a simplified analysis that disregards capital mobility or treats capital movements as exogenous. Formally that is the framework of the following necessarily highly elliptical account, which considers the costs of monetary integration in the light of three over-sharply differentiated strands of macroeconomic analysis: (1) the traditional Keynesian-rooted approach; (2) monetarism; and (3) the emergent eclectic approach that has been termed 'convergence' or disequilibrium monetarist (Cobham, 1984).

The Traditional Approach

The traditional case for retaining exchange rate flexibility within a customs union supposes that the member states wish to maintain internal balance in the sense of full employment with price stability and external balance in the sense of balance of payments equilibrium. Tacitly the case rests on three propositions: that the economies of the member states are 'insular', in McKinnon's (1981) sense that prices are determined domestically because of limited financial and commodity arbitrage with the outside world; that flexible exchange rates can therefore provide significant national autonomy in matters of macroeconomic policy; and that national governments require such autonomy because of differences in national objectives.

To achieve simultaneously a given number of independent economic targets, at least a similar number of policy instruments is required (Tinbergen, 1952). The simultaneous attainment of internal and external balance therefore requires the use of two policy instruments. The orthodox Keynesian approach to the role of exchange rate flexibility assumes these to be: (1) demand management policy, which (prices being given) influences the level of employment and is assigned to the internal balance objective; and (2) exchange rate policy, which is designed to influence the composition of expenditure in favour of, or away from, domestically produced goods through its influence on international competitiveness, and is assigned to the external balance target. The basic case for resisting the fixity of exchange rates that is a necessary part of monetary integration is simply that, if the exchange rate instrument is forgone, conflicts between the objectives of internal and external balance are likely to arise for the members of a customs union or common market.

The underlying model (Swan, 1955; Johnson, 1961) postulates that the level of domestic employment and the balance of payments both depend on the level of domestic expenditure and the cost of a country's exports relative to those its competitors. If the ratio of foreign prices to domestic prices is high (which means that a country's competitive position is favourable), a given level of domestic employment can be supported with a relatively low level of domestic demand. If the ratio is unfavourable, employment generated by exports will be relatively low, and a high level of domestic expenditure will be necessary to maintain a given level of employment. Devaluation is the instrument by which the international cost ratio is affected, in order to produce the switching effect.

Consequently, if countries deprive themselves of the possibility of making needed exchange rate adjustments by participation in some form of monetary integration such as a pseudo union, they will inflict costs upon themselves as a result of an enforced departure from internal balance unless their competitiveness happens to be just right and remains so.

That conclusion assumes that no alternative means are available for altering competitiveness. Any expenditure-switching measures that take the form of discriminatory restrictions would, as already noted, be ruled out in a common market and, in any case, would generally be undesirable on resource allocation grounds. As to more general measures, it is conceivable that incomes might be additionally taxed and the proceeds used to subsidize the prices of domestic production – a fiscal operation that would have similar effects to devaluation. But this too would almost certainly be excluded by international and customs union obligations. The only possible general alternative for bringing about a required adjustment in competitiveness that would not be inconsistent with the obligations of customs union would be to directly change the level of domestic wages and prices. But, as Friedman (1953) has tellingly observed, even if this could be brought about, in just the same way as it is more efficient to change the clock by one hour than to reschedule the time of every activity if the benefits of daylight saving are sought, so single changes in nominal exchange rates are likely to be a more efficient way of producing any required adjustment than the revision of thousands or millions of individual wages and prices in terms of national currencies that would otherwise be needed to produce the same effect. Changes in exchange rates may also accomplish needed real wage and price changes that could not be brought about by market forces or by attempts to operate directly on wage and price levels.

But, in any event, exchange rate flexibility can be successful in maintaining balance in this model only if real wages can be reduced by devaluation, so permitting the real rate of exchange to adjust. If this cannot be done, then in the absence of other solutions, perhaps of a structural kind, external equilibrium will be incompatible with internal balance, no matter whether exchange rates are fixed or flexible. The loss of the option to make exchange rate adjustments that is necessarily involved in monetary integration would then not of itself be of any significance. No 'cost' would be involved.

If monetary integration takes the form of a monetary union with a single currency, rather than a pseudo union, essentially similar considerations arise but they would present themselves in a different form. In a monetary union, the need to settle deficits and surpluses in foreign currency would not arise for individual members. But intra-union current deficits and surpluses would still have to be regulated. If a member state were in deficit, the correction of this deficit would require the same kind of downward real wage adjustment if employment is to be maintained as would occur in the absence of a monetary union with an effective currency devaluation. But inside a monetary union such an adjustment could only be brought about by a relative fall in the deficit country's wage and price levels. The need for such adjustments might, of course, be postponed by a redistribution of private financial assets within the union. If the member states of the monetary union had attained a significant level of fiscal integration as well, it might also be substantially reduced by automatic or discretionary fiscal transfers, as discussed in Chapter 7.

A later approach to the analysis of the implications of exchange rate unification for internal and external balance in a similar analytical tradition has focused attention on a different aspect of the problem, namely the cost of unifying policy targets in a monetary union in which the objectives of national economic policies differ. This approach, initiated by Fleming (1971) and Corden (1972a), crucially assumed an inverse relationship between the rates of change of money wages and prices and the level of unemployment of a kind first postulated by Phillips (1958). A stable Phillips curve relationship of this kind would imply that governments confront a trade-off between unemployment and inflation. The policy problem was then viewed as being that of achieving an optimal combination of compatible rates of inflation and levels of unemployment that in their turn would be consistent with the objective of external balance. In this formulation of the problem, the national authorities were assumed to have a particular preference ordering between alternative achievable levels of unemployment and wage rate changes. A particular welfare-maximizing combination of unemployment and wage rate changes could thus be chosen that represents the point of internal balance on this approach. However, since countries with permanently fixed exchange rates or a common currency cannot maintain different inflation rates, some might be compelled to depart from their optimal positions if a uniform rate of change of costs and prices is to ensue. Some might be compelled to accept more inflation than they would choose while others would have to accept more unemployment. For those countries that were obliged to suffer additional unemployment, its excess (valued by the corresponding loss of output) would be one significant measure of the cost of monetary integration.

Monetarism and Monetary Integration

A very different view of the significance of monetary integration is implied by monetarism and by the theories of expectations put forward by monetarists and other economists that have been such a prominent theme of theoretical macroeconomics since the beginning of the 1970s. Monetarists see the role of monetary policy in terms of the control that it affords, in principle, over nominal targets – the price level, the exchange rate or the rate of inflation. Whether and, if so, to what extent changes in such targets have effects on real variables such as output, employment and the real rate of exchange and competitiveness is seen to depend largely on the behaviour of suppliers of labour and goods. In this connection, monetarists and others have pointed out that the Phillips curve relationship fails to distinguish between changes in real and nominal wages rates, and implicitly assumes that labour suppliers expect the price level or its rate of change to be constant and do not change their price expectations and their willingness to supply at different nominal rates even when, as an inevitable result of monetary policy changes, those price expectations turn out to be false. A more rational theory of the formation of expectations leads to a denial of any long-run trade-off between inflation and unemployment.

The alternative hypothesis proposed by monetarists and many other economists claims that the rate of unemployment is in the long run independent of the rate of inflation. On this view, there is at any moment some level of unemployment that is consistent with the structure of real wage rates. Other things given, at that level of unemployment, the rise of real wage rates in the long term is governed by capital formation and technological change. The natural rate is essentially the rate that is consistent with general equilibrium, defined as the absence of excess demand in all markets or as a state in which all expectations are realized. The natural rate is determined by the structural characteristics of the labour (and

product) markets, including market frictions, minimum wage legislation, unemployment benefit rates and labour mobility. Many of
the characteristics that determine it are thus, as Friedman has put it,
'man-made and policy-made' (Friedman, 1968, p. 9) and it is not
immutable. Natural rate theorists accept that it may not be optimal
and that it may be desirable to aim to reduce it. But their fundamental contention is that it is largely determined by structural and
microeconomic phenomena, that it can be reduced only by appropriate structural policies and that it will be largely invariate with
respect to macroeconomic policies.

On this view, raising the rate of inflation once and for all lowers
the rate of unemployment only temporarily. A corollary of this is
that the only way to keep the unemployment rate permanently
below the natural rate is by continuously increasing the rate of
inflation. Each time the authorities raise the inflation rate they
achieve a temporary increase in employment. Ultimately, however,
this process must be self-defeating. A further corollary is that a
single exchange rate change will not have lasting effects on employment, because it will be neutralized by induced inflation, so that the
ability of a country to achieve relatively low unemployment by
depreciating its exchange rate is also a short-term matter. The
implications of the natural rate hypothesis for the evaluation of
monetary integration are quite profound, for, in contrast to the
traditional approach, the policy stance it suggests is that such
regimes could be adopted without incurring any lasting cost in terms
of unemployment.

The bearing of this analysis on monetary integration may be
illustrated with the aid of a quadrant diagram, first used in this
connection by de Grauwe (1975). In Figure 9.1 the upper half refers
to the home country (H) and the lower half to the partner country
(P). The north-east quadrant shows the long-run Phillips curve for
country H, and the south-east quadrant the corresponding curve for
country P. The positions of these curves are assumed to differ prior
to monetary integration, but both are vertical. The curves are the
locus of all points at which the economy is in full equilibrium in the
sense that actual inflation equals expected inflation. The north-west
and the south-west quadrants determine the inflation rates that
correspond to the wage rate changes in countries H and P respectively. This relationship is denoted by the lines WI_H and WI_P. The
intercepts of these curves with the y axis are equal to the rate of
change of the productivity of labour. In the figure the intercepts are
positive, denoting a positive rate of increase in productivity. It is
assumed that rates of productivity growth differ in the two countries, being higher in country H than in country P. Thus, the

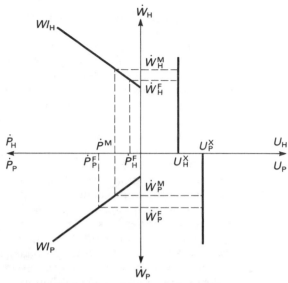

Figure 9.1   Monetary integration

intercept of WI_H is larger than the intercept of WI_P. It follows that, for a uniform wage increase in the two countries, the equilibrium price increase will be lower in country H than in country P.

In the absence of monetary union the inflation rates in the two countries would be equal only by chance. In the example, country H is assumed to have chosen an inflation rate $\dot{P}_H^F$, which is lower than that of country P, in which it is $\dot{P}_P^F$. Equilibrium requires that country P's currency should depreciate continuously relative to that of country H. The system would then attain a new equilibrium, and both countries would be able to achieve their preferred rate of inflation. In Figure 9.1 the equilibrium rate of depreciation of currency P is represented by

$$\dot{E} = \dot{P}_P^F - \dot{P}_H^F.$$

It can be seen that, in the absence of an exchange rate union, the national authorities can determine their national rates of inflation independently, exchange rate changes (the depreciation of country P's currency in this case) making the two national inflation rates compatible. If the two countries should establish a monetary union, they would lose this power to determine their own rates of inflation.

If a monetary (exchange rate) union is constituted between the two countries, irrevocably fixing exchange rates, then, assuming the absence of non-traded goods, the inflation rates in the two countries will not be able to diverge; that is

$$\dot{P}_\mathrm{H} = \dot{P}_\mathrm{P} \; (E = 0).$$

If a union inflation range $\dot{P}_\mathrm{M}$ is assumed that lies between the national inflation rates that would separately be chosen in the absence of the exchange rate union, each country would clearly have to accept a rate of inflation that js sub-optimal from its national standpoint. If, on the other hand, one country's currency is dominant, that country may be able to impose its chosen inflation rate on the other and so maintain its optimal position at the latter's expense. At the same time, no loss of employment would be associated with the latter's loss of autonomy. The higher target rate of inflation in country P ($\dot{P}_\mathrm{P}^\mathrm{F}$) would not achieve a lower rate of unemployment in the long term since that rate is fixed at its natural rate; nor would country P be able to enjoy a higher growth rate of real income as a result of its higher inflation rate. Consequently, the authorities of country P could fix its domestic inflation rate at that of country H ($\dot{P}_\mathrm{H}$) without incurring a loss in employment or in real income.

In the more general case in which non-traded goods exist it would be possible for national inflation rates to diverge in such a union because it is only identical price changes of traded goods that are implied. If rates of growth of productivity in the traded goods sectors differed in the two countries while there were equal growth rates of productivity in the non-traded goods sector, the measured rates of inflation of the two countries would necessarily differ. In this event, price stability in a dominant partner could even require a fall in the price level of the other country. This consideration, which may have some practical importance in the context of the European Monetary System (EMS), complicates the model but does not alter its essential implications and will therefore be disregarded.

The simple two-country model illustrated in Figure 9.1 is also useful to draw out other important aspects of monetary integration. In the first place, the institution of a monetary union that would entail the acceptance of a common rate of inflation clearly would not necessarily imply the balanced growth of the member countries. In the example illustrated, the rates of growth of nominal wages (and therefore of real wages) in the two countries differ. At the same time, given a divergence in rates of growth of real wages that corresponds to the differences in rates of productivity growth, those productivity differences in themselves would not generate later problems of internal balance. A low productivity growth member

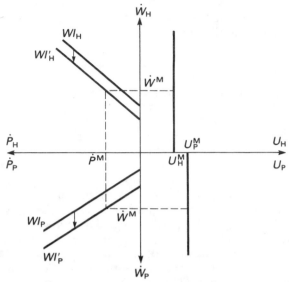

Figure 9.2   Monetary integration with balanced growth

state could be competitive with a high productivity growth member and could remain so if it accepted a lower increase in real wages.

It is not inconceivable that the unbalanced growth in this sense of the prospective partners might be unacceptable. Political considerations may make it essential that the high degree of economic integration that is involved in monetary union should also be accompanied by the balanced growth of its member countries. One possible justification for such a requirement in a common market would be that, otherwise, divergent growth rates of real wages would ultimately lead to large-scale movements of labour towards the high productivity growth countries. The political and economic costs for member states of such intra-group migrations might be perceived to be unacceptably high and to threaten the cohesion of the union. If for any such reasons it were required that a monetary union should also be accompanied by balanced growth, it would be necessary to bring about shifts in curves WI_H and WI_P, so that at a given union inflation rate the changes in nominal wages, and therefore in real wages, would be equalized in the two countries. This is the situation depicted in Figure 9.2, where curves WI_H and WI_P are respectively shifted downwards to WI'_H and upwards to WI'_P in order to satisfy the condition of equal wage rate change, that is, of balanced growth. How might such shifts be effected?

One possibility would be to introduce fiscal transfers from country

H to country P, without attempting to affect national productivity growth rates. Redefining $\dot{W}_H$ and $\dot{W}_P$ as national growth rates of nominal wages after tax subsidy, the downward shift of WI_H could be effected by a wage tax in country H and the upward shift of WI_P by a wage subsidy in country P. Equilibrium would be attained when the fiscal transfer was such that net wage rate changes ($\dot{W}^M$) were equalized in the two countries.

A second possibility would be to introduce structural policies at union level designed to equalize the growth rates of productivity in the two countries. Some of the policies that might be employed to promote an equalization of productivity growth rates, or to limit their divergence, are discussed in Chapter 10, which deals with regional problems and policies in a common market. The limited success of regional policies within nation states suggests that within an economic community an equalization of national productivity growth rates by union policies might be very difficult to achieve. A still more difficult task would be presented if it were a goal of policy that monetary union should be accompanied by a convergence of real wages, which would imply a relatively rapid rate of growth of productivity in the lagging areas.

If it cannot be assumed that 'regional' policies at the union level can be made to produce the required results, monetary union among countries with significantly different productivity growth rates may not be politically feasible without transfer payments from the high- to the low-productivity members. At the same time, if an equalization of the growth rates of productivity among the member states implies a reduction of the growth rate of net incomes in high productivity growth countries, they will be less likely to see monetary union in itself as an attractive proposition. A decision on their part to join such a union would presumably turn on whether other benefits that might be associated with a monetary union, such as trade gains or gains of a political nature, might be expected to compensate for their loss in real income growth.

In the second place, it may be noted that, although a monetary union may enjoy balanced income growth, this does not imply that unemployment rates are equalized throughout the union. If a convergence of unemployment rates were regarded as a further essential part of a programme of monetary integration, policies aimed at harmonizing conditions in the national labour markets would also be called for in order to move the Phillips curves into identical positions.

Convergence and Monetary Integration

The depiction of the effects of monetary integration in Figures 9.1 and 9.2 and the immediately preceding discussion has focused on the role of exchange rate adjustments in terms of an equilibrium model. No attention was given to the implications of the process of adjustment to demand shocks or supply side disturbance such as raw material shocks or productivity changes. This has the effect of obscuring a range of disequilibrium and adjustment problems that may be of considerable and enduring significance for policy choices. These problems are not merely those that would be encountered in a transition towards monetary integration or to a system of fixed intra-bloc exchange rates of the kind discussed in the concluding parts of this chapter, but ones that may arise and persist even when a pseudo union or a complete monetary union has been established.

The underlying model can indeed be interpreted to mean that policy can have no real effects in stabilizing and improving the performance of the economy in the face of such disturbances, thus justifying this neglect. If, for instance, as in the new classical approach, the hypothesis that expectations are formed rationally is combined with the assumption that markets clear instantaneously, then the economy cannot be shifted from its natural rate of unemployment (which may itself undergo shifts as a result of supply shocks) by systematic monetary policy intervention and the aggregate supply curve is vertical even in the short run. The conclusion can then be drawn that activist monetary policies targeted at stabilizing the economy in the face of cyclical fluctuations in aggregate demand or supply shocks that affect the position of the aggregate supply curve and the natural rate of unemployment are completely impotent. Participation in either a pseudo union or a real union would then entail no real cost even in the short run.

Empirical evidence for the particular type of macroeconomic model that is assumed in this interpretation of the issues is not wholly persuasive (Sheffrin, 1983; Carter and Maddock, 1984). Although markets for financial assets may adjust rapidly and efficiently with expectations being formed rationally, labour markets do not seem to clear quickly and smoothly in the face of internal and external shocks as is required to support the conclusion that stabilization policy is impotent.

Policy intervention may thus in principle be able to influence employment and output favourably in the short run if the economy experiences an upward departure from its natural rate of unemployment as a result of shocks whose source and nature are correctly identified by the authorities and appropriately responded to. Moreover, the natural rate of unemployment may itself be adversely affected over time by the workforce's experience of protracted unemployment (Cross, 1987). This 'hysteresis' effect may provide a further ground for policy intervention. In their views on these and a number of other significant theoretical and policy issues, some Keynesians and some monetarists have come together in their analyses and policy stances in a process of convergence.

In terms of that more eclectic approach, which may justify the adoption of an activist stance in relation to monetary policy and the money supply rather than the pursuit of a steady and predictable growth rate target for the money supply irrespective of the current state of the economy and the existence of disequilibria, there would evidently be costs attached both to the fixing of exchange rates within a pseudo union (thus subordinating monetary policy to the pursuit of an exchange rate target) and to the establishment of a common currency in a complete monetary union. These costs may be seen as falling into two categories: (1) the adjustment costs of the transition to monetary integration involved in the achievement of a common rate of inflation; and (2) the adjustment costs associated with later shocks and disturbances.

With respect to the transitional costs of monetary adjustment, if there are differences between the short-run Phillips curves of the prospective member countries, adjustment costs would necessarily be imposed on some members as a result of the adoption of a common target inflation rate, even if the members were initially on their long-run Phillips curves. The magnitude of these costs will be determined by a number of factors, including (1) the time horizon adopted for the achievement of the common rate of inflation; (2) the speed at which expectations adjust to actual inflation; (3) the form of the short-run Phillips curve; and (4) the initial discrepancies between the target rates of inflation that each member country would otherwise choose and the union-adopted rate. If, for instance, a member country initially had a higher target rate of inflation than the union-adopted rate, the downward adjustment required on its part could be brought about only by maintaining its unemployment rate at above its natural level for a period. More-over, the extent of the required rise in unemployment would increase as the time period for bringing inflation rates into line was shortened. The firm adoption of the target of convergence to part-ner countries' inflation rates might itself facilitate the adjustment of expectations and thus reduce the transitional real cost. In principle, however, it would be desirable for monetary and fiscal policies to be coordinated for a sufficiently long period prior to monetary integra-tion to bring about a high degree of convergence, if not an equaliza-tion, of inflation rates; for reasons mentioned later this might not be operationally feasible.

After monetary integration has become effective and inflation rates are harmonized, costs may continue to be incurred by individual members as a result of the constraints imposed on monetary policy responses in the face of adjustments required by later localized shocks and disturbances. Their magnitude will again depend primarily on the speed with which expectations adjust, and on institutional and contractual rigidities, which will affect the degree and duration of disequilibria. In a different analytical tradition, the various elements stressed in different optimal currency area theories are pointers to factors that may ameliorate the impact of adjustment costs.

In terms of an eclectic view, the issue of the costs of monetary integration appears to remain closely bound up with the issue of the optimal rate of inflation – who determines it – and with the issue of the extent to which the monetary supply of the pseudo or complete union should and would be allowed to vary in an attempt to accommodate short-term adjustment problems of employment or output, perhaps at the cost of creating or enhancing long-term problems by discouraging or postponing necessary adjustments and alignments, rather than targeted to grow at a fixed and predictable rate. These long-term effects operate through the effects of short-run stabilization policy on such factors as (1) the long-run allocation of resources by way, for example, of its impact on the investment–consumption split; and (2) future macroeconomic performance by way of its impact on future wage and price behaviour (for instance by permitting real wage stickiness to be perpetuated in real wage rigidity). These familiar but complex issues are illuminatingly explored in Calmfors (1983).

Some Specific Issues of Monetary Integration

The analytical framework referred to above, although essential to an understanding of monetary integration, does not address several issues that may be significant in relation to such arrangements, of which three merit particular mention. First, it will often be relevant to relax the small-country assumption and to take specific account of structural and perhaps policy interdependence amongst the countries contemplating jointly fixing their exchange rates or entering a monetary union. This raises complex questions, some of which are referred to in Chapter 7. Second, it may be significant to consider also the implications of alternative exchange rate regimes of the union or the zone for the rest of the world. The two-country model presented above cannot allow for the union's interaction with the rest of the world. Thirdly, it is desirable to consider the extent to which capital mobility affects the ability of the union's monetary policy, or of union or national fiscal policies, to deal with the problems of stabilization and adjustment that have been considered earlier in this chapter.

These and many other issues are addressed by Allen and Kenen (1980) in their exhaustive analysis of monetary integration which rests on the modern, interactive theory of exchange rate determination in the context of capital (i.e. bond) market integration. Labour mobility and the intra-union transfer of ownership of equity capital that would be unobstructed if a monetary union were superimposed on a common market are, however, both excluded. Their analysis is used to elucidate the implications of monetary integration in both Keynesian and new classical contexts. In the context of structural and policy interdependence, highly restrictive assumptions have to be introduced to limit the otherwise unmanageably large number of possible outcomes. Three conclusions may be mentioned that have an important bearing on monetary integration with respect to the second and third issues distinguished above.

First, in the case of a disturbance (such as, for instance, a decline in productivity in one country), the direction of change of price, real product and nominal income of that country are unaffected by the choice between a pegged external exchange rate for the union and a flexible rate, whether wage rates are fixed or not, and this is the case both on impact and in the long run. The directions of change of the union price index and of real product moreover remain the same in Keynesian or new classical versions (Allen and Kenen, 1980; Allen, 1982). Nevertheless, nominal changes in union income can be offset by flexible rates and evidently, in a non-classical world, some real differences may still arise, depending on which of the policy options is followed.

A second important issue in the specific context of full monetary union relates to the possibility of using union monetary policy to facilitate adjustments to disturbances affecting a particular member state. It is concluded that there would be a limited possibility of exercising a nationally differentiated impact through monetary policy if (1) capital market integration is not perfect so that the bonds of the countries are not perfect substitutes and (2) the goods of the countries are not perfect substitutes either. Even so, the central bank can affect the incidence of its policies on the national incomes of member states (prices and perhaps output) only in the short run. If the external rate of the union is pegged, there can, of course, be no effective long-run monetary policy. If, instead, the union adopts a flexible external rate in order to retain some degree of monetary independence, differences in member states' current account balances must still be adjusted by a redistribution of assets within the union. The long-run requirement that current accounts should be balanced globally will imply specific intra union relative prices and a specific distribution of the union's money supply. These requirements cannot be altered by monetary policy. This conclusion accords with that of earlier analyses.

A third important issue concerns the extent to which fiscal policies can be used to compensate for any possible costs that arise from the loss of the exchange rate as an instrument of national policy under monetary integration. It is concluded that national fiscal policy may be able to exercise some differential impact and provide some short-run scope for the alleviation of disturbances and facilitating adjustments – so long as asset markets are not perfectly integrated and the goods of one member country are not perfect substitutes for those of another. This conclusion also accords with orthodoxy.

The opportunity for exercising differential impacts through fiscal policy in the interests of adjustment would be greater if there should be a relatively large community budget, coupled with a substantial degree of integration of fiscal instruments. Not only might the budget constraint on fiscal action then be less binding, but in any case, even within a balanced budget, expenditures could, in principle, be shifted amongst member states in the face of asymmetrical shocks or other potentially destabilizing factors.

It is principally a process of this latter kind that must be relied upon to alleviate differential adjustment problems within full economic unions and nation states. In these contexts, what limits the impact of adjustment problems and provides a mechanism for their alleviation although regions, like the member states in a monetary union, cannot devalue, is not the fact that foreign currency deficits and surpluses cannot arise, but the inter-regional fiscal adjustment mechanism that is built into their systems of public finance as a result of the combined operation of progressive taxation and the character of public expenditures. Such a mechanism would be absent in a monetary union unless at the same time there were a strong community fiscal authority disposing of a relatively large budget and significant tax powers. Since the emergence of asymmetrical adjustment problems can never be excluded, complete monetary union may thus be recommendable and feasible only if it is accompanied by a degree of fiscal integration that would suffice for dealing with them. The MacDougall Report's (Commission, 1977a) attempt to quantify what that might imply in an EC context is briefly discussed in Chapter 7.

STRATEGIES FOR MONETARY INTEGRATION

If the net benefits of complete monetary integration in an economic community are perceived to be positive, what strategies might be adopted to bring it about? Vaubel (1978) has distinguished two main strategies – the strategy of *coordination* and the strategy of *centralization*, each of which is seen as having three variants. These strategies are appraised principally in terms of two criteria, namely gradualism and automaticity. For currency unification to be feasible, progress towards it must be gradual, otherwise the associated transitional adjustment costs may be prohibitive. At the same time, there is a need for automaticity to limit the discretion of participants once they have opted for a particular strategy. In the interests of the crucial objective that underlies monetary integration, which is to eliminate uncertainty about future exchange rates, automaticity is seen to be needed to prevent renegotiation, violation of agreements or opting out of them.

Under the head of coordination strategies, Vaubel distinguishes: (1) agreements to reduce the variability of exchange rates by *ex post* intervention in foreign exchange markets; (2) agreements to harmonize *ex ante* monetary policies so as to produce exchange stability without the need for intervention in the foreign exchange markets; and (3) agreements involving a combination of (1) and (2). Major technical difficulties confront each of these approaches. That consideration apart, although all are capable of conforming to the criterion of gradualism, they all lack the attribute of automaticity and therefore cannot guarantee progress towards monetary integration.

The alternative to a strategy of coordination would be one of centralization, of which Vaubel distinguishes three variants: (1) the 'big leap' solution involving the replacement of national currencies by a community currency at once and completely; (2) free competition amongst the currencies of all member states for any contracts; and (3) the introduction of a parallel currency – such as a newly created community currency – that would compete with purely national currencies. The 'big leap' would clearly conflict with the requirement of gradualism unless it were to follow on from a phase of successful coordination. The other two variants of the centralization strategy envisage a gradual but automatic centralization of monetary policy whose pace would be dictated by market forces as the most useful currency displaces purely national currencies.

A choice between these options cannot be made on the basis of purely technical criteria. Indeed, strategies of coordination and centralization are essentially looking at different issues. On the one hand, coordination strategies seek to establish the preconditions for political agreement on monetary integration. Centralization strategies, on the other hand, are essentially to be viewed as relevant alternatives for achieving monetary union once a political agreement on establishing it has been arrived at. Arriving at that agreement, with its implied transfer of political authority, remains the nub of the problem. Ultimately this is the leap that has to be made.

MONETARY INTEGRATION AND THE EC

L'Europe se fera par la monnaie ou ne se fera pas. (Jacques Rueff)

The Treaty of Rome was primarily concerned with the liberalization of trade and factor movements and with establishing a common commercial policy and a common agricultural policy. It contained no specific provisions for the adoption of a common monetary policy. Apart from general statements on the need for coordinating economic policies, the treaty confined itself to asserting that counter-cyclical policy and changes in exchange rates should be treated 'as a matter of common concern' (Articles 103 and 107). No prior commitment or understanding existed from which negotiations on monetary integration could start.

The initiative for economic and monetary union (EMU) in Europe that subsequently developed in the late 1960s was predominantly motivated not so much by any obviously pressing economic necessity for the conduct of the common market itself but rather by a political desire to provide a focus and a driving force for European integration in the next decade, when the initial task of establishing the customs union and the common agricultural policy would have been completed. Nevertheless, impending developments were soon to underline dramatically the immense difficulties of operating the common market, and particularly its CAP, if exchange rates, which under the Bretton Woods system had hitherto been fairly stable, were to fluctuate markedly. Indeed, from 1969 onward, special provisions in the shape of monetary compensation amounts (MCAs) had to be introduced in an attempt to deal with the problem of CAP. The operation and impact of MCAs are discussed in Strauss (1983).

The monetary integration initiative of the EC has been interpreted by some in terms of a 'neofunctionalist' strategy through which spillover effects would force governments to extend their cooperation to new fields of economic activity, culminating ultimately in political union. Whatever its rationale, its proponents were forced to admit that many practical problems would arise during the process. In the ensuing debate over strategy and timing, two main viewpoints emerged among the member states. On the one hand, a group that included France, Belgium and Luxemburg argued that positive steps towards monetary integration (in the shape of an arrangement to fix exchange rates irrevocably) would themselves strengthen and accelerate the process of economic integration. Member nations would then be compelled to coordinate their economic and financial policies, thus reducing disparities in wage and price trends and making full monetary union easier to achieve. The other group of countries, which included West Germany and the Netherlands, took the view that policy harmonization and economic convergence must come first, and that major steps towards monetary integration should not be taken – and indeed would not be feasible – until wage and price changes had converged and structural adaptations to intra-Community free trade had been completed. West Germany and the Netherlands also argued that premature attempts to fix exchange rates irrevocably might impede rather than stimulate a further liberalization of trade and of capital markets, because some member states would be obliged to retain controls in order to maintain those rates. Their opponents countered by contending that, if capital liberalization were introduced while exchange rates were merely pegged, massive speculative flows could develop with which official reserves could not cope, forcing exchange rates to move in the anticipated directions. The solution, they suggested, lay in taking a decision to fix exchange rates irrevocably rather than in attempting to approach the objective by a succession of small steps.

The compromise ultimately worked out between these two views is reflected in the Werner Report (Werner, 1970), which was broadly accepted by the Council of the European Communities early in 1971. The Werner Report proposed the establishment by stages of an economic and monetary union by 1980. There was by then to be a single EC currency, or at least a rigid fixing of exchange rates and the irreversible inter-convertibility of all such currencies. In addition, all capital movements were to be completely liberalized, and a common central banking system was to be established. Until the last moment, however, the separate monetary authorities were to stay in existence, and would retain the right to follow their own monetary policies, to withdraw from the arrangement and to refuse to finance partners in deficit. The first stage of the plan aimed to narrow the margins of exchange rate fluctuations.

The feasibility of the approach proposed in the Werner Report was never put to the test, since the succession of monetary crises that accompanied and succeeded the break-up of the fixed exchange rate system of Bretton Woods effectively removed it from the agenda. Although specific arrangements to limit exchange rate fluctuations were introduced by the member states of the EC in the early 1970s, these are to be seen more as a response to developments in the international monetary system than as the first steps towards the implementation of plans for economic and monetary union. In any case, even they soon proved to be too much for certain member states.

An alternative approach to economic union was thus advocated in the next important policy document, the Tindemans report on European union (Tindemans, 1976). On the specific issue of monetary integration, its proposals differed from those of the Werner Report mainly in its recognition of the obstacles that at the time hindered certain member states from making any advance towards monetary integration, while at the same time seeking to maintain some momentum towards that objective. It therefore suggested that the various steps towards monetary union in Europe need not be taken simultaneously by all countries, but that member states could join as and when they were ready. Specifically, a two-tier Community was envisaged: one tier being made up of those adhering to a 'snake' or narrow margin agreement, limiting exchange rate fluctuations and moving towards monetary union; and the other made up of those not taking part.

The *de facto* position that had been reached at the end of 1978 was that West Germany, Belgium, Luxemburg, the Netherlands and Denmark adhered to such a narrow margin or 'snake' agreement, essentially based on the Deutschmark and in operation from April 1972, whereby the monetary authorities of these countries intervened in order to keep exchange rate fluctuations within certain narrow limits. Britain, Ireland, Italy and France, although originally members, had all opted out.

The snake did not need justification as a strategy for monetary union but, if it is so viewed, its main weakness and that of any similar system is simply that, until an irrevocable commitment is made to staying within it (as evidenced for instance by the pooling of reserves and the establishment of a common central bank), there can be no certainty that national monetary developments will produce uniform inflation rates and stable exchange rates. This would be the case even if the system were to be operated in conjunction with an *ex ante* harmonization of monetary policies involving the adoption of supposedly consistent monetary growth rate targets. In operational terms there is no means of ensuring that even the full implementation of *ex ante* monetary targets would be consistent with exchange rate objectives, since the relationship between such intermediate targets and the policy objectives is variable and difficult to predict. In any event, in the last resort, participants can opt out.

Since the appearance of the Tindemans Report, little attention has been paid by European policy makers to the issue of monetary union. It is true that Mr Roy Jenkins, when President of the European Commission, did attempt in his 1977 Monnet lecture to relaunch public debate on the subject and to stimulate action (Jenkins, 1978). But the subsequent EC proposals for the creation of a new monetary zone, which finally resulted in the establishment of a new European Monetary System (EMS) in March 1979 (Her Majesty's Government, 1978b), were motivated primarily by a desire to mitigate the increasingly disruptive effects on intra-EC exchange rates that had resulted from pressure on the dollar rather than by any interest in monetary union. Although the EMS might facilitate a later move towards monetary union if it should succeed in promoting a close convergence of economic policies *and* performance in the EC, which was one of its aims, its principal declared objective was to establish a greater measure of monetary stability in the Community. There is nothing to suggest that any of the protagonists of the scheme saw the initiative as one that, if successful, would *necessarily* lead to monetary union. It is not appropriate to evaluate the structure and performance of the EMS only in terms of its accord with the supposed requirements for monetary union.

The essential feature of the system is the creation of an enlarged system of fixed but adjustable exchange rates. Four Community countries – the UK, Greece, Portugal and Spain—have so far chosen not to participate in the system's exchange rate mechanism (ERM). Each participating currency has a central rate expressed in terms of the European Currency Unit (ECU), the value of which is calculated as a basket of determined amounts of each member state's currency, excluding only the peseta and the escudo. These central rates determine a grid of bilateral central rates around which permissible fluctuation margins of ± 2.25 per cent have been established (6 per cent for the weaker Irish punt and the Italian lira). At these margins, intervention by all participating central banks is obligatory and unlimited. Intervention limits are supplemented by a novel indicator, which measures the degree of divergence of each currency from its central rate. If a currency crosses a threshold of divergence, set at 75 per cent of the maximum permissible spread, the country concerned is expected to take corrective measures, which may include intervention, measures of domestic monetary policy, changes in central rates or other measures of economic policy. Adjustments of central rates are subject to mutual agreement by a common procedure involving all countries participating in the exchange rate mechanism and the Commission itself. Eleven such realignments took place between 1979 and January 1987.

The ECU has a central role in the new system. It serves as a *numéraire* for the exchange rate mechanism, as the denominator for operations in both the intervention and credit mechanisms, as a reference point for the divergence indicator, and as a means of settlement and a reserve asset for EMS central banks.

At the start of the EMS, the central banks participating in the exchange rate mechanism deposited 20 per cent of their gold and dollar reserves with the European Monetary Cooperation Fund on a revolving three-month swap basis, receiving in return drawing rights denominated in ECUs. To support the operation of the EMS, previously established European credit mechanisms have been strengthened. These include the mutual credit lines between the participating central banks for the financing of interventions (the 'very short-term financing facility') and the short-term and medium-term support and assistance credits, which were substantially enlarged with the establishment of the EMS from 10 billion ECU to 25 billion ECU. The introduction of the EMS was linked with a separate arrangement to provide subsidized loans through the European Investment Bank under the so-called New Community Instrument (see Chapter 10) to two less prosperous member states (Italy and Ireland) for the period 1979–83 to finance infrastructure projects in the countries concerned. This was designed to strengthen their economic base and to encourage their acceptance of the disciplines that the EMS would impose.

The initial phase of the EMS was to have been consolidated within two years by the creation of a European monetary fund (to replace the EMCF) as well as by the full utilization of the ECU as a reserve asset and a means of settlement. There was also to have been a permanent transfer of a certain portion of member countries' reserves against ECUs in place of the swap arrangements. So far, it has proved to be impossible to advance much beyond the initial transitional phase. In particular, it has proved to be impossible to design an acceptable EMF because of basic differences of opinion amongst the member states with respect to its structure, tasks and powers and the extent to which it should be independent of governments.

The establishment of the EMS was attended by considerable scepticism. Some of its critics argued that the system would exercise a deflationary influence, while others insisted that it would encourage inflation by serving as a vehicle for the expansion of liquidity and would thus help to make economic divergences more persistent. It was widely predicted that divergent national economic developments would encourage speculative capital movements that would rapidly disrupt the system. That certainly has not happened; the system has not only survived, but is widely regarded as having achieved some of its objectives.

Any attempt to assess the performance of the EMS since 1979 confronts the difficulty that it is impossible to know how events would have developed in its absence. Enthusiasts are inclined to base their judgements on favourable movements of certain key indicators of policy and performance in the EMS since its establishment, which are imputed to the system. More sceptical observers have sought to judge success partly by comparing EMS experience with that of the principal non-participating countries during the same period, namely Japan, USA and UK. The judgements of some sceptics on the role of the EMS are also coloured by their mistrust of the argument that exchange rate volatility has had harmful effects upon trade.

Taking first the central issue of nominal exchange rate variability, and using standard deviations based on quarterly exchange rate changes as the indicator, it is indisputable that in these terms the ERM countries have experienced a substantial reduction in exchange rate variability within the system over the period 1979–85. However, the same currencies have not become less volatile when measured against the principal non-ERM countries.

A reduction of intra-EC exchange rate volatility is not the only criterion by which success should be judged. It had also been hoped that the operation of the EMS would promote a convergence of economic policies and of performance within the Community, thus facilitating its further integration. In the event, any such convergence has so far been limited. The coordination of policies amongst EC members, particularly of their monetary and budgetary policies, has clearly not sufficed to maintain complete exchange stability and in key respects there has been a marked failure of economic performance to converge.

In terms of standard indicators of economic policy such as monetary growth, and using standard deviations as the measure of convergence and divergence (House of Commons, 1985a), the post-1979 period appears to have seen little convergence either in the monetary or in the fiscal dimension. This is particularly so for nominal monetary growth rates and interest rates.

In the realm of economic performance there has certainly been some improvement in the degree of convergence amongst the ERM countries in respect of inflation rates, but this specific development cannot be attributed entirely – and perhaps not even mainly – to the system, since the shift in economic priorities that it reflects has been a world-wide phenomenon. Indeed, the improvement in the ERM countries has not in fact been as great as that which has occurred in the principal non-member countries. Furthermore, the improvement in intra-EC convergence that has occurred with respect to inflation must be weighed against a deterioration in certain other respects, notably for rates of unemployment, where the performance of ERM countries has diverged. Their performance has also been worse in this respect than that of the non-ERM reference countries, although not worse than that of other non-ERM European countries – perhaps the more significant comparison. It is indeed possible that the greater convergence of certain nominal variables that has occurred in the EC, notably with respect to the rate of inflation, may have been achieved at the price of less convergence amongst real variables such as unemployment and real growth. This does not mean that the existence of the ERM and the constraints that it has imposed may not have helped to prevent even greater disparities in economic performance from developing among the member countries.

A traditional argument for seeking to strengthen the EMS, namely the presumed adverse effect of exchange rate volatility on trade, might appear to have been weakened by the results of a recent study (International Monetary Fund, 1984) that reports little evidence so far of a negative relationship between real exchange rate variability and trade flows. However, the effects of exchange rate uncertainty are particularly difficult to measure. In any case, its direct trade impact is only one part of the persuasive case that underlies the continued concern of policy makers with the stability of exchange rates in the EC. But if that objective is to be more fully attained in the future, the record suggests that fresh mechanisms will have to be developed for ensuring that the policies of member states are fully consonant with it. This will not be easy to achieve even with a high degree of political commitment for, as already noted, the connections between monetary targets through which an *ex ante* coordination of policies might be attempted and the inflation and exchange rate objectives are variable and difficult to predict. Moreover, although monetary policy convergence will be necessary to bring about a convergence of economic performance, almost certainly it will not be sufficient. Other EC policies of a structural nature could have an important role to play in support of national policies.

It is sometimes suggested that, in order to bring about effective monetary policy coordination, the establishment of a strong EMF is needed, endowed with explicit rules of intervention and given the task of monitoring national policies and interventions. Evidently such a body would run into similar problems in formulating clear intervention rules as do the authorities in the member states themselves. An EMF would suffer from the additional disadvantage of lacking effective sanctions to enforce its rules, since in the last resort, as long as there is scope for borrowing in private international markets for credit-worthy governments, it is difficult to see how a recalcitrant member could be constrained to adjust. The fundamental problem stems from the difficulty of designing an EMS that would be more effective than the present informal methods of cooperation for reducing exchange rate uncertainties without requiring national politicians to accept some transfer of authority and ultimately a commitment to the adoption of a common currency – which at the present juncture is clearly impracticable. The Council's two-year delay in accepting even the first stage of the Commission's modest 1984 proposals (*Bulletin of the European Communities*, 11/1984) for strengthening and expanding the EMS by more effective surveillance procedures, a further liberalization of capital movements and the promotion of the already substantial and growing use of the ECU merely underlines the determination of the member states to retain their perceived autonomy in this field, however nominal and tenuous it may be.

Britain and the EMS

Should Britain join the exchange rate mechanism? Of late a growing body of opinion inside and outside the UK has expressed the view that the time is ripe for the full participation of the UK in the EMS, both in its own interest and in that of the EC as a whole. If the issue is considered purely from the UK's viewpoint it is generally accepted that the force of many of the domestic obstacles that prevented entry at the outset has diminished considerably, in some cases to vanishing point. In particular, monetary policy in Britain has recently moved away from sole reliance on money supply targets (which effectively ruled out participation initially) and has given weight to managing the exchange rate. Moreover, since 1979, the UK's inflation rate and money supply growth rates have moved into line with those of the ERM countries. It is far from clear that any substantial 'transitional' adjustment costs would now be imposed upon Britain if she were to enter.

Looking to the past, it is possible to take the view that substantial positive benefits might have accrued to Britain from participation. For instance, membership would almost certainly have avoided the extreme over-appreciation of sterling that occurred in 1980–1, with its damaging effects on economic performance, since monetary growth would necessarily have been higher. Participation in the future, it might be argued, would be another matter because differential rates of growth of productivity are still evident and provide grounds for concern. The reserve currency role of sterling (if it is to be maintained) would suggest an additional need to retain flexibility. But the EMS does not demand a rigid fixity of exchange rates, in any case, and it seems reasonable to suppose that acceptable technical adjustments could be negotiated to take care of the special position of sterling, for instance by providing for wider fluctuation bands in its case. Nevertheless, there must be substantial reasons for a realignment; decisions are now truly collective, leaving no 'scope for obtaining trade advantages by unilateral exchange rate management' (Padoa-Schioppa, 1985, p. 351).

From Britain's viewpoint there seem now to be few solid economic arguments against entry, though equally, perhaps, there are no very strong economic arguments in favour. If that is so, it might have been expected that the important political arguments for entry that are bound up with the UK's membership of and position in the EC should be allowed to prevail. That was not the judgement of the Parliamentary Committee that reviewed this issue in 1985 (House of Commons, 1985b). It concluded that the status quo should be maintained in the short and medium term, although it did not rule out participation at some future date.

CONCLUSION

Any purely economic assessment of the merits of monetary integration and of monetary union must be related primarily to the magnitude of three principal elements of a cost–benefit appraisal and the weight that is attached to them by its prospective participants.

The first element is made up principally of the lasting beneficial impact on the efficiency of industry and finance – and so on output – that can be expected to result from improved capital mobility and investment decisions in the area when exchange risks are eliminated (in a complete union) or reduced.

The second element is made up of anticipated real adjustment costs. These take the form of (1) the loss of output and employment that some members may incur in the transition to monetary integration during which inflation rates have to be aligned, and (2) any differential short-term costs of adjustment to localized or union-wide disturbances that would arise even in the longer run after the monetary union has come into effect. Other possible costs may be associated with the choice of the target inflation rate, not only during the transitional period but in the longer run. These costs and their intra-union distribution would depend on the monetary policies adopted by the monetary authority or authorities with respect to inflation and short-term stabilization problems.

The third element in the appraisal consists of the potential costs entailed for certain members by the need for intra-union transfers of resources in order to ease adjustment costs that might otherwise be perceived to be unacceptably high for certain other members. In the transitional period, such transfers might be a necessary political condition for a commitment to monetary integration. If the union is to endure, such transfers might well be needed indefinitely to facilitate structural adjustments to asymmetrical real disturbances or to promote a convergence of economic performance in the community. Their costs would inevitably fall mainly on its economically stronger members and would from their standpoint reduce any potential economic attractions that monetary integration might otherwise possess in terms of its efficiency-promoting effects.

Evaluations of the merits of monetary integration and of monetary unions in the light of these conflicting considerations cannot usefully be made in general and in the abstract. Judgement must be related first to the structural behaviour and characteristics of particular economies for which the magnitude of the effects and the weight to be attached to them may be concretely evaluated from the standpoint of the union and its constituent member states; and, secondly, to the policies that could be expected to be pursued by the monetary authority or authorities of an integrated area. Those policies could to some extent be constrained and predicted by the treaty or monetary agreement that would necessarily have to be negotiated for any form of monetary integration that was not merely a *de facto* arrangement resting on the hegemony of a pivotal currency.

CHAPTER 10

Regional Problems and Policy in a Common Market

Regional problems are difficult to define but easy to recognize. Essentially, they express themselves in marked geographical disparities in levels and rates of growth of output, incomes and employment. These disparities are often coupled with a high degree of inter-regional labour migration, and, for some areas, an extreme susceptibility to economic fluctuations.

Regional problems at the level of the member states vis-à-vis each other and regional problems at the level of designated regions within member states are not identical; but many of the fundamental factors at work are similar, and economists have found it fruitful to approach the problems by similar analytical methods. Among the important differences between the problems of regions within countries and those of nations within economic communities, two in particular stand out. First, factor mobility is likely to be greater within member countries than between them. Secondly, members of economic groups often retain control over their monetary and exchange policies, whereas regions within states do not. The principal implication of these differences is that, if exchange rates are flexible, trade among member countries takes place on the basis of comparative costs. Inter-country differences in factor earnings can be matched by exchange rate adjustments, permitting full employment to be maintained but not necessarily resolving the problem of income disparities. On the other hand, trade within a nation takes place on the basis of prices in the national currency; but, because labour is mobile, it is less easy for differences in regional productivities to be matched by differences in earnings. As groupings progress along the spectrum that ranges from common markets to economic union, these differences between the contexts of the two regional problems gradually become obliterated.

This chapter discusses the problem of regional policy in an economic community under the following heads: (1) the source of the regional problem; (2) the rationale for regional policy in an economic community; and (3) the implementation of a community regional policy. Lastly, policy in the European Community (EC) is briefly reviewed.

THE SOURCE OF THE REGIONAL PROBLEM

What is the source of the 'regional problem'? It seems clear that the regional disparities that now exist within advanced countries, amongst advanced countries and between advanced and less developed countries cannot be explained in terms of differences in initial natural resource endowments, for only a relatively small part of these divergences originates in activities based on land or mineral resources. Present-day regional disparities have largely emerged during the process of modern economic growth – during the last 150 years – and are mainly to be explained in terms of the unequal development of industrial activities. High-income areas are almost invariably those that possess a developed and efficient modern industry.

In a fundamental sense the regional problem is caused by disparate movements in industrial productivity growth rates. Regions or countries with lagging productivity rates will tend to experience lower levels of per capita income and lower growth rates. If, moreover, factor remuneration rates are not kept in line with productivity, unemployment differences will also tend to arise. There is room for debate over the precise weight to be attached to the different factors that are important in explaining trends in productivity, and these may in any case be expected to vary between regions and countries.

In seeking a theoretical explanation for the regional problem, economists today place much emphasis on a factor that orthodox trade theory still largely neglects, namely, the process of increasing returns. This is central to the theories offered by Myrdal (1957), Hirschman (1958) and Kaldor (1970, 1971).

To explain the persistence of regional divergences Myrdal has invoked 'the principle of circular and cumulative causation', which is closely bound up with increasing returns. In Kaldor's words:

These are not just the economies of large-scale production commonly considered, but the cumulative advantages accruing from the growth of industry itself – the development of skill and know-how; the opportunity of ever-increasing differentiations of processes and specialisation in human activity. (1970, p. 340)

On this view, initial differences become perpetuated by a cumulative movement that is reinforced rather than offset by factor movements and trade. Factor movements themselves can generate increasing returns; thus, flows of labour, capital, goods and services from poor to rich regions may occur, which serve not to ameliorate disparities in per capita incomes and growth rates, as neoclassical theory may seem to suggest, but rather to enhance them. In the presence of increasing returns, trade between regions may also operate so as to widen, not narrow, differences in comparative costs and may not necessarily be beneficial to all. The solution to regional disparities is therefore not to be found in the indiscriminate promotion of factor mobility. The process by which the initial advantage of the growing region is sustained and reinforced has been termed 'polarization' by Hirschman and 'backwash' by Myrdal.

For the lagging areas an important influence on their rates of growth is the induced effects of growth in the prosperous centre. These effects are of two kinds: (1) the unfavourable effects that result from polarization; and (2) the favourable effects, termed 'spread' by Myrdal and 'trickle-down effects' by Hirschman. The latter include such repercussions as the increased demand for imports generated by growth at the centre, and the effects of the diffusion of the technology of the more advanced centres.

If spread effects were sufficiently strong, all countries or regions could benefit from growth at the centre, and the problem of inequalities would become one of differential rates of progress. Myrdal has taken the view that spread effects are likely to be weak, so that, failing government intervention, the success of fast-growing areas will actually inhibit the development of the others. Myrdal has seen this process as operating for long periods of time until ultimately, perhaps, natural checks are imposed on the growing areas as a result of diseconomies associated with high rates of industrial growth, including environmental problems.

A more developed version of the cumulative causation theory has been presented by Kaldor (1970, 1971). Its essential features may be briefly summarized. Resource increases are primarily self-generated, being determined by the rate at which technical progress is embodied in capital equipment, which in turn is primarily determined by the rate of growth of output. The long-run growth of output is governed by the rate of growth of autonomous demand. In a regional context the main autonomous demand factor is the demand for exports, which in turn induces new investment in the region.

The behaviour of exports, and of a region's production, depends on two factors: (1) the rate of growth of world demand for the region's products; and (2) the movement of 'efficiency wages' in the region relative to other producing regions. The movement of efficiency wages depends on the relative movement of money wages and of productivity. If this relationship (the index of wages divided by the index of productivity) moves in favour of the area, it will gain in competitiveness, and vice versa.

There is empirical evidence to suggest that money wages can be expected to move in a similar fashion in each region, even though regional growth rates of employment vary widely. However, because of increasing returns, higher growth rates of productivity will be experienced by regions with faster growth rates of output – the relationship known as Verdoorn's law (Verdoorn, 1949). Thus, efficiency wages tend to fall in areas where output and productivity are increasing relatively rapidly, allowing those areas to acquire a cumulative competitive advantage over relatively slow-growing areas. This is the mechanism through which, according to Kaldor, the process of cumulative causation works.

A formal model of regional growth differences on Kaldorian lines has been set out by Dixon and Thirlwall (1975). This makes it possible to clarify the role of the Verdoorn effect in contributing to regional growth differences, throws light on the question of whether regional growth rate differences will tend to narrow or diverge through time, and helps to elucidate the role of structural factors in explaining growth rate differences.

The model shows a region's equilibrium growth rate as depending on four main factors: (1) the income elasticity of demand for exports; (2) the price elasticity of demand for exports; (3) the rate of inflation; and (4) the Verdoorn effect, which itself operates through the price elasticity of demand for exports. Regional differences persist because of the sustaining influence of the Verdoorn effect, which provides the link between exports and growth via prices and completes the circle of circular cumulative causation. The model may be specified as follows.

Let

$$r_t = r_a + \lambda(g_t) \tag{1}$$

$$P_t^d = W_t + \tau_t - r_t \tag{2}$$

$$X_t = \eta(P_t^d) + \epsilon(Z_t) + \delta(P_t^f) \tag{3}$$

$$g_t = \gamma(X_t) \tag{4}$$

where, at time t, r is the rate of productivity growth; r_a is the rate of autonomous productivity growth; g is the rate of output growth; λ is the Verdoorn coefficient; P^d is the rate of domestic inflation; W is the rate of growth of money wages; τ is the rate of growth of $1 +$ the percentage markup on unit labour costs; X is the rate of growth of exports; Z is the rate of growth of 'world' income; P^f is the rate of growth of 'world' prices; η is the price elasticity of demand for exports; ϵ is the income elasticity of demand for exports; δ is the cross-elasticity of demand for exports; and γ is a constant (equal to unity if exports are a constant proportion of output). Combining equations 1–4 to obtain an expression for the growth rate gives

$$g_t = \frac{\gamma[\eta(W_t + \tau_t - r_a) + \epsilon(Z_t) + \delta(P_t^f)]}{1 + \gamma\eta\lambda}. \tag{5}$$

Several points emerge. First, the Verdoorn effect is a source of regional growth differences only to the extent that the coefficient varies between regions or, if not, that initial differences exist with respect to other parameters and variables such that the Verdoorn effect serves to magnify the effect of the differences. The dependence of productivity growth on the growth rate is not in itself sufficient to cause differences in regional growth rates unless the Verdoorn coefficient varies between regions or unless growth rates would differ for other reasons. It is clear, however, that it is the Verdoorn relationship that makes the model circular and cumulative and gives rise to the possibility that, once a region obtains a growth advantage, it will, other things being given, keep it.

Suppose, for instance, that a region obtains an advantage in the production of goods with a high elasticity of demand, which causes its growth rate to rise above that of another region. As a result of the Verdoorn effect, productivity growth will be higher, the rate of change of prices will be lower (assuming W and τ to be the same in both regions), the rate of growth of exports (and hence the rate of growth of output) will be higher, and so on. Moreover, the fact that the region with the initial advantage will obtain a competitive advantage in the production of goods with a high income elasticity of demand will mean that it will be difficult for other regions to establish similar activities.

Secondly, whether growth converges to an equilibrium or diverges depends on the product of the price elasticity of demand for exports and the Verdoorn coefficient. Assume that growth is a lagged function of export demand, such that equation 4 may be written

$$g_t = \gamma(X_{t-1}) \tag{4a}$$

Substitution (assuming $\gamma = 1$) gives the first-order difference equation

$$g_t + \eta\lambda g_{t-1}1 = \eta(W_t + \tau_{t-1} - r_a) + \epsilon(Z_{t-1}) + \delta(P^f_{t-1}) \tag{6}$$

the general solution of which is

$$g_t = A(-\eta\lambda)^t + \frac{\eta(W_t + \tau_t - r_a) + \epsilon(Z_t) + \delta(P^f_t)}{1 + \eta\lambda} \tag{7}$$

where A is the initial condition.

The second term on the right-hand side of equation 7 gives the equilibrium growth rate. Since $\eta < 0$ and $\lambda > 0$, the system will converge to or diverge from the equilibrium growth rate depending on whether $-\eta\lambda \gtrless = 1$. If a two-regional model is assumed, a necessary condition for the growth rates to diverge will be that the growth rate of one of the regions diverges from its own equilibrium rate. This will also be a sufficient condition if the growth rate of the other region is stable or diverges from equilibrium in the opposite direction. Since the price elasticity of demand for exports rarely exceeds -2.0 and the Verdoorn coefficient rarely exceeds 0.5, and $\gamma=1$ if exports are a constant proportion of output, it may be concluded that regional growth rate divergence is unlikely to occur. To explain why growth rates differ between regions it is thus necessary to explain why equilibrium growth rates differ between regions. On this view, Kaldor's model is best interpreted as predicting different equilibrium growth rates rather than cumulatively diverging growth rates. Of course, constant persistent growth-rate differences will be sufficient to generate a widening of regional per capita income levels if population growth is the same in each region and each region starts at the same level.

The formal model just described rests on a partial equilibrium approach in the sense that each region is considered in isolation from the others, inter-regional relations being taken into account only through the Verdoorn effect. From this point of view it is narrower than the theories of Myrdal, Hirschman and Kaldor, who all have explicitly recognized the importance of inter-regional relationships that operate through the spread effect. The less formal approach of those writers has also enabled them to encompass more of the complexity of the development process than is possible in a formal model, and their analyses contain many useful insights. Kaldor, for instance, has argued, by analogy with oligopoly theory, that cumulative causation is likely to lead to the concentration of industrial development in several successful regions rather than one. It is then possible that these regions may hold each other in balance through increasing specialization between them, some becoming more prominent in some industries and some in others.

Despite its neglect of spread effects the Dixon–Thirlwall model has the great merit of clarifying the role of structural factors in determining the equilibrium growth rate, which is illuminating in any consideration of the instruments of regional policy. Disregarding inter-regional differences in W and τ, regional growth rate differences are explained by differences in η, δ, r_a, ϵ and λ. The price and income elasticities of demand for regional exports will depend on the nature of the products produced. The rate of autonomous productivity growth and the Verdoorn coefficient will depend on the technical dynamism of productive agents in the region, that is, on their ability to invent and introduce new techniques of production, coupled with the extent to which capital accumulation is induced by growth and also embodies technical progress. The determinants of r_a and λ may vary between industries, and so they may vary between regions depending on the industrial structure of the region. It is thus made clear that raising a region's growth rate is fundamentally a question of making regions more competitive by increasing the rate of autonomous growth of productivity or by altering the industrial structure so that goods are produced that are subject to higher income elasticities of demand and higher Verdoorn coefficients. The process is not automatic once started, however. Continued success requires a continuous adaptation to changing needs and requirements.

The analyses of the regional problem that have been presented in this chapter do not distinguish between regions within countries and inter-country comparisons. There are nevertheless important differences between the two cases, which must be borne in mind in applying such analyses to the explanation of regional disparities and a discussion of policy issues. Some of these differences may usefully be mentioned in concluding this section.

One important point specific to Kaldor's model is that it assumes that growth is demand-led and unconstrained by factor supplies. Such models may be criticized on the grounds that growth is often constrained, at least in part, by factor supplies rather than by demand considerations and that, even where demand is the constraint, exports are not the sole or even the major autonomous demand component of regional demand.

If it is regional problems within a country that are at issue, these are perhaps not strong arguments. Within countries, where capital is perfectly mobile, demand in expanding regions does tend to create its own supply. Even in lagging regions, to view economic growth as being constrained by factor supplies will often be inappropriate.

At the national level, however, the arguments for neglecting supply constraints, particularly with respect to investment and the constraints that affect its productivity, are less compelling. Under-lying Kaldor's theory of regional development is a particular theory of growth and income distribution. It is implied that the necessary rate of accumulation will automatically be financed out of profits, irrespective of the rate of profits taxation. In the presence of price and profit controls and collective bargaining this is unlikely to be a satisfactory hypothesis of the savings-investment mechanism. It does, moreover, seem to belie the important role of capital move-ments in the history of economic development.

Other important differences that may be briefly noted are, first, that the tendency for money wages and their rate of increase to be similar within countries is much less noticeable between countries, although, as Kaldor (1971) has noted, even internationally 'the dispersion in the growth of money wages as between different industrial areas tends always to be considerably smaller than the dispersion in productivity movements'. Finally, countries, unlike regions, may have separate currencies. This may make it possible at a national level for devaluation to counteract the effects on employ-ment of adverse trends in efficiency wages. By the same token, in considering the problem of growth at a national level the introduc-tion of a balance of payments constraint would be desirable.

THE RATIONALE FOR REGIONAL POLICY IN AN ECONOMIC COMMUNITY

It may appear that a regional policy involving attempts to reduce disparities will necessarily conflict with the basic rationale of eco-nomic integration, namely, improved resource allocation, by inter-fering with market forces. This is not necessarily so; but even if it were, other economic goals would clearly have to be taken into account in formulating an optimal economic policy in an economic community, including in particular those concerned with the level of resource utilization and economic stabilization, and distribu-tional considerations.

At a national level the economic case for the pursuit of regional policies rests on three principal considerations. The first is a resource allocation argument, which asserts that market forces alone cannot be relied upon to operate satisfactorily in relation to location decisions. The argument is in part a structural one. It is contended that the external economies and diseconomies of location decisions are such that regulatory action is called for in order to ensure an efficient economic framework within which private locational decisions can operate optimally. Congestion in central areas is a notable example of the need for control. Since the diseconomies of congestion are external to the individual producer and may not be fully reflected in selling costs or prices, concentration in growing areas may be carried much further than is socially defensible on efficiency grounds. The second argument is a resource utilization argument, which orthodox integration theory abstracts from by its assumption of full employment. Output and growth-maximization considerations require that the economy's resources should be fully utilized. If labour is immobile and its price fails to reflect its opportunity cost, this may justify intervention to influence the level of utilization. The third argument derives from stabilization considerations. The avoidance of inflation and the achievement of steady growth may be compatible only if large differences in regional unemployment rates are avoided. Acute regional disparities in unemployment rates are likely to affect a country's ability to control inflation, by making it difficult to devise general fiscal measures that avoid excessive inflationary pressures in some areas without imposing an unacceptably high rate of unemployment in others. Regional policy measures may be regarded in part as an attempt to manage the level of aggregate demand on a more selective basis than the use of orthodox fiscal and monetary measures allows.

The practical justification of regional policies at a national level rests, not only on purely economic arguments, but on political and social considerations as well. The political argument for regional policies is basically one of cohesion. Wide economic divergences generate political tensions and are felt to be inconsistent with the equality of economic opportunity that a common citizenship implies. The inhabitants of depressed areas also have votes. It is useless to expect that factor mobility will necessarily alleviate regional problems. Even if, by increased factor mobility, income disparities may be reduced, the political and social costs of major geographical movements of the population may be too great. It is a combination of such political, social and economic arguments that has in practice led to the adoption of regional policies in many advanced countries.

The force of the arguments for the adoption and maintenance of regional policies at the national level is not diminished by the formation of an economic grouping. Indeed, the case for regional policy *per se* may be strengthened, in as much as there are reasons to suppose that the formation of a community may accentuate regional problems. The establishment of an economic community does, however, raise the question of whether a community regional policy is required in addition to national policies and, if so, how it is to be related to the latter. In general, most of the arguments used to justify national regional policies can also be used to justify a community policy, although the weight attached to the different arguments may be different and the appropriate role of community policy vis-à-vis national policy in terms of character and importance will vary with the level of integration.

Perhaps the fundamental argument for the adoption of a regional policy at the level of an economic community is the distributional or political one. However satisfactory the initial integration arrangements may be for all member states, the dynamic effects of integration cannot be foreseen. Although they will no doubt be favourable for the group, they may not benefit each member. For a variety of reasons the formation of an economic grouping is likely to enhance the forces of polarization at country level. If disparities grow between countries, then, even if this is not attributable to integration, the necessary political basis for integration may be eroded or disappear.

Moreover, even if national economic performances continue to be satisfactory, existing regional problems within member states will not disappear with integration. Indeed, with the passage of time they may be made more acute. New regional problems may be generated by the evolution of the group's sectoral policies. Even if national interests are adequately safeguarded in the formulation of such policies, any adverse regional impact that is attributable to them will be obvious and difficult to disregard. Also, in practice it may be difficult, without introducing distortions, for sectoral policies to be operated in such a way as to leave particular national interests unaffected when those sectoral policies have a strong regional impact. The case for a separate adjustment through regional policy measures taken at the union level may then be a strong one.

Finally, irrespective of any deterioration in the regional situation, the mere existence of national regional policies will pose problems for the group, which provides an argument for a community policy on harmonization grounds. Some kinds of national regional aids may be incompatible with the working of the common market by directly discriminating against intra-community trade. Others, while not involving significant discrimination, may nevertheless fail to contribute to the alleviation of the regional problem. Competition among member states in national regional aids may result only in the reciprocal neutralization of their effects. National regional aids in terms of the level of assistance or methods may not correspond to the relative seriousness of the regional problem in different national regions when viewed at the level of the group. For all these reasons there will be a legitimate interest on the part of the community in national regional aid systems, and a specific need for a community policy to coordinate national policies both to prevent regional aids from causing undue distortion of competition and to make regional policies more effective.

A regional policy thus seems to be required at community level in economic groupings for three main reasons:

(1) to ensure that the distribution of costs and benefits among members continues to be equitable in the long run in the face of the operation of structural forces and unforeseen changes;

(2) to ensure that national regional aids are consistent with the objectives of the group from the standpoint of competition policy and regional policy;

(3) to ensure that specific regional problems within countries are not aggravated by community policies.

The relative importance attached to group regional policy vis-à-vis national regional policy, and also its specific character, must clearly depend on the nature of the countries integrating and on the degree of integration aimed at or achieved.

For instance, in contrast to the case of advanced countries, regional policy in groupings of less developed countries is concerned principally with relative national developments and in particular with the inter-country distribution of modern sector industrial growth. National aids are more concerned with attracting investment to the country rather than with influencing its internal geographical distribution. Internal disparities are rarely a matter of primary concern, even though they are often much wider than those found in advanced countries. In groupings of less developed countries the danger of reciprocal neutralization may be particularly important. Harmonization of national incentive legislation to influence the location of new enterprises amongst the different countries is then a crucial issue.

Apart from this basic distinction, the degree of integration aimed at or attained is also important for the character and extent of community policy. In a simple customs union, a policy limited to avoiding distortions by measures of fiscal harmonization may suffice. In a common market where large-scale labour and capital flows may occur, there may be a greater need to introduce community instruments to influence the scale and character of those flows or to deal with their physical and financial repercussions. In a common market in which national fiscal and monetary policies are also harmonized, there would be additional justification for attaching a still greater role to community regional policy, since national policy instruments for dealing with adjustment problems will then be greatly reduced or constrained. Regionally differentiated community monetary and fiscal policies may then be desirable until the member states have moved towards a common cycle, although the use of monetary policy for this purpose is subject to severe limitations (Allen, 1983).

THE IMPLEMENTATION OF A COMMUNITY REGIONAL POLICY

The implementation of a community regional policy requires: agreement on objectives; agreement on criteria or indicators of qualification for benefit; the choice of instruments; and the provision of financial resources for carrying out the policy. The problem of assigning instruments of regional policy between the community and the national authorities also arises.

The choice of instruments is a central issue. There are three broad approaches that may be employed: (1) the use of market incentives; (2) administrative controls; and (3) public investment in infrastructure or productive investment. In a discussion of integration among market economies, the use of fiscal or financial measures merits special consideration. What general conclusions are suggested as to the use of such measures by the theories discussed in this chapter?

One solution that has been suggested for overcoming regional disparities in economic groupings is to subsidize labour in depressed regions. This policy has been supported by both Kaldor (1970) and Balassa (1975a). How would such subsidies operate? For a region within a country, the payment of a regional wage subsidy would be equivalent to the combination of a regional devaluation plus a transfer payment to the region. The cost of labour would be reduced, which would have an effect on exports that was akin to devaluation, but the adverse effects that devaluation would otherwise have on regional expenditures would be offset where the wage subsidy was financed by the national budget.

In the context of such regional aids operated at the national level, it can be envisaged that a payroll tax or social security contributions could be allowed to vary from region to region, being low as a percentage of wages in regions of high unemployment and high in regions of full employment and congestion. Such a policy might also be applied by community agencies – perhaps by the introduction of a supplementary tax or subsidy, which would be varied according to the seriousness of the problem viewed from a community level. This approach would have many merits. It could alleviate the regional unemployment problem by providing a stimulus to regional exports; it could provide an inducement to the use of labour rather than capital in those areas; it could discourage production in areas of excessive concentration; and, finally, it would have the great merit of not discriminating against existing activities as do orthodox investment incentives, which apply only to new investment. If the problem were a static one of overcoming given disparities in rates of unemployment, wage subsidies would have much to be said for them, although it may be noted that a device of this kind, in the form of Britain's Regional Employment Premium, has nevertheless been condemned by the European Commission and it has been withdrawn.

However, the regional problem is not merely one of disparities in employment rates and in levels of per capita output. It is particularly one of divergences in growth rates. Wage subsidies at given rates can have a permanent effect only on the price level, not on the rate of change of prices. Consequently, in the context of an export-led model of expansion, the growth rate of the benefiting regions will not be affected permanently unless the structural parameters determining growth are favourably affected. Wage subsidies in themselves clearly do nothing to alter the industrial structure and, indeed, may even hinder desirable adjustments. If, therefore, the object of regional policy is not merely to increase the level of employment but also to improve the growth rate of incomes in the region, attention will have to be given to the determinants of growth, which means giving attention to the structure of regions and the determinants of productivity growth.

This points to the desirability of relating regional fiscal incentives to activities that have favourable structural characteristics rather than to particular factors of production, whether labour or capital. If trade is the mainspring of growth, and if activities with high income elasticities of demand can be identified, it will be advantageous to encourage greater concentration on such activities in depressed regions or countries by means of capital or labour subsidies, or even both.

More fundamentally, a strategy for raising the growth rate of a region or a country and its level of income should be directed towards encouraging a relatively rapid rate of growth of labour productivity in lagging regions. Ultimately, in the absence of ever-increasing budgetary transfers between regions and countries, it is only by such means that divergences in real incomes can be reduced. Policies aimed at increasing labour productivity in the lagging regions will confront the familiar conflict between short-term employment growth and long-term output (and real income) growth, so that it will be necessary to formulate them in such a way as to ensure that they do not unduly worsen short-term unemployment disparities while encouraging a convergence of regional incomes.

It will be plain that rather similar considerations can be applied to the use of devaluation as a means of dealing with the regional problems of whole countries in an economic community. There are clearly some differences, because the cost of devaluation is borne by the devaluing country and is not offset by an income transfer. Devaluation is the equivalent of a uniform *ad valorem* duty on imports and a uniform *ad valorem* subsidy on exports. The impact effect should increase competitiveness and lower the static level of unemployment in a country. However, there is no reason to suppose that a single act of devaluation will of itself have any permanent effect on the rate of growth of productivity and income in a country. This conclusion is obviously important in considering the possible implications of the loss of monetary sovereignty involved in monetary integration.

REGIONAL POLICY IN THE EUROPEAN COMMUNITY

From its inception the EC has had a concern with regional development. One of the expressed objectives of the Treaty of Rome is to promote 'balanced expansion'. Its attainment, by reducing the difference between the various regions and by mitigating the backwardness of the 'less favoured', implies the need for action at the Community level in the area of regional policy.

Up to the present time, that policy has been mainly concerned with the backward regions of member countries that are areas of relative poverty, high unemployment, underemployment and outward migration, and which are in receipt of national aid. The backward regions of the EC initially fell into two principal categories: (1) underdeveloped peripheral agricultural regions typified by the Mezzogiorno of Italy and southwest France; and (2) industrialized regions where traditional industries are in decline, such as

182   *The Economics of International Integration*

some of the assisted areas of the UK and parts of northern France and Belgium. With the enlargement of the EC, whole countries – Ireland, Greece and Portugal – must be considered as falling into the former category, which is characterized by per capita incomes markedly below the average for the Community as a whole. Regional problems of a different kind are found in a third class of region, namely the prosperous industrial conurbations of the EC's heartland. Their difficulties are partly environmental – those of congestion, with its many economic and social costs, pollution and other forms of deterioration in the qualify of life. Underdevelopment and congestion are two aspects of the same problem whose solution ideally calls for a coordinated approach.

Although the problem regions of Western Europe existed long before the EC was established, it was perceived that, if they were permitted to continue, severe constraints would be placed upon the future operation and development of the Community. It was, in any case, widely expected that the inception of the EEC might aggravate their problems – thus reinforcing the need for a regional policy – principally as a result of one or more of three effects: (1) a tendency for increased competition to drive inefficient enterprises out of production; (2) an enhanced tendency for factor earnings throughout the EC to become equalized; and (3) the adverse repercussions on the peripheral areas resulting from the shift in market centres that would accompany the abolition of customs frontiers.

It was, of course not inevitable that the problems of the regions would be adversely affected. In principle, the static effects of the customs union might have favoured the problem areas to the extent that their products were largely competitive with those of countries outside the EC, and trade diversion in their favour resulted. It was also possible that the spread and homogenization of production techniques might have operated to offset any impact of further polarization upon the backward regions. Despite the possibility of such countervailing forces, a relative deterioration of the position of the problem regions of the Community was generally thought to be a likely initial outcome of its formation. There is, as it happens, little overall evidence in the empirical estimates noted in Chapter 13 that trade diversion took place in the EC and nothing to suggest that the regions benefited from any that there might have been.

The Treaty of Rome recognizes the Community's interest in the resolution of its existing and emergent regional problems concretely by authorizing member states to provide certain normally unacceptable incentives so long as this is done for the purpose of dealing with regional problems. Thus, although Article 92 states that state aids that distort competition are incompatible with the common market, exceptions are allowed, principally in the interests of regional policy.

Under the treaty, the Commission was merely assigned the 'negative' function of overseeing such state regional aids. On a somewhat more positive note, it was later charged to ensure that the regional repercussions of sectoral Community policies in agriculture, and elsewhere, were taken into account in pursuing those policies. Apart from these two aspects, regional policy found expression in the limited amount of aid that was provided from the outset in the interests of regional development through the European Investment Bank (EIB), the European Social Fund, and the European Agricultural Guidance and Guarantee Fund. Of these three Community agencies, however, only the EIB had a clear commitment to aid regional development, and, although it has regularly allocated a large proportion of its funds to support regional development, until 1978 no element of subsidy was involved.

In the context of regional policy, none of the operations of these three Community agencies was particularly significant, for they possessed no powers of initiative; they merely responded to national initiatives or implemented sectoral policies. Moreover, their actions were coordinated neither with those of the other agencies nor with those of the Commission itself, within which responsibility for matters affecting regional policy was in any case divided. These arrangements scarcely provided an adequate basis for the implementation of a positive Community regional policy.

Progress towards the development of a positive and coherent Community policy was in fact initially slow. Measures to harmonize national regional aid policies were not introduced until 1971, and it was not until 1975 that provision was first made for regional subsidies from the EC's own resources.

Inter-country and Inter-regional Disparities in the EC

Before outlining these developments, the extent of the regional disparities in the EC and the implications of its recent enlargement from this point of view may be briefly noted. In its review of the evolution of the regional problem in the EC, the Commission's *Report on the Regional Problems in the Enlarged Community* (Thomson Report) remarked of the period 1959–70:

> It cannot be said that economic activity throughout the Community has developed evenly, nor has expansion been geographically balanced. Indeed, despite interventionist policies by Member Governments, the gap with regard to comparative

incomes between the regions has not shown any noticeable degree of change. (*Bulletin of the European Communities*, Supplement 8/73, p. 6)

As far as income disparities are concerned however – a major, although not the only significant dimension of the problem – it is generally accepted that comparisons of national and regional GDP per head at current exchange rates do not adequately reflect relative real purchasing power over goods and services and generally exaggerate the differences between richer and poorer countries. The Statistical Office of the European Communities endeavours to overcome this problem for policy evaluation purposes by assessing relative price levels in the different member states and, on their basis, computing per capita GDP in 'purchasing power parities'. These are the best available indicators of relative real incomes in the EC.

Estimates of nominal and real per capita incomes in the twelve countries of the EC are summarized in Table 10.1. It can be seen that whereas in nominal terms the per capita income of the richest country (Denmark) in 1983 was five times as large as that of the poorest (Portugal), in real terms the difference between the richest country (Luxemburg) and the poorest (which remains Portugal) narrows to about two and half to one.

In terms of comparisons amongst the regions of Europe, at the time of the initial enlargement of the Community to nine members in 1973 the real incomes of about three-quarters of the EC's population lay in a band of 80–120 per cent of the Community average. The top 10 per cent lived in regions whose average real per capita incomes were comparable with the highest living standards achieved anywhere in the world. The bottom 10 per cent – Ireland and the Mezzogiorno of Italy – had incomes well below the European average, ranging between one-half and two-thirds respectively, as shown in Table 10.2, which aggregates data for major (level 1) regions in the EC.

In the 1970s it was widely expected that the adverse effects of slower growth, the decline in world trade and structural unemployment in Europe would inevitably be felt more severely in the poorer regions of the EC, thus serving to widen the range in economic prosperity in the Community. For the decade 1973–82 that expectation has not been borne out by experience. In terms of the grouping of regions distinguished in Table 10.2, the EC's poorest regions had not become worse off vis-à-vis the Community average by 1982 than they were in 1973. Over this period, indeed, there is some indication of convergence, income levels at the upper end of the scale

Table 10.1 European Community: relative nominal and real GDP per capita

Country	Population 1985 (million)	Relative GDP[a] per capita				Relative real GDP[b] per capita			
		1973	1981	1983	1984	1973	1981	1983	1984
Belgium	9.9	115	106	96	96	104	105	106	105
Denmark	5.1	142	127	130	134	115	110	114	116
France	55.2	118	106	113	111	107	110	111	109
Germany	61.0	136	123	126	125	111	114	113	115
Greece	10.0	45	42	42	42	55	56	54	54
Ireland	3.6	55	54	60	62	61	68	66	67
Italy	57.1	70	68	73	76	86	89	86	87
Luxemburg	0.4	121	109	103	115	139	116	113	124
Netherlands	14.5	112	110	109	106	107	104	101	101
Portugal	10.2	30	27	26	..	48	48	47	..
Spain	38.6	52	54	49	52	74	71	69	72
United Kingdom	56.6	79	99	95	94	100	93	97	96
Europe	322.2	100[c]	100[c]	100	100	100[c]	100	100	100[c]

.. not available
[a] At current prices and current purchasing power parities
[b] At current prices and current exchange rates
[c] The Ten
Source: Statistical Office of the European Communities.

Table 10.2 The European Community regions: relative real GDP per capita

Region	Relative real GDP per capita[a]						Population 1982	
	1970	1973	1975	1977	1978	1982	Millions	Percentage
Ile ce France	160.0	164.0	195.0	162.6	160.0	163.4	10.1	3.7
'Prosperous' Germany[b]	134.9	133.8	133.1	135.5	136.5	130.3	13.5	5.0
Luxemburg	127.0	130.0	116.0	110.7	115.0	116.8	0.4	0.1
Denmark	120.0	121.0	119.0	119.0	114.0	112.5	5.1	1.9
UK – south east	112.0	111.0	105.0	102.8	102.0	109.6	17.0	6.3
Germany – remainder[c]	111.0	109.9	111.3	110.5	113.0	107.9	48.2	17.7
Belgium	102.0	107.0	109.0	107.2	104.0	106.7	9.9	3.6
Netherlands	107.0	106.0	108.0	106.2	103.0	102.1	14.3	5.3
France – east & central less Paris[d]	100.9	105.6	104.7	107.4	104.7	103.5	25.2	9.3
Ital – northwest[e]	99.8	96.0	94.1	102.2	101.7	111.6	19.2	7.1
UK – remainder	91.0	90.6	87.9	85.7	85.6	87.1	39.3	14.5
France – western & southern[f] periphery	83.8	87.0	80.8	90.5	88.6	93.9	19.0	7.0
Ital – northeast & central[g]	79.0	76.3	75.1	80.7	82.5	93.0	17.2	6.3
Ireland	61.0	65.0	61.0	59.5	61.0	67.6	3.5	1.3
Ital – Mezzogiorno[h]	50.6	49.7	50.5	52.4	52.8	61.2	20.1	7.3
Greece – Athens region						63.3	4.0	1.5
Greece – remainder						49.3	5.7	2.1
Europe[i]	100.0	100.0	100.0	100.0	100.0	100.0	271.8	100.0

[a] GDP per capita in purchasing power parities
[b] Hamburg, Bremen, Baden–Württemberg, West Berlin
[c] Schleswig-Holstein, Niedersachsen, Nordrhein-Westfalen, Hessen, Rheinland-Pfalz, Bayern, Saarland
[d] Bassin Parisien, North, Pas-de-Calais, East, Centre–East
[e] Northwest, Lombardia, Emilia Romagna
[f] West, Southwest, Mediterranean
[g] Northeast, Centre, Lazio
[h] Campania, Abruzzi-Molise, South, Sicilia, Sardegna
[i] The Ten

Sources: Wabe, Eversley and Despicht (1983) Tables 1 and 2; Statistical Office of the European Communities, *Regional Statistics Yearbook*, 1985.

having moved a little closer to the Community average, while those of most of the poorer regions have moved substantially in the direction of the EC average.

As a result of the accession of Greece to membership in 1981, followed in 1986 by that of Portugal and Spain, some 55–60 million inhabitants have been added to the EC, bringing its total population to more than 300 million. From the standpoint of regional policy, the importance of the EC's expansion from nine to twelve members is evidently that it has increased substantially the proportion of the Community's population living in regions whose average per capita real incomes are much below (less than two-thirds) the Community level. Prior to the accession of Greece, some 23 million inhabitants of the EC had incomes below that level, namely the inhabitants of the Mezzogiorno and the whole of Ireland. By 1982, Ireland had become a borderline case, but the accession of Greece, none of whose regions attained an income level of two-thirds of the EC average, meant that some 30 million of the EC's population nevertheless still lived in such low-income regions. Commission statistics (Commission, 1984b) suggest that about one-third of the total population of Spain dwelling in its peripheral areas, and the whole of the population of Portugal (including the Lisbon region) would also fall currently into this category. Thus the enlargement of the EC that has resulted from the accession of Greece, Portugal and Spain has much more than doubled the total number of persons living in low-income regions, bringing it in 1986 to some 50 million. The regions in question are all underdeveloped in a structural sense. Their problems evidently differ greatly from those of the regions of industrialized Western Europe that are experiencing industrial decline and a need for reconversion and to resolve their difficulties will demand different policies.

The Coordination of National Regional Aid Systems

From the time of the Community's establishment in 1957 until its first enlargement in 1973, the principal achievement of the Commission in the area of regional policy was the development of principles for the coordination of national regional aids and the overcoming of national and operational problems that hindered their implementation. The Commission's primary concern has been to prevent national aids from causing undue distortions of competition and to render regional policies more consistent with Community objectives. A major goal of the Commission has been to avoid a competitive bidding-up of the regional financial incentives offered by some member states not only to investors from other member states but more particularly to those from outside the Community, notably those from the United States. The Commission has also been concerned with the disparities between the levels of national aid and the relative seriousness of the various regional problems when viewed from the level of the Community as a whole.

The principles first laid down on regional aid harmonization in 1971 (*Bulletin of the European Communities*, 11/71) reflect these and other concerns, and have been gradually redefined over the years. Those currently in force are broadly as follows:

(1)   Aids to new investment should not be allowed to exceed a certain ceiling expressed either as a percentage of the value of the investment or in terms of cost per job created. Four categories of regions are distinguished according to the severity of the regional problems and different ceilings are imposed for each, being higher in the least-favoured regions. In the more favoured central and industrialized regions, the ceilings are 20 per cent of initial investment costs or 3,500 EUA (European Units of Account) per job created subject to an absolute maximum of 25 per cent of initial investment costs. These ceilings rise to 75 per cent of initial investment and 13,000 EUA per job created in such regions as Ireland and the Mezzogiorno.

(2)   Aid is expected to be 'transparent', that is it should be capable of being measured and related to the ceilings. This is clearly necessary if any principles of coordination are to be generally applied. The significance of this issue can be gauged from the Commission's estimate (1979) that nearly 50 per cent of all regional assistance granted by member states had not hitherto been covered by the ceilings that were first laid down under the coordination machinery agreed in 1975 (Commission, 1976). The redefined principles agreed in 1978 (*Bulletin of the European Communities*, 11/78) introduce new techniques for measuring forms of aid (such as loan guarantees and rent rebates) not hitherto controlled against the ceilings, and in principle, all forms of regional aid are in future covered.

(3)   A system of supervision is provided for that involves a general scrutiny of national aid measures. In this connection, the Commission has confirmed its objections to those operating aids that are not conditional on initial investment or job creation. Such aids are to be frozen in their present forms until their compatibility with the common market has been decided.

(4) Sectoral repercussions are considered. This involves an evaluation of the effects of regional aid on competition and trade.

The Emergence of a Positive Community Regional Policy

It is only in the course of the past decade that a positive Community regional policy has begun to emerge. At the Paris Summit of October 1972, which preceded the first enlargement of the Community, the Heads of State, urged by two of the prospective new entrants, agreed to give high priority to correcting structural and regional imbalances in the EC. They also specifically agreed to coordinate their regional policies and to establish a special regional development fund to be financed from the Community's own resources. The Commission's subsequent report (1973a) on regional problems in the context of an enlarged Community highlighted the issues, documented the serious disparities existing in the EC, and provided initial guidelines for the new policy.

The principal instrument of the new policy is the European Regional Development Fund (ERDF), which was established in March 1975 with an initial three-year (1975–7) budget of 1,300 million gold parity units of account (u.a.), that is, £540 million at an exchange rate of £1 = 2.4 u.a. The Fund was empowered to make supplementary grants to support the costs (up to a ceiling, currently 55 per cent) of investment projects in the industrial and service sectors that create new jobs or safeguard existing jobs, of infrastructure investment linked to such productive investment and of infrastructure investment in less favoured rural areas. To be eligible for assistance, projects had to be located in areas that qualify for regional assistance from national authorities, and that actually receive such support.

The Fund's resources are shared out amongst member states on a basis that reflects the extent of their individual regional problems. Fund quotas for the first decade of its operation, and those in force from January 1986, are set out in Table 10.3.

The main limitations of the new policy have been apparent from the outset: the size of the ERDF is modest in relation both to the scale of regional problems and to the level of regional expenditures by the member states; the criteria for assistance are such, moreover, that projects in parts of every member state are eligible for benefit, although many of the assisted areas in the richer countries cannot justly be viewed as problem areas in a Community context; it is in practice difficult to ensure that Community funds are truly additional, and do not merely lead to an offsetting reduction of

Table 10.3   European Regional Development Fund: quotas

Member state	1975–78	1978–80[a]	1981–84[a]	1984–85[b]	1986[c]
Belgium	1.5	1.39	1.11	0.90– 1.20	0.61– 0.82
Denmark	1.3	1.20	1.06	0.51– 0.67	0.34– 0.46
France	15.0	16.86	13.64	11.05–14.74	7.47– 9.96
Germany	6.4	6.0	4.65	3.76– 4.81	2.55– 3.40
Greece	—	—	13.0	12.35–15.74	8.35–10.64
Ireland	6.0	6.46	5.94	5.64– 6.83	3.81– 4.61
Italy	40.0	39.39	35.49	31.94–42.59	21.59–28.79
Luxemburg	0.1	0.09	0.07	0.06– 0.08	0.04– 0.06
Netherlands	1.7	1.58	1.24	1.00– 1.34	0.68– 0.91
Portugal	—	—	—	—	10.65–14.20
Spain	—	—	—	—	17.95–23.93
United Kingdom	28.0	27.03	23.80	21.42–28.56	14.48–19.31

[a] including the 'non-quota' element (5%).
[b] The division between quota and non-quota elements is abolished, and quotas themselves are replaced by indicative ranges.
[c] The revised indicative ranges allow for the accession of Portugal and Spain.

Source: Bulletin of the European Communities.

national aid expenditures; areas adversely affected by Community decisions and in particular by its sectoral policies are not necessarily located within nationally assisted regions; grants for investment projects are not necessarily the most effectual means of utilizing the limited resources available for Community assistance. Finally, the Fund could respond only to national initiatives and decisions in the field of regional policy. It was not empowered to support initiatives of the EC itself. In an attempt to overcome these constraints and to provide a basis for a more active and comprehensive Community regional policy, the Commission has put forward a number of important proposals for reform since 1975.

The first of these (Commission, 1977b) involved, *inter alia*, the establishment of a 'non-quota' section of the Fund to operate in conjunction with a system of subsidized loans to be provided through the EIB and designed specifically to finance Community-initiated programmes in support of regional development outside the nationally assisted regions. The Council accepted the proposal for a non-quota section in 1978 and during 1978–84 5 per cent of the Fund's resources was allocated to such assistance. At the same time, the Council empowered the Commission through the EIB to borrow on the European capital market to finance the new loans to be made available through the Bank under the so called New Community Instrument (NCI). This is designed to provide expanded support for regional development projects and for other projects that would contribute to greater convergence and integration such as the subsidized loans made to Ireland and Italy to facilitate their entry into the EMS (see Chapter 9).

Further important changes were proposed in 1981 when the Commission put forward new regional policy guidelines (the Giolitti proposals; *Bulletin of the European Communities*, 10/81) aimed at making the instruments of Community regional policy – and in particular the Fund – more effective. With respect to the Fund itself, it was proposed that its expenditure should be concentrated on regions suffering from especially severe structural problems, instead of dispersing it over as much as one-third of the EC's total population as was then the case. The principal regions identified for benefit and their proposed shares of Fund quotas were: the Mezzogiorno, 43.67 per cent; the Greek regions other than Athens and Thessalonika, 15.97 per cent; Ireland 7.31 per cent; and the UK Assisted Areas 29.28 per cent. At the same time it was proposed that areas suffering from serious industrial decline should be eligible for assistance from an expanded non-quota section of the Fund, to which a ceiling of 20 per cent of the Fund's resources would be attached. The proposals – and notably the exclusion of the less favoured zones of relatively prosperous member states from eligibility for quota assistance – proved to be extremely controversial, and the Council failed to adopt them.

Currently the Fund operates on the basis of the latest reforms adopted in 1984 (*Bulletin of the European Communities*, 6/84), which came into effect at the beginning of 1985. The new system is marked by three main features: (1) an emphasis on increasing coordination of member states' regional policy; (2) the replacement of national quotas by a system of indicative ranges; and (3) an emphasis on an integrated approach to regional development. One of the objects of replacing the quota system is to provide the EC with greater influence over the regional allocation of expenditures. An important feature of the reforms is the decision to reduce the proportion of expenditure that is made on a project basis, which is very largely under the control of the member states, and to increase the proportion that is provided through coordinated multi-annual programmes, jointly agreed by the EC and the member state involved. The intention is to increase such programme financing to 20 per cent of the total over a three-year period. There are, however, to be two sorts of programme: Community Programmes will be initiated by the EC and largely under its control; National Programmes will be initiated by the member states, and, as was the

case prior to the reform in the case of non-quota aid, only programmes in regions eligible for national assistance will be eligible
for National Programme assistance. Apart from these developments, the EC has also become increasingly involved in devising
integrated development schemes that depend on several agencies
and instruments. The first of these were the schemes for depressed
urban areas, such as Naples and Belfast. The most recent are the
Integrated Mediterranean Programmes (IMPs), which were
approved in June 1985 for the specific purpose of helping the poorer
Mediterranean regions of France, Greece and Italy to meet the
problems created for them by the enlargement of the Community to
include Portugal and Spain. Assistance under the IMPs will be
provided not only from the ERDF but also from the Social Fund,
the CAP Guidance Section and by loans through the EIB from its
own resources and from the already established NCI. In addition,
specific additional resources are to be allocated by the EC from the
budget. The total assistance from EC budgetary funds amounts to
4,100 million ECU (£2.3 bn) over seven years. Of this sum 2,500
million ECU comes from the various existing funds and 1,600 ECU
takes the form of specific additional resources.

   This brief review of regional policy in the EC demonstrates the
Commission's concern since the mid-1970s to develop a more
coherent and independent approach. Its proposals have consistently been a matter of considerable controversy. Member states
have resisted any encroachment on their own role but the Commission's efforts can nevertheless be said to have met with some
success. On the negative side, principles have been laid down and
largely implemented to harmonize and rationalize national aids to
assisted regions. On the positive side, the Community has established the ERDF, and the latest reforms that came into effect in
January 1985 somewhat increase the discretion and influence of the
Commission and should make a contribution to overcoming some
of the administrative and other deficiencies of Community regional
policy that have been pointed out in this chapter.

   It remains true, however, that the still modest size of the ERDF
and the basis on which most of its aid will continue to be furnished
even after the most recent reform suggest that the improvements so
far made and assistance through other channels will not be sufficient
to bring about a major lessening of regional disparities. The severity
of those problems has in any case inevitably been increased by the
accession of Greece, Portugal and Spain to the EC. More substantial progress towards the goal of reducing disparities would demand
a greatly enlarged Fund, altered criteria for eligibility and the
development of more general Community policies to deal with

imbalances at state level, which would almost certainly point to Community involvement in other policy areas. As an example of what might be required, a Commission study group (Commission, 1977b) has cited the imposition of fiscal disincentives on regions that fulfil the obverse criteria to those used for determining eligibility for regional aids. The establishment of a Community regional development corporation has even been envisaged in the context of a more vigorous regional policy.

At the present time, the EC's degree of political cohesion is such that no major strengthening of existing Community regional policy measures seems in prospect in the short term, still less the adoption of any major new instruments. At the time of the Community's first enlargement in 1973 it was emphasized in the context of the then new regional policy that measures to strengthen the economic potential of less prosperous member states and of their regions were to remain primarily the responsibility of the member states concerned. The EC's new measures were seen as supportive. That view of the EC's role in regional development was again expressed in the different context of the EMS at the time of its introduction in 1980. It evidently continues to colour policy today in many areas. In the specific field of regional policy, the relatively limited current commitment of the EC to a reduction of regional disparities expresses itself in the small size of the ERDF – only 2,456 million ECU in 1986, a mere 7.5 per cent of the EC's draft budget for that year.

The general case in favour of promoting a greater measure of regional convergence not only for its own sake but in order to promote a smooth functioning of the EC and to prepare the way for further advance, nevertheless remains as strong as it ever was, and it appears still to command widespread assent. As the constraints of the current recession are relaxed, the reduction of divergences may thus assert itself as a more prominent objective of the Community.

CHAPTER 11

Economic Integration Among Developing Countries

Although the economies of Europe provide the principal examples of international economic integration, the most numerous are those involving less developed countries. Of the seventeen instances of integration mentioned in Chapter 1, fourteen concern developing countries. Four of these are in Latin America and the Caribbean, eight are in Africa, and two are in Asia. This chapter considers the rationale of economic integration among developing countries, the special difficulties that confront it, and the various mechanisms employed or advocated to deal with those problems.

THE RATIONALE OF ECONOMIC INTEGRATION AMONG DEVELOPING COUNTRIES

It will be recalled that the orthodox theory of customs unions is concerned with the gains that may be derived from changes in the existing pattern of trade. Full employment and given inputs of resources are assumed, and, apart from the tariff, domestic prices are assumed to reflect opportunity costs, so that the chief domestic grounds for interference with the market allocation of resources do not arise. The orthodox theory was evolved with the developed countries of Europe in mind and expressly for the purpose of throwing light on the problems of integration in Western Europe. It is natural to ask how far, if at all, the theory is also relevant to the rather different circumstances of developing countries. To answer this question requires a consideration of two principal issues: (1) to what extent the characteristics of less developed countries favour trade creation; and (2) whether trade creation is the significant criterion for evaluating customs unions among such countries.

Although it is difficult to generalize usefully about the circumstances that favour trade creation, it appears more likely to arise when the existing external trade of prospective members is small relative to their domestic production and where a high proportion of external trade is already undertaken with prospective partners. This proposition is virtually self-evident. Where external trade is unimportant relative to domestic production, union offers more scope for creating intra-union trade by the displacement of high-cost domestic products. Similarly, where external trade with non-union members is relatively unimportant, the union can have little effect in diverting imports to higher-cost sources within the union.

The conditions that favour trade creation are thus precisely the opposite of those typically found in developing countries, whose existing external trade is usually large relative to their domestic production but whose intra-group trade is a minor component of their total trade. Developing countries rely heavily on the exportation of primary products, which are freely traded on world markets. Integration is unlikely to affect significantly the volume of resources allocated to the production of such commodities. On the other hand, the imports of developing countries consist chiefly of intermediate products and final manufactures, which many such countries either do not produce at all or produce only to a very limited extent. In terms of the criterion of gain of orthodox customs-union theory, therefore, integration among developing countries may appear at best to be irrelevant and at worst to be positively harmful, except possibly for the more developed of such countries.

To accept this conclusion, however, is to suppose that the rationale of market integration among developing countries lies in the gains to be derived from changes in their *existing* pattern of trade, which is necessarily based on their *existing* pattern of production. Yet, this is not the case; or rather, it is so only to an extent that will vary inversely with the level of development of the countries concerned. The rationale of integration among developing countries rests mainly on the effects of the creation of regional markets on their more fundamental problems, which include the need to increase the opportunities for profitable domestic and foreign investment and the need to mobilize unemployed resources. In evaluating the merits of integration among such countries, what is relevant is not so much its impact on the existing patterns of production and trade, as its impact on those patterns that are likely to emerge in the absence of the formation of regional groupings.

The argument for regional integration among developing countries is thus largely based on the prospective gains from rationalizing the *emergent* structure of production. The lower is the level of development attained by the integrating countries at the time of integration, the greater will be the importance of the gains from *prospective* rationalization.

The case for economic integration must still rely on the validity of one or more of the several arguments justifying protection in the partner countries, and in particular on the case for import substitution. If there is such a case for protecting industry, then, as explained in Chapter 3, integration may offer the prospect of reducing its costs, thus freeing resources for further investment and offering the prospect of increased output and a faster rate of economic growth. A further important argument for regional integration among developing countries is that it may increase the group's bargaining power in its external economic relations, and this in practice appears to have been an important consideration. In this perspective the conventional static criteria of trade diversion and trade creation lose some of their relevance, and a policy of integration among developing countries may be warranted even if the conditions for static trade creation do not exist.

Moreover, it must be emphasized that the merits of integration still need to be demonstrated for any proposed grouping. No *a priori* case can be made for integration among developing countries from the perspective just suggested, any more than when the policy is being evaluated for situations to which the assumptions of the classical analysis apply. The strength of such a case, in so far as it rests on economic considerations, will depend on the empirical significance of a variety of factors. The more important of these will be: (1) the weight attached to industrialization in economic development; (2) the possibilities, if any, of exporting manufactures to world markets rather than to protected regional markets; (3) the magnitude of scale economies in prospective regional industries; (4) the differences in the costs of producing industrial products in the different member countries; (5) the location of markets in member countries; and (6) the costs of transporting raw materials and finished products within the region.

In the light of these factors, an optimal policy for some developing countries of course, would be to seek to develop by first supplying their domestic markets and then moving directly into world markets without relying on the support of preferential arrangements at any stage. However, in the economic conditions of the late twentieth century, the countries for which such a path would be indicated may be the minority of relatively large ones. For many less developed countries, and particularly for those with very small domestic markets, regional economic cooperation may offer an indispensable experience and discipline for making a transition to a more balanced development and a more open economy. The case for regional integration as a useful strategy for numbers of less developed countries in the conditions of the 1980s is not undermined by the impressive, but possibly exceptional, experiences of countries such as Hong Kong, Singapore, South Korea and Taiwan.

TECHNIQUES OF ECONOMIC INTEGRATION AMONG DEVELOPING COUNTRIES

Three principal approaches to international economic integration have been employed in groupings of less developed countries, sometimes in combination.

(1) The classical approach involves across-the-board trade liberalization for all or most products, through the formation of customs unions or free trade areas.

(2) The 'complementarity agreement' approach involves trade liberalization for certain existing industries or product groups in the context of a deliberate planned rationalization of production.

(3) The third approach, also limited to specified products or industries, takes the form of measures to promote and regulate investment in new regionally based industries that enjoy economies of scale, so as more economically to meet the combined demand of member countries.

In each case the objective is to bring about profitable specialization. The difference is that, in the case of across-the-board trade liberalization, the procedural emphasis is on attaining the objective through the operation of market forces by the negotiation of a suitable tariff structure, which is expected to work broadly in the desired directions. In the case of the other two techniques, the emphasis is on first determining the appropriate scope for specialization in existing or new industries, perhaps on the basis of detailed feasibility and social cost–benefit studies, and then utilising a variety of policy instruments, such as tariffs, fiscal incentives and administrative controls, to implement the desired changes in the pattern of production.

The classical mode of integration was the basis of the integration arrangements established among developing countries in the various regions of Africa, in Central America and the Caribbean. Few of these arrangements have survived to the present day without the introduction of major modifications.

Complementarity agreements, which have been widely used in

the Latin American Free Trade Association (LAFTA), represent a narrower form of regional integration. Their object is to promote specialization among the limited number of existing plants or processes in order to exploit scale economies and to utilize excess capacities. This approach has considerable attractions in principle, particularly where structural distortions render the price system an unreliable guide to regional specialization. Its practical disadvantage is that it is administratively and operationally complex, and it demands much time-consuming inter-firm and inter-industry negotiation. If the experience of LAFTA is any guide, its successful use is to be looked for only where the sectors involved are fairly narrow and where a reallocation of production can take place without adversely affecting the interests of particular enterprises.

The third approach to integration among developing countries calls for inter-governmental agreement on the establishment of designated new plants or industries, coupled with the adoption of tariff or other policy measures to ensure implementation. Agreed specialization has been attempted in several groupings, including the East African Community, the Central American Common Market (CACM) and the Andean Group. The proposed measures for sectoral industrial cooperation among the countries of the Association of South-East Asian Nations (ASEAN) also rest on this basis.

On a broad view of the progress and experience of integration among developing countries in the past quarter of a century, one of its most striking features is the gradual but marked change of emphasis that has taken place with respect to approach. Although all the earlier integration schemes relied largely or entirely on trade liberalization, in almost every instance attempts have subsequently been made to plan or regulate specialization or to influence the location of industrial activity. In more recently established groupings, such as the Andean Group, the regulation of industrial development constituted an integral part of the arrangements from the outset. The gradual resort to a more regulated approach has accompanied a recognition of the special problems confronting integration among developing countries, which render trade liberalization on its own an inadequate, and sometimes even an inappropriate, strategy even when the potential for fruitful cooperation exists.

THE SPECIAL PROBLEMS OF ECONOMIC INTEGRATION AMONG DEVELOPING COUNTRIES

The principal policy issues of integration among developing countries centre on three issues disregarded by orthodox analysis: (1) the determination in operational terms of the appropriate scope and direction of regional trade, development and specialization; (2) the issue of equity in the distribution of benefits; (3) policy towards foreign investment and multinational enterprises. Some of these issues may obviously be important in any integration arrangement, but the structural features of typical developing countries often render them of overriding importance. In combination these issues produce a situation that dictates a different approach to integration among developing countries from what may be appropriate in advanced market economies. In the latter, the market can largely be left to take care of the integration process; in developing countries a more positive integration strategy is called for.

Comparative Advantage, Regional Specialization and Investment

The first issue, to ascertain the desirable extent and direction of industrial development and the character of regional specialization, is basic. It requires an appreciation in operational terms of the comparative advantages of the group as a whole and of particular countries within it. If, as is typically the case, money costs do not reflect social opportunity costs because of unemployment, infant industry considerations, external economies and diseconomies, economies of scale, foreign exchange shortages and, in particular, fiscally induced price or cost distortions, the price system will not provide such a guide, and desirable patterns of trade and development will have to be directly evaluated.

The problem of ascertaining the operational scope for regional specialization and development when distortions are severe and widespread arises both for trade liberalization in the context of the existing industrial structures of member countries, and for new investment opportunities and needs created by the unified market, including community joint ventures. Social cost–benefit analysis will have an important role to play in the evaluation of major new investments, but it is not a method that can be used for determining the comparative strengths of whole economies and of their existing industrial sectors. For that purpose – of vital importance for imparting a proper direction to integration policy – alternative approaches must be devised.

A useful approach to the problem can be based on estimates of effective protection and domestic resource costs. Since the late 1960s, these have been widely used for broad evaluations of trade policies. An extension of the method to throw light on desirable patterns of specialization in economic groupings is overdue.

In essence, the effective protection approach assumes that the combined effects of tariffs, quantitative restrictions and other protective measures on a domestic producer's output and inputs can be represented by the effective protection coefficient (EPC). This coefficient expresses the impact of protection on domestic value-added in production. Specifically, it is defined as the ratio that domestic value-added after applying protective measures bears to value-added expressed at world market prices. (The latter amount corresponds, on certain assumptions, to the domestic currency equivalent of the net foreign exchange saved through import substitution or earned through the exportation of the products of the protected industry.) An EPC of a value greater than unity means that, at the existing exchange rate, protective measures provide positive incentives to the firm or activity. An EPC of less than unity indicates that, on balance, protective measures discriminate against the firm or activity. A negative EPC would signify that the firm or activity produces a loss of foreign exchange to the national economy.

In calculating the EPC, domestic value-added is expressed in terms of actual domestic market prices. This may overestimate the resource cost of production to the national economy for two main reasons: (1) if above-normal profits are being earned; or (2) if, because of unemployment, market wages exceed shadow wages. If domestic value-added is corrected for these points in an attempt to arrive at the social opportunity cost of the activity, and the corrected amount is then compared, as before, with the value-added at world market prices, a coefficient is arrived at that is termed the domestic resource cost of foreign exchange (DRC). The DRC represents the value of domestic resources expended in saving a unit of foreign exchange by import substitution or earning a unit of foreign exchange by export activity, expressed as a proportion of the actual exchange rate.

DRC coefficients can be used to provide a ranking of activities in terms of comparative advantage. A coefficient of less than unity indicates that the activity is socially profitable. A coefficient of more than unity indicates that the activity is socially unprofitable. A negative coefficient would signify that the activity actually results in a loss of foreign exchange. DRC coefficients require correction if the exchange rate is overvalued. Coefficients of DRC corrected for the equilibrium value of foreign exchange are sometimes termed coefficients of real costs of production.

Calculations of this kind may be particularly useful for giving direction to integration policies in the short and medium run, but their limitations must be borne in mind. They are derived from historical data relating to industries set up primarily to serve national markets alone and at different times, whose technologies may not be the most up to date or the most appropriate to serve a unified market in which scale economies can be more fully exploited. Essentially such estimates provide a snapshot of the position at a point in time, whereas a moving picture would be more useful for eliciting trends and directions. They must therefore be supplemented by information on the structural changes in process in the different member countries.

Policies for Equity and Balance

The second crucial policy issue that confronts regional groupings of developing countries is to design and implement measures that will produce an equitable distribution of the benefits of integration. Until a relatively advanced level of economic development is attained, domestic manufacturing industries in developing countries normally require a significant level of protection if production is to be commercially viable, even when tariff-free access to a regional market is assured. If this protection is provided principally by tariffs or by other 'second-best' price-raising devices, as is normally the case, any conflicts of interest over the intra-regional distribution of the costs and benefits of integration are likely to be greatly exacerbated.

Tariff protection necessarily results in a situation in which the direct costs of import substitution, which are represented by the excess private cost of domestic production over the cost of imports from the outside world, are borne by union members in proportion to their consumption of import substitutes. On the other hand, the benefits of import substitution (which may include an enhanced rate of return to capital and labour, expanded employment and wage incomes, a more balanced economic structure, savings in foreign exchange and an increased rate of economic growth) will accrue primarily to those countries in which the new productive capacity is located.

In these circumstances, if the protected activity justified by regional integration does not spread itself over the regional market so that each country attracts an equitable share, conflicts of interest are bound to be perceived. The experience of Third World regional groupings in which the distribution of industry is left to the working of market forces suggests that an equitable regional balance is unlikely to occur. On the contrary, a marked 'polarization' of development has tended to take place that has disproportionately favoured regions and states with relatively high per capita incomes or relatively large domestic markets. Typical examples of this phenomenon are the concentration of industry, commerce and services found in and around Abidjan and Dakar in the CEAO, in Nairobi in the defunct East African Community, and in Guatemala City and San Salvador in the CACM. Polarization is reflected in marked imbalances in intra-regional trade in manufactures.

If economic integration is to endure, it must not only result in a situation that improves allocational efficiency and growth, but it must also be perceived to be equitable. If the market itself cannot be relied upon to produce such an outcome, corrective policies will have to be employed to promote balanced development and appropriate instruments will have to be devised to implement them. Some of these policies may involve a trade-off between considerations of efficiency and those of equity. The choice essentially lies between (1) income transfers, and (2) instruments to effect a change in the emergent patterns of resource allocation, trade and development, which income transfers do not do. Under (2) there is a further choice between methods that principally rely on the market and methods that rely on a deliberate planned rationalization of industrial development. The objective of both methods is to bring about profitable specialization, subject to the requirements of balanced development. The difference is that in the first case the emphasis is on the attainment of the objective through the operation of market forces by the negotiation of a suitable generally applicable structure of fiscal and other incentives, which is expected to work broadly in the desired directions. With the other approach the emphasis is first on determining the appropriate scope for specialization in new industries and then utilizing administrative controls in an attempt to implement the desired changes in the pattern of production.

FISCAL COMPENSATION

Fiscal compensation by intergovernmental financial transfer through the budget is one possible mechanism for promoting equity. It is an element that is found in the financial arrangements that underpin UDEAC, CEAO, ECOWAS, and the Southern African Customs Union.

A commonly advocated criterion for compensation is the net tariff revenue forgone as a result of buying the products of other member states. The rationale for a transfer on this basis is that in certain circumstances such losses will correspond to higher import prices and therefore to the static loss of national income suffered by an importing country from its extension of a preference to member countries. Likewise, in certain circumstances, the preference measures the lowest value that attaches to the benefit that the exporting country receives in terms of national income for its opportunity to export to a partner on preferential terms, and it may thus serve also as a basis for determining contributions.

Fiscal compensation, whether based on 'revenue' losses or some other indicator, can certainly facilitate the trade liberalization process of integration by reducing or removing one of its major potential costs for the less advanced countries, but it is for several reasons an unsatisfactory approach. In the first place, from a free trade point of view, a country that is merely compensated for its customs revenue losses (that is, roughly for the cost of trade diversion) would not necessarily be better off within a customs union than it would be if it instead pursued a non-discriminatory policy of tariff reductions. Secondly, from the alternative and more relevant standpoint of the objectives of a protectionist trade policy, this measure is unsatisfactory in its disregard of the benefits of development that a country forgoes, notably in the shape of increased value-added and employment in manufacturing, when it imports from its partners instead of producing import substitutes for itself, where that option exists. In other words, from this point of view even the part of trade expansion that involves trade creation – actual in the case of existing industries, potential in the case of new ones – may involve a cost. A country that loses established industries as a result of trade liberalization may suffer a loss of real income for which there is no counterpart in tariff revenue losses. (There may be direct tax losses as taxable income falls also.) These considerations justify the refusal of the more recently established regional economic groupings to rely solely on fiscal compensation to deal with the problem of the distribution of benefits. Where compensation is provided – as it is in UDEAC, CEAO and ECOWAS – it is seen as one element in a package of policies designed to alter the distribution of benefits by influencing the regional distribution of industry. A discussion of compensation in CEAO and ECOWAS will be found in Robson (1983).

The measures potentially available for influencing industrial development, regional specialization and location within an economic grouping, for whatever reason, operate either indirectly through the market system through the provision of incentives or directly through the adoption of planned industrial specialization agreements backed by administrative or legislative sanction. The following sections assume that justification for interference by these means with the market's allocation of resources is based on a need to promote more equitable and balanced development, but these instruments may equally be used to promote desirable specialization patterns disclosed by direct evaluations of regional comparative advantage.

FISCAL INCENTIVES TO INFLUENCE THE LOCATION OF INDUSTRY

Fiscal mechanisms may be used to influence the location of new enterprises in an economic grouping, either with or without the support of inter-country fiscal transfers. In the first case, fiscal compensation may be linked to the promotion of productive investment in less favoured member countries through the provision of supplementary fiscal investment incentives financed by the community. Alternatively, compensation funds may be used to finance the provision of loan finance on a subsidized basis for investment in industry or in infrastructure through the medium of regional development banks, as was done by the Central American Bank for Economic Integration and the East African Development Bank, as happens to a limited extent in the Entente countries of West Africa and in CEAO, and as is envisaged in the ECOWAS Fund.

Even if inter-country fiscal transfers are not utilized for these purposes, an agreed harmonization of national fiscal incentives can still be a way of influencing the distribution of industrial activity. By this means, less developed member countries may be authorized to provide more generous investment incentives (from their own budgetary resources), while harmonization excludes a counter-productive bidding-up of incentives by more advanced members. Several economic groupings of LDCs have formulated measures of incentive harmonization with these considerations in mind and, at the level of regional policy, the EC itself operates such a system. All of the West African groupings envisage a harmonization of incentives, but it is not yet clear whether this will result in agreed differentials to serve the interests of regional policy, or merely in measures that will avoid competitive distortions.

Remedies for inter-country imbalances might also be sought through the limited retention of intra-group tariffs. In newly formed groupings, less developed member countries could be permitted to adopt a slower pace towards full trade liberalization than their more advanced partners, as was provided in the Andean Group arrangements, and as is envisaged in ECOWAS. Indeed, the indefinite retention of moderate intra-group duties by less developed members may even be defensible in certain circumstances, since that procedure might be less costly to the group (Cooper and Massell, 1965) in producing a desired regional balance than would a simple customs union.

REGIONAL INDUSTRIAL POLICY AND AGREED INDUSTRIAL SPECIALIZATION

The alternative to relying on fiscal harmonization in conjunction with the forces of the market to influence the emergent pattern of industrial development is to attempt to shape developments positively by the adoption of a regional industrial policy involving some agreed specialization for new industrial development, whether that takes place in the private sector or on the basis of joint ventures operated by agencies of the member states themselves. The adoption of regional industrial policies and industrial harmonization measures is increasingly given greater weight in emergent regional integration initiatives.

The history of earlier initiatives on agreed specialization is one of failures both of negotiation and of implementation. There are many reasons for the poor record, including uncertainty as to the outcome, differing evaluations of the costs and benefits involved on the part of different participants, and differing concepts of equity. These problems will never disappear. There are, however, two other contributory factors that often handicapped earlier attempts, and that may be partly remediable.

The first possibly remediable factor is bound up with negotiating procedures. Often the choice of location for each new industry has been the subject of separate negotiation. This is a relatively uncomplicated procedure. Negotiations can be undertaken as projects come forward, and do not have to be held back until a portfolio of well-developed project studies is built up. Nevertheless, this approach has the defect that it does not necessarily provide an immediate benefit from each new development for each participant. Governments have been understandably reluctant to agree to the establishment of industries in partner countries partly to serve their own markets, when by so doing they impose tangible and immediate costs upon themselves in the shape of real income losses (reflected in revenue losses), in return for the prospect of uncertain benefits at some future time if and when some other project in its turn is assigned to them. One way of dealing with this problem is to prepare an indicative regional programme for a specific range of industrial projects. Member countries could then be invited to endorse such a programme, the projects in which would be allocated amongst the member states in such a way that each receives an acceptable share. This approach has the practical advantage of providing an incentive for each participant to agree on each programme. Its practicability would, however, require the simultaneous availability of several well-worked-out projects. If the procedure is not to hold back, rather than encourage economic development, it will demand a considerable and sustained planning effort on the part of a community's institutions and close cooperation with the planning agencies of the member countries.

A second remediable reason for the lack of success of attempts at agreed industrial specialization is that, although a particular regional allocation of industries may be negotiable at governmental level, that alone does not ensure the implementation of the projects in the largely market economies that characterize less developed groupings. Agreed specialization almost by definition usually implies the allocation of industries to country locations that investors regard as sub-optimal. Investment that is excluded by means of licensing or some other device from the privately preferred country location may well not be undertaken anywhere else in the region, unless the perceived disadvantages are offset. Past attempts to operate industrial cooperation agreements among developing countries have usually given insufficient weight to this consideration. The resolution of this second aspect of the implementation problem requires measures to ensure that the envisaged investment will be commercially profitable, either by the provision of adequate fiscal incentives or by other means. Evidently this point would apply equally to attempts to promote specialization patterns that reflect true regional comparative advantage.

The planned industrial specialization approach and its implications for specific groups or sectors of less developed countries has been explored several times since the 1970s. Notable examples are provided by a study of LAFTA (Carnoy, 1972), the United Nations study for ASEAN (UN, 1974), the study by the UN Economic Commission for Asia and the Far East (1973) of selected countries in South-East Asia and the Pacific, and the sectoral study by Mennes and Stoutjesdijk (1985) with reference to the Andean Group. Each of these studies provides confirmation of the substantial economic gains that can be derived from this partial form of economic integration. The methodology itself has been fully discussed by Mennes (1973).

The study of LAFTA utilized a modified linear programming approach in a partial equilibrium framework in order to ascertain the cheapest way of satisfying LAFTA's projected demand for six product groups: nitrogenous fertilizers; methanol and formaldehyde; paper and pulp; dairy products; lathes; and tractors. Essentially, the exercise involved balancing the economies of scale made possible by the expansion of production at a single point against the increased costs of transporting the products to their final markets. The resource cost of importing from the minimum-cost location was compared both with the cost of importing from the United States and with the cost of production on a national scale. The cost to the region in terms of increased production costs resulting from producing on a regional scale but at various sub-optimal locations was also computed. The study attempted in this way to quantify the welfare gains from integration, defined as resources saved, that would result from importing from the least-cost location and to compare these gains with those that would result from various specified alternatives. The size of the potential gains from integration appeared to be quite significant. For instance, whereas without integration none of the Latin American products could at the time compete with imports in the production of these manufactures, the analysis suggested that the formation of a customs union would make the designated products competitive and would also free 3–4 per cent of the aggregate gross domestic product each year to be used for further investment. It was also found that several alternative locational patterns could be adopted without causing great losses of economic efficiency – a consideration that is obviously very important from the standpoint of the feasibility of measures to distribute the gains from integration acceptably.

As one of the earliest attempts to quantify the orders of magnitude of prospective gains from an optimal investment programme for an actual economic grouping, the study of LAFTA is of much interest, although the estimates themselves may be criticized on several grounds. In particular, differences between private and social costs were disregarded, and the estimates of private costs appear to rest on tenuous foundations.

The United Nations' study, which attempted to surmount some of the difficulties left unresolved in the study of LAFTA, was undertaken for the countries of ASEAN: Singapore, Thailand, Malaysia, the Philippines and Indonesia (UN, 1974). Like the study of LAFTA, this took as its starting point the presumed advantages of regional cooperation for establishing a number of new industries in which economies of scale were important. The industries selected as *prima facie* suitable for an integrated regional market were: nitrogenous fertilizers; phosphatic fertilizers; carbon black; caprolactam; dimethyl terephthalate; ethylene glycol; soda ash; sheet glass; newsprint; sealed compressor units; small engines; typewriters; and steel. The study estimated total unit costs for these products in regional and national plants, and these costs were then compared with the costs of imports. Several alternative locational packages for the regional plants were then compared, assuming given demands for the products in the different national markets.

The calculations indicated clearly that, if production were undertaken in national plants, production costs would always be higher than world c.i.f. prices, the excess amounting, for instance, to some 40 per cent in the case of steel and caprolactam and to as much as 70–80 per cent in the case of sheet glass and compressor units. If, instead, production were undertaken in regional plants, most of the products could be produced at about the world price, and some more cheaply. Moreover, except for sheet glass, small compressors and steel, a very modest tariff preference (10 per cent) would enable the regional products to compete in the regional market, assuming that they would require a 10 per cent price advantage to enable them to do so.

A particularly interesting feature of the ASEAN study is the close attention that it gives to the problem of equity in regional industrial cooperation. In this connection a broader range of welfare indicators was utilized than the conventional ones of unit cost differentials and cost savings. For each assumed locational pattern, indicators were computed of a variety of objective costs and benefits that would accrue to each country. These included: capital costs of constructing the plants; employment generated; value added; foreign exchange costs; and, finally, the cost of concessions given and received (in terms of tariff preferences) to make feasible the trade pattern assumed in each programme.

The report went on to suggest that any programme in which a country's relative share of costs and benefits in terms of these enumerated respects were broadly in line with indicators such as that country's share in the ASEAN market for the products, its relative national income, etc. might be regarded as *prima facie* acceptable on equity grounds. No attempt was made to estimate any special benefits or costs that a country might subjectively judge particular projects to have for itself (because, for example, of its employment situation or a special preference on political or other grounds for certain types of industry). It is apparent that if such special costs and benefits were taken into account, a country might rationally prefer an industrial allocation that did not perform well on the rather limited test of equity proposed in the study.

The agreed industrial specialization approach to regional integration has many merits, and it has justifiably received much attention in recent years. Its application to concrete situations has provided ample confirmation of the substantial gains that may be derived from properly conceived integration initiatives, even those of limited scope. It remains to refine estimates of the cost implications of various alternatives so as to bring out clearly the objective trade-offs involved in various alternative patterns of location. The adoption of this approach could then make an important contribution to constructive policy making on economic integration by facilitating decisions that minimized the costs of regional production, subject to any necessary equity and political constraints.

Transnational Enterprises and Regional Integration

The third policy issue or set of policy issues confronting integration groupings of developing countries has to do with foreign direct investment, monopolistic practices and access to technology. With negligible exceptions, the orthodox theory of integration disregards these matters by assuming that technology is constant, that competition is perfect, and that capital is immobile internationally. In developing countries the issues that arise when these conditions are not satisfied have a common focus in the activities of multinational or transnational enterprises (TNEs), whose operations have assumed a dominant role in nearly all present-day regional groupings.

The implications of the operations of TNEs for the practice of integration in developing countries need careful consideration. The issues are considered at a general level in Chapter 6 in their bearing on improved resource allocation (static and dynamic efficiency), and on equity considerations. It is also necessary – in developing countries in particular – to consider the bearing of TNE operations on the ability of member states to attain other policy objectives that may underly their integration initiatives. In developing countries these objectives include notably the promotion of inter-industry linkages, the reduction of dependence and the enhancement of external bargaining power. Without question the operations of TNEs have important implications for the attainment of efficiency, equity and other policy objectives in many countries, but they are likely to be of particular significance for developing countries because of the dominant importance of TNEs in many of those economies. In their case, indeed, the relationship between integration and the operations of TNEs is so close that the policies of the group and of its individual members towards TNEs might well be regarded as the primary issue in contemporary integration processes (Vaitsos, 1982).

On *a priori* grounds a TNE might be expected to promote integration where national markets are small and it is not itself involved already in other member countries through parallel direct investments. This was the situation both in the countries of the Central American Common Market prior to their integration and in those of the smaller African groupings. In groupings of medium or larger-size developing countries by contrast, the attitudes and behaviour of a TNE may well be less favourable to integration if it is already involved in several member countries or if it is faced by potential competition from other TNEs located in other member states. The resulting pattern of oligopolistic rivalry may generate behaviour designed to preserve a balance of interests. The accompanying patterns of trade and investment may then not be efficient, and integration itself may not ameliorate the situation. Moreover, even when market conditions present favourable opportunities for TNEs to stimulate integration among developing countries, it may operate principally at the level of final products. With respect to inputs, it may be more advantageous for a TNE to promote links with its parent firms outside the region than with locally based enterprises in other member countries. The task of developing intra-industry linkages within the region may then be rendered more difficult to the extent that the integration process relies heavily on the operations of TNEs. Likewise, the typically high dependence of TNEs on often highly specialized imported inputs helps to maintain and may enhance the degree of external economic dependence of the member countries and the influence of TNEs in the group. In these ways some of the broader objectives of integration and development policy may be frustrated, unless effective countervailing policies can be implemented.

Apart from its possible effects in limiting efficient patterns of trade and investment, the behaviour of transnationals in developing countries with respect to transfer prices may also have an important impact on the ability of smaller enterprises to survive, with consequent implications for the viability of a competitive market structure.

A further problem is that the pricing practices that are used for competitive purposes may also serve to influence the distribution of benefits between the host countries in the region. For instance, profits may be transferred by such practices to member states having more liberal tax or profit repatriation policies towards business enterprises. Similarly the distribution of benefits between the region and the country of origin of the foreign direct investment may also be influenced by the decisions taken by TNEs concerning the prices at which technology and specialized intermediate inputs and other factors are bought in from the parent enterprises.

There are virtually no satisfactory studies of the operations of TNEs in regional groupings. However, two recent studies of integration groupings in Africa do present some incidental material that bears on the impact of TNE affiliates on resource allocation and benefit distribution in the blocs.

In the West African Economic Community (CEAO) the large and medium-sized enterprises are mostly affiliated to foreign corporations that own between 60 and 100 per cent of their capital. Many of these – Bata, Peugeot, Air Liquide, Wonder – operate in several countries. In some industries, as in textiles, a complex system of interlocking financial participations both within and between member states has also been created between different transnationals operating within the community, such as Gonfreville, Texunion, Riegel, Schaeffer.

It seems clear that the outcome of this pattern of development within CEAO has been a marked lack of country specialization, whether particular products or product ranges are considered. In most industrial sectors, plants are replicated, and production takes place on a smaller scale and on a less specialized basis than the size of the regional market as a whole would permit (Robson, 1983). As a result, the opportunities for inter-country trade are reduced, and the advantages of integration that derive from specialization and the exploitation of scale economies are dissipated, even allowing for the relatively great importance of transport costs in limiting the scope for profitable specialization in this region. Uneconomic replication has occurred notably in textiles (despite the interlocking links of many of the enterprises involved), and also in batteries, pharmaceuticals and plastics. Only in rare industries does a limited degree of product specialization occur – as in footwear, where Bata does not produce a complete range at each of its plants.

A similar lack of industrial specialization and limited intra-group trade is found in UDEAC, where TNEs also have a major role – and where indeed a number of the TNEs found in CEAO also operate (such as Bata, Riegel, Schaeffer and CFAO). Market segmentation is widespread in UDEAC also, and plants and products are replicated throughout the region. These and other aspects of the operation of the UDEAC market have been severely criticized in a report (United Nations Economic Commission for Africa, 1981) that lays the blame for the lack of specialization primarily at the door of the transnational corporations.

The ECA report condemns the operations of the transnationals as unconstructive, and as contributing to the disintegration of the regional economy. Inter-regional trade flows are claimed to respond not to conditions in the UDEAC countries but to the global and regional strategies adopted by the TNEs, which are seen as the principal beneficiaries of such limited intra-regional trade as there is. Market segmentation has been produced by the extensive use of intra-union tax barriers between the national markets, which has resulted in oligopolistic or monopolistic market structures. Combined with tax incentives, segmentation has, it is argued, strengthened the market dominance of foreign enterprises, has eliminated incentives to efficient production and has encouraged a replication of plants throughout the region. The report concludes that the member states themselves derive little benefit from the operations of the transnational enterprises that locate subsidiaries within their borders.

There can be little doubt that the pattern of investment and trade in manufactures that has resulted in both CEAO and UDEAC is far from optimal, or that market fragmentation – the proximate cause – is excessive. However, it is certainly not apposite to lay the primary blame for this outcome on the multinationals. The root of the problem – which is present in most groupings – lies in the failure of the member states themselves to agree on programmes of regional specialization and on a suitable industrial and fiscal strategy to underpin it. The intra-union taxes in the two African groups that make market segmentation possible are essentially national devices enabling member states – in particular the less developed ones – to protect themselves from the consequences of this failure. In other groupings, unharmonized investment incentives produce similar results.

The conduct of the transnationals in both of these African groupings is that of any profit-maximizing enterprise that operates by reference to distorted market signals, although it is true that the market power of the transnationals does enable them to exercise influence and pressure on the member states and the group; they do not merely respond to exogenous provisions. The basic remedy, however, must be sought mainly in the adoption of a regional industrial strategy and a related fiscal incentive policy for all enterprises, and partly in the adoption of more rational pricing systems throughout the regions so that commercial self-interest and community objectives are better harmonized. It does not by any means follow that the adoption of such a strategy would of itself fully resolve this and related problems arising from the operations of transnational enterprises, but it can hardly be gainsaid that it would be the single most important step towards encouraging a more rational allocation of investment within such economic groupings.

Regional integration among developing countries undoubtedly provides TNEs with additional scope for promoting efficient resource allocation, but it may well also be accompanied by an increase in their market power if other national policies are not harmonized. The result then could be that both resource allocation and the distribution of benefits are affected in ways that are adverse to the interests of some or even all of the member countries. Harmonized investment codes geared to the attainment of the developmental objectives of industrial strategy are thus important, and may be crucial if integration is to serve the policy objectives of the member states. Where TNEs have a major role, as they do in most developing countries, their operations thus provide further important reasons for supposing that market integration and trade liberalization constitute inadequate and inappropriate techniques for promoting improved resource allocation, an equitable distribution of benefits and other sought-after developmental objectives.

CONCLUSION

When measured against the economic benefits that might have been expected from integration among developing countries, or even against the implementation of formal commitments, the progress and achievements of integration in many less developed areas since the mid-1960s must be judged to have been less than satisfactory. Although only one bloc – the East African Community – has actually broken up, overt progress elsewhere has been slow and sometimes interrupted. This is reflected in the levelling-off in the rate of growth of intra-group trade that has occurred in most groupings in the past few years – despite the low initial shares – and in an actual fall in the ratio in some cases. Table 13.2 shows that, by 1983, intra-bloc trade as a percentage of total exports exceeded 20 per cent only in ASEAN and in the CACM. In CEAO it amounted to 12 per cent, in LAIA (the successor to LAFTA) to 10 per cent, and in CARICOM to 9 per cent.

The reasons for the difficulties experienced by the various integration schemes are many and complex. Some of them are specific to particular groupings and originate in such factors as the personal relations between national leaders, or differences in economic philosophy with respect to the roles of the market and the state. An important factor of widespread relevance, however, is quite simply that, at low levels of development, not only are the benefits of classical integration on the basis of trade liberalization limited, but also, because of widespread distortions, trade liberalization itself gives rise to major problems. Successful economic integration among less developed countries therefore seems likely to call for a more deliberate approach than has been found necessary in advanced economies. Moreover, since it finds its rationale largely in the gains from coordinating and stimulating investment, it must be accompanied by measures to create or strengthen the production structures. It is here that planning will have an important role to play. To the extent that economic integration in less developed countries has its effect largely through its impact on future investment and future production, it is necessary to consider integration as a part of development policy, subjected to a planning process and utilizing appropriate planning techniques.

At the same time, across-the-board planned integration is not in general a practicable approach. It is difficult, if not impossible, for participants accurately to estimate the impact of such far-reaching arrangements. Moreover, the administrative skills and the expertise required to operate comprehensive regional-planning arrangements are likely to be particularly scarce in developing countries. Narrower arrangements limited to particular sectors or industries may well be more suitable. Many of the difficulties encountered by integration arrangements among developing countries can reasonably be said to have arisen from attempts to proceed on a very broad front too rapidly, before the preconditions for effective integration have been created, with the almost inevitable result that the outcome has been unproductive.

If effective means (direct or indirect) can be devised for rationally coordinating productive activity on a regional basis, a growing number of empirical studies suggest that the benefits from integration among developing countries can be substantial. In the absence of effective coordination, any benefits will be limited. In more advanced regions, such as Central and South America, the outcome is likely to be an intense and unprofitable competition for foreign capital and technology, producing a proliferation of competing plants, each operating with excess capacity. In less advanced regions such as Africa, a more probable outcome is the creation of ultimately destabilizing industrial imbalances. In the longer run, the adoption of more rational pricing systems and systems of protection should enable a greater role to be assigned to market forces in promoting integration among developing countries. This would have the merit of reducing the at times paralysing process of international negotiation on which, at present, it often depends. In the meantime, for most groupings of less developed countries it is unrealistic to expect that trade liberalization by itself would produce a pattern of integration that was necessarily either equitable or socially profitable.

CHAPTER 12

Integration among Centrally Planned Economies

Earlier chapters have dealt with the theory of economic integration among predominantly market economy countries. Even in these circumstances there may be arguments for planning and agreed specialization where significant economies of scale and interdependence are present. These considerations often do underlie initiatives for the joint planning and harmonization of structural policies among such countries.

Integration also takes place among centrally planned economies. The instruments and processes of integration under these two systems of organization differ markedly. This chapter outlines some of the characteristic features of integration under central planning and looks briefly at some aspects of integration among the centrally planned economies of Eastern Europe.

TRADE AND INTEGRATION UNDER CENTRAL PLANNING

The differences in the instruments of integration between market and planned systems are apparent. The principal instrument of integration among market economies is the creation of identical competitive conditions for producers, consumers and traders in the member countries. The resulting pattern of trade integration should then largely reflect differences in absolute or comparative costs among the member states. In centrally planned economies, by contrast, most enterprises are publicly owned, and the economies are organized on the basis of comprehensive development plans, which lay down detailed targets for production, investment and prices. In such a situation many commercial barriers of the types emphasized in customs union theory are irrelevant. Foreign trade is regulated not by the instruments employed in market economies but by administrative means in accordance with the provisions of the plan. Centrally planned economies generally conduct their foreign trade through state trading organizations, which introduce elements of monopoly power into the conduct of foreign trade.

In the short run, the amount and composition of trade among centrally planned economies must be largely determined within the limits of the annual plan. In the longer run, intra-group trade can develop as the outcome of a coordination of production plans. The process of coordination might consist of the establishment of a single plan for the whole region, drawn up by a supranational authority, or by national planning agencies working together. Such a plan would allocate specific production goals to the different member states, and trade among them would reflect the specialization of production that is implicit in the plan. In the absence of a supranational authority or agency with executive powers, which the centrally planned economies of Eastern Europe have not so far found it possible to agree on, a single plan will be impossible to attain. The pattern of integration then found will reflect the outcome of political pressures, bargaining strengths, to some extent the comparative production advantages of different members, and their perceptions of their separate national interests.

Given that the trade and integration patterns of centrally planned economies are determined by direct controls, an important practical question is how policy makers actually determine what is to be produced and exported. The problem is that, under central planning, domestic production and prices are not determined by supply and demand, and prices are not necessarily rational indicators of the relative values of goods to planners or of their real costs of production. Furthermore, foreign exchange rates are to a greater or lesser extent arbitrary and serve chiefly as a unit of account. In these circumstances planners lack a rational basis for determining the extent and pattern of foreign trade.

The importance of this problem should not be exaggerated. There are many export and import lines that are obvious, even to planners – for instance, oil and gas in Soviet exports, and coal in the case of Poland. It is when processed manufactures and complex machinery are in question that the problem becomes acute. It is in this area that the problem increasingly became felt in centrally planned economies during the 1960s and 1970s, and much effort was devoted during this period to providing a basis for rationalizing foreign trade decisions. Initially, this was approached principally through the development of foreign trade effectiveness indicators, of which many varieties exist. Basically, these seek to indicate, in the case of exports, which domestically produced products will earn the largest amount of foreign exchange per rouble of expenditure of domestic resources; in the case of imports the object is similarly to determine which commodities will save the largest amount of domestic resources per dollar of foreign exchange expended.

In earlier calculations of this kind, given productive capacities were assumed. Later attempts recognized that for the optimal planning of integration over the long run it is necessary also to evaluate the efficiency of investment in new capacity from the standpoint of foreign trade. Attempts to do this for particular commodities have been discussed by Wilczynski (1965). However, although particular indexes may facilitate a more rational choice in particular areas of foreign trade, the question of foreign trade efficiency is ultimately integrally connected with the efficiency of the whole economy. With this in mind, optimization models for foreign trade have been constructed, utilizing linear programming techniques (Trzeciakowski and Mycielski, 1976). Wilczynski has claimed that there is little evidence that efficiency calculations led to the modification of trade patterns, uneconomic trade being typically justified by advantages not reflected in the indexes.

Planning models for economic integration, involving both production and trade, have also been developed by Western economists and are reviewed in Mennes (1973). Mennes himself has developed a general equilibrium model for this purpose, the use of which in principle is highly desirable as it can allow for the impact of new projects on the cost structure of the economies into which they are to be imbedded. However, it is not yet possible to solve such models when economies of scale are present (necessitating mixed integer programming methods), except for a few projects for division among a few countries. For programmes involving the coordination of considerable numbers of trade-justified projects for allocation among several countries therefore, it is necessary to resort to partial equilibrium methods. Of course, even to be able to utilize this simpler planning approach for the solution of practical integration problems requires much data, in particular of input requirements. The principal practical difficulty is that input requirements can only be determined approximately, and it is also very difficult to determine *ex ante* how these requirements may vary for any one industry from one country to another, although this is crucial to regional efficiency calculations.

Planning models, whether for national planning or for integration planning, can evidently be used in a variety of ways, and they can be formulated to embody any chosen criteria of efficiency and preference function. At one extreme they can be used to generate an optimal competitive-equilibrium solution, given free trade or implicit tariffs at particular levels. This solution will correspond to optimal integration by market forces. Alternatively, planning models can be used to generate an integrated joint optimization solution employing some kind of preference function for the group. This would correspond to integration with supranational planning. The essential issue that arises in relation to integration under central planning is not therefore about the role of the plan as opposed to the market but rather it is about the criteria that are to be the basis for the planned coordination (Csikós-Nagy, 1976). However, there is evidently an important difference between national planning and planning for integration. In the absence of supranational planning, the criteria employed to determine production and prices domestically (which reflect the interaction of a variety of domestically relevant criteria) are largely irrelevant to the determination of what the country should export; and they are also irrelevant to the partner countries, which normally have a different scale of preferences and will be interested *ceteris paribus* in obtaining their commodities on the most favourable terms.

Plainly, central planning in itself contains nothing to resolve the interest conflicts that arise among planned economies where preference functions differ and the welfare of a person in each country is not weighted equally by the policy makers. In these circumstances it will not be rational to evaluate the merits of an international integration programme mainly by reference to differences in unit processing costs (a commonly suggested criterion of efficiency) under alternative specialization patterns, even if (1) there is agreement on how these costs are to be measured; and (2) these costs are also relevant to the procurement and supply of goods in intra-bloc trade. Interest conflicts arise because member countries are not indifferent to the location of economic activity over the region and because they normally differ in their preferences for different types of economic activity, reflecting in part differences in their national circumstances. Ultimately, where integration is planned, each country's negotiators have to: (1) assess the merits of the projects that could be allocated to them under alternative programmes; (2) compare these with the value of the concessions that they would have to offer as a result of adopting a particular import programme; and (3) relate these to their national policy objectives and development strategies. This is an immensely difficult task.

In principle, planned integration should have considerable advantages in making it possible to avoid the costs involved in reaching a solution by trial and error and in enabling the interdependence of different projects to be taken into account. In practice, however, the politicization of the integration process that is inevitably involved may render the process much more difficult, no more optimal and, with respect to its pace, certainly slower than the outcome under the market approach. Wiles has remarked: 'It is thus tempting . . . to attribute the quicker economic integration of the Six to their economic model; which integrates quietly and impersonally while prime ministers are in bed' (1968, p. 328).

Some of the problems of integration in practice under centrally planned economies may be illustrated by a summary account of the history of integration among the socialist countries of Eastern Europe. Unless otherwise indicated, the reference for all official documents and agreements is the compendiums periodically produced by the Secretariat (CMEA, *Basic Documents*).

THE EVOLUTION OF COMECON

The Council for Mutual Economic Assistance (CMEA), better known in the West as Comecon, is an economic grouping established in 1949 by the socialist countries of Eastern Europe with the objects of accelerating economic development and establishing a more rational division of labour among member countries. At present, its full members are formally Albania, Bulgaria, Czechoslovakia, the German Democratic Republic (GDR), Hungary, Poland, Romania and the Soviet Union, together with three developing countries, Cuba, Mongolia and Vietnam. In practical terms, regional economic integration is only in question for the European members of Comecon excluding Albania, and the following discussion is therefore limited to those countries. In these terms the bloc consists of one dominant member (the Soviet Union) and six much smaller members – a feature that gives the grouping a distinctive character because of the enormous influence that the Soviet Union can exercise over the affairs of the group by virtue of its economic, political and military power.

Following the economic ferment of mid-1949–50 that accompanied the establishment of Comecon, four main phases can be distinguished in its history: a dormant phase until 1954; an active phase that lasted from 1955 until 1963; a phase of stagnation between 1964 and 1969; and a reactivized phase lasting from 1969 to the present day. During this last phase, several marked changes of emphasis have occurred. These are notably the redirection that took place in the mid-1970s as a result of the decision to introduce integration plans and targets and the emphasis of the early 1980s on coping with external problems. A new phase may currently be developing with the prominence given by Gorbachev to scientific and technological progress, which is the focus of the latest blueprint for CMEA.

In the years immediately following the establishment of Comecon, intra-bloc trade developed rapidly until 1953, but this was mainly attributable to political factors and had little to do with the Council's activities. Despite its extent, moreover, intra-bloc integration was for several years of a primitive character. Trade resulted from a year-by-year exchange of surpluses, and no attempt was made *ex ante* to gear production plans to each other. Until the mid-1950s, indeed, the Council itself performed no real function in relation to trade, which resulted almost entirely from bilateral agreements entered into outside its aegis.

A new phase began in 1954 with the commencement of the Khrushchev era, during which attempts were made to strengthen Comecon 'as a device to substitute for Stalinist control in the economic sphere' (Holzman, 1976). Several innovations were made, mainly in the later 1950s, such as the conclusion of the first joint investment and joint enterprise agreements. Progress was slow, but Soviet interest in strengthening the Council continued, stimulated in part by the formation of the rival groupings of the European Economic Community (EEC) and the European Free Trade Association (EFTA) in the West and by fear of their potentially adverse implications for any attempt on the part of the Comecon nations to expand their trade with the West. These efforts to strengthen the Council were eventually reflected in the publication of two formal documents: the Comecon Charter itself, which did not go into effect until 1960 – a whole decade after the Council's formation; and the important 1962 statement on goals and methods entitled 'Basic Principles of the International Socialist Division of Labour'. Both documents stressed the desirability of coordination and cooperation in the economic, technical and scientific spheres; the importance of improving the division of labour by the multilateral coordination of the separate national development plans; the desirability of achieving high rates of industrialization and development, especially for the less developed members; and the eventual elimination of differences in levels of development. Like the original statement of principles, they also stressed that each member was to be fully independent and sovereign and was not to be bound by decisions with which it disagreed. Despite this emphasis on sovereignty, attempts were made by Khrushchev in 1962 to advance the cause of supranational planning. These had their immediate roots in difficulties with Romania, which went back to 1957 when Romania had insisted on producing a type of truck not allotted to it – an insistence that culminated in the dispute over the Galati Steel Works, which Romania wished to build (Brown, 1963).

From the early 1960s, the issue of supranational planning in connection with coordination and specialization has been intermittently debated in Comecon and has from time to time generated protracted conflict between its more and less industrially developed members. In the earlier stages of the Council it had been assumed that each member would industrialize as rapidly as possible. By 1954 this approach was leading to raw materials shortages throughout the bloc, and its more advanced members began putting pressure on the less advanced, especially on Romania and Bulgaria, to concentrate more on agriculture and extractive industries and less on manufacturing. The advanced countries took the view that industrialization should be accomplished on a bloc-wide basis, with comparative advantage dictating the direction of specialization of each nation. The less developed countries of the bloc, on the other hand, continued to maintain that each nation was entitled to industrialize as rapidly as possible and should do so.

The controversy was reflected in a diversity of attitudes towards the use of the foreign trade profitability indexes, which were being developed at this time by some member countries as an aid to guide the desirable composition of imports and exports. In general the less developed countries were opposed to the use of such indexes – essentially on the ground that comparative advantage must be viewed dynamically, not statically. Romania's opposition also rested on its desire to take account of other policy objectives, such as full employment and balance of payments equilibrium (Montias, 1967). Much of the practical debate between the nations of the bloc over the implementation of integration thus centred on the issue of static efficiency versus equalization of development (Holzman, 1976).

In the event, although the debate went on vigorously, by the early 1960s the advocates of national sovereignty appeared to have carried the day. The debate, however, came to the fore again in 1968.

Throughout the 1960s it appears that little major progress was in fact made towards the more effective economic integration of the Comecon countries. With respect to factors of production, capital, labour and technical knowledge moved to only a small extent across national frontiers. As to products and trade, integration was held back by the lack of progress towards solving the problems of inconvertibility and bilateralism that had hampered trade from the start. An International Bank for Economic Cooperation (IBEC) was established in 1963 with the principal purpose of multilateralizing intra-bloc trade. This was supposed to be achieved by the introduction of the so-called transferable rouble, in which all Comecon trade was to be transacted. Scant progress was made towards this objective then or subsequently. The conditions that had initially resulted in 'commodity inconvertibility' in the bloc still existed. Commodity inconvertibility refers to the fact that a bloc country with a trade surplus in a bloc currency or in transferable roubles is unable to spend that currency freely on unplanned imports from other Soviet bloc countries because most commodities are allocated in advance and free access to internal markets by foreigners is not permitted. Not surprisingly, IBEC compensations have remained relatively small. Moreover, although a certain number of joint investment projects were undertaken during this period (Romania and the GDR cooperated in a chemical complex; Hungary and Czechoslovakia cooperated in a paper-making mill) and, partly as a result, trade in certain items expanded, the share of intra-bloc trade as a whole in total trade stagnated or fell. For Romania it fell particularly sharply, being offset by a rise in the percentage of its trade with the Western industrialized countries (from 16 per cent in 1958 to 45 per cent in 1969).

The internal economic difficulties experienced by all the Comecon countries during the 1960s, which were reflected in slower rates of economic growth, also had their repercussions on the integration process. First, internal economic reforms were introduced by most Comecon countries following the end of the Khrushchev era, and their importance in some countries has continued to increase. Although these reforms were by no means uniform, generally they involved some decentralization and a rationalization of pricing procedures. In some countries enterprises were allowed limited authority to trade in foreign markets without having to go through foreign trade monopolies. Although such changes were ultimately capable of being beneficial to the Comecon integration process, their immediate effect was to make it more difficult for the planned role of trade in the Comecon countries to be fulfilled. Secondly, the economic slowdown and emergent difficulties in the area of technology were creating a strong incentive for the Eastern bloc nations to look towards the West.

Despite the economic difficulties experienced by Comecon countries during this period and the pull of potential East–West trade, or perhaps because of them, Soviet concern with making Comecon integration more effective was renewed in 1966–8. This was reflected in renewed Soviet criticism of Romania, whose interest in Comecon integration appeared to have ebbed to a low point. Romania's opposition to any attempt at supranational planning was supported by Czechoslovakia and Hungary, which were both experimenting with reforms leading in the direction of market socialism.

Progress on specialization in the Comecon countries during the 1960s had been summed up by Heiss (1970):

> In practice, most specialization agreements have consisted of an allocation of production responsibility by type or size among countries already producing the items involved, permitting some economies of scale. Although several thousand products concentrated in the engineering, chemical, and ferrous metal industries are covered, the share of total output affected, even within these industries, is small (e.g. 6 to 7 percent of CMEA's machinery output).

The invasion of Czechoslovakia in August 1968 halted what some saw at the time as the incipient disintegration of Comecon and ushered in the most recent phase of the Council's history. With the enunciation of the Brezhnev doctrine in 1968 the political motivation for seeking to confer supranational powers on the Council was no longer so urgent. Nevertheless, the economic rationale for attempts to improve the working of the Council continued to be valid. An expansion of foreign trade, in particular of bloc trade, was widely seen in Eastern Europe as a major source for accelerating economic growth. Debate on integration strategy continued against that background, and the outcome was the adoption in 1971, at the twenty-fifth session of the Council, of the 'Comprehensive Programme for Socialist Economic Integration'.

The programme, which was to be implemented over a period of fifteen–twenty years, attempted to lay down guidelines for the extension of integration in the areas of production, trade, currencies, pricing and administrative procedures. National interests and the needs of the whole socialist community were to be integrated in order to take maximum advantage of economic cooperation between member countries. Closer coordination of investment policies and of research and technological development were envisaged. Although governments were to continue to play a key role in coordination, more importance was to be attached to direct relationships at the intermediate and enterprise level. The mechanism of integration would continue to be based mainly on the coordination of long-term national plans and the conclusion of bilateral and multilateral agreements. However, the impact of coordination was expected to be reinforced by the fact that it would take place before the final completion and approval of national plans and not by way of *ex post* adjustment. An overhaul of national price relations and a realignment of exchange rates between national currencies and the transferable rouble were envisaged, together with a move to convertibility in mutual payments. Emphasis was given to narrowing and eventually eliminating the gaps in industrial development between the various members. To facilitate this the programme envisaged incentives of a preferential nature for the benefit of the less industrialized socialist countries (UNCTAD, 1972).

In the context of the emphasis on multilateralism in the Comprehensive Programme, two specific measures in the financial field may be noted. The first is the increased role that was assigned to IBEC, which was to use measures of credit and interest more actively to promote trade. The possibility of increasing the bank's capital with convertible currency was raised. Comecon members already traded certain goods among themselves on a hard currency basis, notably gold – as they still do. Other goods, for example oil and meat, command hard currency payments if deliveries exceed the quotas set in long-term agreements. According to some Eastern European estimates, such trade accounts for up to 20 per cent of total intra-bloc trade, and it is growing in importance. Secondly, an International Investment Bank (IIB) was established and commenced operations in January 1971 with a capital of 1,000 million roubles, 30 per cent of which was in gold or convertible currencies. Its task is to grant credits for Comecon joint ventures that are capable of promoting the international division of labour. Although the establishment of the new bank could help to multilateralize capital flows, intra-bloc capital transfers are effectively implemented by commodity transfer. So long as 'commodity inconvertibility' continues, the capital transfer process will be hindered.

A further stage in the progress of integration was represented by the adoption in 1975 of the first Concerted Plan for Multilateral Integration Measures. This was designed to integrate several sectors, including mechanical engineering, petrochemicals, agriculture and transport, by a range of integration projects and further specialization agreements. The plan envisaged about thirty key projects, for the implementation of which the Comecon countries allocated some 9,000 million transferable roubles. Among the larger projects were a pulp and paper combine, an asbestos combine, iron and ferro-alloy production and polyisoprene rubber. At the thirtieth session of the Council, five long-term 'target' cooperation programmes were also agreed; but even today these appear still to be in their initial stages, and it is unclear what measures will be adopted for their practical implementation and how effective they are likely to be.

Nevertheless, the Comprehensive Programme appears to have generated a certain number of projects involving industrial specialization and cooperation, and these were clearly central to the attempts to coordinate the national economic plans for 1976–80. By the beginning of 1977 more than ninety multilateral agreements on cooperation in production had been concluded. Particular attention had been given to engineering, for which fifty-five agreements covering 5,000 items had been made. Trade flows under specialization agreements still appear to represent a modest share of overall intra-Comecon trade – perhaps 10 per cent – but the share appears to be substantially higher in the case of trade in machinery and equipment where it may attain 25 per cent. Within their limits, these agreements should help to secure the advantages of large-scale specialized production and lower production costs. Often cited examples of achieved specialization include the production of: battery-driven fork-lift trucks in Bulgaria; buses and automobile components in Hungary; shipbuilding, chemical and textile machinery and passenger coaches in the GDR; shipbuilding and repairing in Poland; chemical machinery building and heavy trucks in the Soviet Union and Czechoslovakia; and oil equipment and locomotives in Romania. Some of this merely recognizes already established production advantages. Otherwise (van Brabant, 1980) the significance of specialization agreements for integration is limited. What is strongly suggested by analyses produced for the 1986 NATO economic colloquium (North Atlantic Treaty Organization, 1987) is that no significant sectoral or industrial integration has yet been achieved in CMEA.

ASPECTS OF INTRA-COMECON TRADE

In 1938, trade among the Eastern European countries (Bulgaria, Czechoslovakia, Hungary, Poland and Romania) amounted to only 11 per cent of their total trade. The USSR had virtually no trade with any of these countries except Czechoslovakia, for which it accounted for 2 per cent of trade. The most important trade partner of the Eastern countries was Germany, which accounted for 28 per cent of total trade (Wiles, 1968). By 1950, intra-bloc trade, including the USSR and the GDR, exceeded 60 per cent of the total, and by 1953 it had risen to almost 80 per cent. The redirection of trade towards the USSR accounted for the largest part of the change in trade patterns, but increased trade among the six smaller members themselves was also important and has become still more so of late. Since 1953 the relative importance of intra-bloc trade has fallen significantly: in 1983 it constituted only 54 per cent of total trade (see Table 13.1, p. 235). The Council's experience may be compared with that of the EEC Six in which the share of intra-community trade grew steadily over the period from 1959 until the first enlargement, at which date it accounted for some 50 per cent of total trade.

Two interrelated questions have received considerable attention in connection with the restructured trade patterns of Comecon:

(1)   To what extent did these altered trade flows represent trade creation, and to what extent trade diversion?
(2)   How have the gains from trade been influenced by the intra-bloc pricing policies pursued?

Trade Creation and Trade Diversion

It is impossible to estimate quantitatively the effects on intra-bloc trade of the discrimination involved in Comecon by the more commonly used methods discussed in Chapter 13 since the trade barriers in these countries take the form of implicit quotas and flow from planning decisions. A second factor that would in any case hinder systematic analysis is that the dramatic redirection of trade among the socialist countries that took place after 1949 occurred simultaneously with, or closely followed, other major policy changes, namely, the introduction of nationalization and of central planning in all the countries of Eastern Europe and the related moves towards rapid industrialization and self-sufficiency along the lines of the 1930 Soviet model. Holzman (1976) has nevertheless suggested that the switch in trade flows noted above 'must largely reflect trade diversion', although no evidence is presented to support that assertion. Elsewhere, Holzman (1985) has characterized Comecon rather as 'trade-destroying'.

The concepts of trade creation and trade diversion are strictly static: they apply to a situation in which there are given productive capacities, supply is equal to demand, and prices net of tariffs reflect opportunity costs. It makes little sense to apply them without qualification to the development of economies to which these conditions do not apply. Indeed, the concepts would lose their relevance even in market economies if the structure of production were changing substantially under the impetus of forced industrialization. In such a situation the relevant concepts would be those of 'development creation' and 'development diversion'. These are much more difficult to quantify; certainly no Western student of Comecon has yet attempted it. Merely on the basis of an analysis of trade flows it cannot be concluded that the redirection of trade that occurred in the Comecon countries was adverse to their economic interests. Certainly, there is no ground for Holzman's conclusion that:

> . . . customs union analysis leads us to infer that the sharp shift from East–West to intrabloc trade undoubtedly imposed large economic losses on all the Eastern European nations, including the U.S.S.R. in the sense that all the nations would have been better off if they could have continued trading with the West. (1976, p. 74)

Two later studies by Broner (1976) and Pelzman (1977) attempted to approach the issue by way of 'gravity' flow trade models of the type originated by Linneman (1966) in order to determine 'normal' trade flows and from them to infer the extent of trade creation and trade diversion. Both studies found substantial and in fact very similar magnitudes of gross trade creation. The net results differed substantially however, because in the case of Broner a very large trade diversion effect calculated for the Soviet Union resulted in a negative figure for net trade creation, whereas for Pelzman trade diversion was negligible, so that substantial net trade creation was reported. Gravity trade models may be useful for drawing conclusions about the nature and extent of trade flows among integrated market economies in the absence of crucial data on prices and costs that rule out a more direct approach. It is, however, questionable if they can be expected to be as useful for this purpose in relation to centrally planned economies when the connection between foreign trade prices and domestic costs will often be tenuous. In any case, there remains the question of how far it is appropriate to impute calculated trade flow changes to integration rather than to the operation of many other factors. One authority, after an exhaustive discussion of conceptual, statistical and methodological aspects of both studies has concluded that the reported magnitudes of trade impacts for CMEA 'border on the fantastic' (van Brabant, 1980).

The Intra-bloc Effects of Comecon Pricing Policies

One aim of Comecon has been to develop its own independent pricing system based upon market conditions in the socialist world. Such prices would be 'fair' prices; in Marxist terminology they would reflect 'equivalent exchange'. Those nations that have received poorer terms of trade for their products under the world-price-related system that is actually used by the Council have argued that such prices reflect 'non-equivalent' exchange. Although Marxists are inclined to argue that capitalist world prices are non-equivalent and unfair in contrast to socialist world prices, differences of opinion have been apparent within the bloc over the choice of a basis on which to determine an 'own' socialist-world price system, each nation favouring the system that would yield it the best terms of trade. Bulgaria, for instance, which has a relatively low productivity of labour within the Soviet bloc, and, moreover, tends to import capital-intensive and to export labour-intensive commodities, would naturally prefer to use man-hours as the basis for pricing intra-bloc trade since such a basis would mean high prices for its exports and low prices for its imports. Advanced member states such as the GDR and Czechoslovakia on the other hand have opposed such a standard and have instead argued for prices reflecting all factors of production. Some members have wished to include demand factors in the system, and others have urged the use of world prices as the basis for intra-bloc trade (Holzman, 1976).

Intra-bloc prices are in fact fixed on a basis that represents an uneasy compromise. The procedure that determines prices is essentially one of bilateral bargaining. The negotiations are supposed to be carried out in the light of the so-called Bucharest principles, which were adopted in 1958 and have regard to the price of comparable commodities on world markets for some previous time period. Because the notion of a world market price is ambiguous for most products, because the negotiations are bilateral, and finally because the principles are anyway not always adhered to, individual prices can and do differ substantially from world market prices. For 1971–75, prices were to have been negotiated on the basis of world market price averages for 1966–70. In 1974, however, following the OPEC crisis, the Soviet Union initiated a renegotiation of the price basis which resulted in an agreement that for 1975 prices would be set on the basis of world market prices existing in 1972–74, and that from 1976 onwards prices would be negotiated every year on the basis of average world market prices during the previous five years. That system is the one in force today.

The use of historic prices in Comecon trade has, among other things, contributed to a rigidity in trading relationships and to a reinforcement of bilateralism. Because prices of raw materials in intra-bloc trade have tended to be below what supply and demand would indicate, raw material suppliers have also attempted to segment their trade so as to be able to exchange raw materials for raw materials and manufactures for manufactures.

Which Comecon countries appear to have benefited most from intra-bloc trade? In the short term the intra-bloc distribution of costs and benefits is largely a function of the pricing arrangements adopted and of the composition of the trade. In this connection it must again be emphasized that much intra-bloc trade takes place in commodities that, being unstandardized, do not have a 'world' price, so that their prices must be arrived at through bargaining. It has already been noted that the bloc has one dominant member. Moreover that member has a relatively low trade dependence, which puts it in a strong bargaining position. Has the USSR taken advantage of its position to exploit the other Eastern nations by imposing unfavourable or discriminatory prices upon them?

There seems little doubt that this did happen for isolated commodities prior to 1956, as with Polish coal and Romanian oil (Holzman, 1976). In the early days of Comecon it was indeed often suggested in the West that Soviet exploitation extended to commodity trade in general. This view appeared to find support in studies by Mendershausen (1959, 1960). On the basis of an analysis of Soviet trade returns for 1955–9, Mendershausen has concluded that, on average, for similar products, the USSR charged the Eastern bloc about 15 per cent more than it charged Western Europe and paid the Eastern bloc about 15 per cent less than it paid Western Europe. In terms of numbers of commodities, Eastern Europe paid more, and sold for less, to the USSR for about three out of every four products for which comparisons were possible. These data appear to provide support for the belief that the Soviet Union was exploiting the nations of Eastern Europe. Mendershausen has explained this as a simple exercise of monopoly power by the Soviet Union in its economic relations with Eastern Europe.

The results obtained by Mendershausen are also consistent with a different hypothesis, namely, that the West discriminates against the USSR. More relevantly, direct tests of Soviet discrimination using data for trade among the six smaller members, and for trade between them and the Soviet Union, undertaken by Holzman (1974) do not suggest that for the period 1955–60 any significant discrimination was present. Nevertheless, quantities and not merely prices are relevant to a judgement. In this connection Wiles (1968) has suggested that exploitation took place because bloc countries were forced to supply an excessive quantity for export to the USSR at world prices, thereby incurring losses.

From the early 1960s, however, the USSR has consistently

claimed to be a loser rather than a gainer from intra-bloc trade. Two academic studies provide some support for this claim. The first (McMillan, 1973) relates to total trade rather than to Comecon trade alone; but, since nearly 50 per cent of Soviet trade is with Comecon countries, the conclusion has been interpreted to apply to intra-bloc trade also. The technique of analysis utilizes an input–output table for the USSR to calculate the quantity of basic factors (capital, labour and natural resources) required to produce 1 million roubles' worth of exports. An estimate is then made of how much of the same factors would be required to produce 1 million roubles' worth of the products that the USSR actually imports. It is to be expected that, if a nation is to benefit from trade, it will cost it less in factors of production to produce its exports than to produce its imports. What McMillan actually found, utilizing the Soviet input–output table for 1959, was that a given value of exports would cost the USSR 15 per cent more capital, 16 per cent more labour and 20 per cent more natural resources than would the same value of import replacements. A similar conclusion has been arrived at in a study by Hewett (1977), who has utilized adjusted input–output tables for all Comecon countries for 1960 to indicate gains and losses for 1960 and 1970. In a country-by-country analysis, Soviet losses on this basis were found to be concentrated in its trade with the more developed Comecon countries, particularly Czechoslovakia and the GDR, and to a lesser extent with Poland and Hungary. Only for trade with Romania and Bulgaria were gains from trade indicated for the USSR. This pattern of gains and losses was associated with the importation by the USSR of relatively costly machinery from the more advanced countries and the exportation in return of relatively cheap food, non-agricultural raw materials and fuels. Subject to the data limitations, which are considerable, these calculations have been taken to suggest that, during this period, the USSR may not have gained much from its intra-bloc trade and may indeed have lost.

Whatever conclusion may be drawn from these estimates as to the absolute gains and losses from intra-bloc trade during the period in question, it is widely accepted that during the early 1970s the Soviet Union experienced losses in its terms of trade with Comecon countries by comparison with the position that would have existed if world market prices had been employed. For the years 1970–4 the loss has been put at equivalent to 1 per cent of Soviet gross national product (Kohn, 1976). The changes introduced for 1975 improved the USSR's terms of trade by about 10 per cent, but even this was only about a third of what would have been required to adjust the

USSR's terms of trade fully for world price movements during 1971–4.

More recent calculations suggest that over the decade 1973–82 the Soviet terms of trade with the rest of the CMEA rose by 42 per cent (Hewett, 1984). Nevertheless, had the official price base for intra-CMEA prices been fully implemented, on an annual basis, the Soviet terms of trade would have risen still further by 61 per cent. Thus the other Comecon countries appear to have continued to benefit economically at the expense of the Soviet Union. These benefits took the form not of improved terms of trade but rather of a deterioration in the terms of trade at a rate well below what world market prices or even CMEA rules themselves would suggest. In addition to this, over the decade 1973–82 the other Comecon countries were allowed to run substantial deficits in transferable roubles, which softened the impact of the terms-of-trade changes that did occur. This is reflected in the smaller increase of the gross barter terms of trade in favour of the Soviet Union from 100 in 1973 to 122 in 1982 (Hewett, 1984). A rapid escalation in implicit subsidies by the Soviet Union to the rest of the CMEA has been documented also by Marrese and Vanous (1983) and Lavigne (1983).

The outcomes discussed in this section have been widely interpreted as evidence of a willingness on the part of the Soviet Union to trade off economic benefits for political influence. The Soviet Union has in effect been willing to accept some economic losses in order to support Eastern European regimes. The price system is a way of paying through economic relations for political gains, or, as Marrese and Vanous put it (1983), it represents the exchange of Soviet subsidies for 'unconventional gains from trade'.

ECONOMIC CONVERGENCE AMONG THE COMECON COUNTRIES

A major objective of Comecon is to equalize the levels of development among its members. How far has this occurred? There are immense difficulties involved in making statistical comparisons among the Comecon countries except in terms of physical units, because of the lack of any satisfactory *numeraire*. It appears, however, that in terms of levels of industrial development there has been some tendency to convergence. Over the period 1950–70, for instance, growth rates of industrial production in Bulgaria and Romania, which were originally less developed members of the Council, have been double those reported for two of Comecon's most developed members, GDR and Czechoslovakia (UNCTAD,

Table 12.1   Relative per capita incomes in Comecon countries

Year	Bulgaria	Hungary	GDR	Poland	Romania	USSR	Czechoslovakia
1950	0.6	1.2	1.3	1.1	0.5	1.0	1.6
1970	0.8	0.9	1.3	0.8	0.8	1.0	1.2

Source: Foreign Trade (April 1972), p. 7; cited in Holzman (1976)

1972). Growth rate figures for 1960–80 published in the World Bank Atlas also point broadly to some convergence but the statistics for Comecon countries are thought to be so unreliable that the Atlas no longer publishes them (except for Hungary). Comparisons of per capita incomes are more difficult to make. Official Soviet statistics suggest that a marked degree of convergence occurred among the European Comecon members over the period 1950–70, as Table 12.1 illustrates. More recent calculations for 1979 (CMEA, 1980) suggest that, as measured by the range of incomes, no further convergence had occurred by the end of the 1970s.

There is little reason to doubt that some degree of convergence has occurred since 1950. Official Comecon commentators habitually attribute a large role in this development to the operations of the Council. At present no adequate studies are available on the basis of which it would be possible to arrive at even an approximate notion of the contribution made by the CMEA to the convergence of levels of economic development in Eastern Europe.

CHAPTER 13

Empirical Studies: Quantifying the Extent and Effects of Integration

Economists wish to measure economic integration for three main purposes: (1) in order to compare the degree of economic integration found in one regional group with that in another, or the progress of integration in a particular grouping over time; (2) in order to quantify the aggregate effects of integration on trade and on other variables that influence the welfare of the group; and (3) in order to quantify the effects of integration on the distribution of the benefits of integration among the participating countries. This chapter outlines some of the principal methods that have been employed to quantify integration from these standpoints and briefly reviews some of the results of the reported studies.

INDICATORS OF THE DEGREE OF PROGRESS OF ECONOMIC INTEGRATION

The institutional conditions affecting the mobility of factors and products are obviously important indicators of the state of integration within an area. Most quantitative economic studies of the degree or progress of integration are, however, not concerned with the institutional conditions themselves and changes in them over time, but rather with the effects that they have, through their impact on mobility, on a variety of variables. The effects of integration-induced product and factor mobility may be gauged both from its impact on relative prices and from the movements of goods and factors that take place. For instance, through its effects on mobility the progress of integration should be reflected in a reduction in the dispersion of the prices of goods and factors of production in the area. This indicator is often used for capital, but difficulties arise in its application to factors such as labour that are not homogeneous. In practice the most commonly used quantitative indicator of the extent and progress of integration or economic interdependence is statistics of trade flows. In this connection attention is usually concentrated on the relative shares of trade with partners and non-partners and on changes in those shares over time.

Tables 13.1 and 13.2 utilize such ratios to indicate the degree of economic interdependence of existing groupings for the period 1960–83. Table 13.1 relates to groupings of developed countries, including groupings both of market economies – such as the European Economic Community (EEC) and the European Free Trade Association (EFTA) – and of socialist countries – the Council for Mutual Economic Assistance (CMEA or Comecon). Table 13.2 provides the same information for groupings of developing countries.

Several significant points emerge from these tables. First, in relation to developed country groupings, intra-bloc trade is evidently of major importance, accounting in both the EEC and Comecon for more than half of total trade. Secondly, intra-bloc trade in the EEC has grown much more rapidly than total trade, its share rising from about one-third in 1960 to about one-half in 1972 for the original six-member grouping. Intra-Comecon trade, although slightly more important in relative terms, stagnated or fell over the period 1960–83, the big increase in intra-Eastern bloc trade having occurred immediately after the Second World War when the economies of the Eastern European countries were forcibly aligned with the economy of the Soviet Union. There are however peculiar difficulties in interpreting trade data relating to the Comecon group; these were discussed in Chapter 12.

In economic groupings of developing countries intra-bloc trade is relatively much less important. Only in the cases of the Central American Common Market and ASEAN does the ratio of intra-bloc to total trade exceed 20 per cent. Even in the East African Community, which was until its break-up in 1977 a relatively well-developed grouping, the ratio never exceeded that level. The other notable feature is the evident stagnation of intra-group trade during the decade of the 1970s, despite the fact that the initial ratios were low. This partly reflects a lack of exportable commodities, particularly of manufactures, in many of these countries; but it also reflects the widespread difficulties experienced in integration arrangements among less developed countries that have been discussed in Chapter 11.

Trade ratios are useful in providing broad indicators of the actual

Table 13.1 Intra-trade of economic groupings of developed countries, 1960 and 1970–83 (selected years)[a]

Economic grouping	Intra-trade (US$bn)						World exports						Intra-trade of group as % of total group exports					
	1960	1970	1972	1973	1980	1983	1960	1970	1972	1973	1980	1983	1960	1970	1972	1973	1980	1983
EEC(6)	10.3	43.4	61.4				8.0	13.9	14.9				34.6	48.9	49.5			
EFTA[b]	2.9	9.4	12.9				2.3	3.0	3.1				15.7	21.8	23.2			
EEC (expanded)[c]				110.5	347.0	298.9				19.4	17.3	16.5				52.3	52.8	52.4
Trade in manufactures between expanded EEC and the residual EFTA member countries				34.8	105.9	85.3				6.1	5.3	4.7				14.0	13.7	12.7
Intra-trade in manufactures of residual EFTA member countries				6.0	14.8	11.9				1.1	0.7	0.7				15.9	12.8	11.4
Comecon	8.1	18.4	24.2	29.9	79.0	93.1	6.3	5.9	5.9	5.2	4.0	5.2	62.3	59.4	60.5	56.5	51.0	53.7

[a] based on export (f.o.b.) data
[b] excluding goods shown in annex D of the Stockholm Convention
[c] The Nine.
Source: UNCTAD (1985), p. 36.

Table 13.2 Intra-trade of economic groupings of developing countries, 1960 and 1970–83 (selected years)[a]

Economic grouping[d]	Intra-trade (US$m)					Exports to developing countries as % of total group exports					Intra-trade of group as % of total exports of each group				
	1960	1970	1976	1980	1983	1960	1970	1976	1980	1983	1960	1970	1976	1980	1983
ASEAN[b]	839	860	3619	11918	17080	32.8	31.7	30.3	35.6	37.7	21.7	14.7	13.9	17.8	23.1
UDEAC	3	33	75	200	80	8.3	11.9	15.0	22.5	10.0	1.6	3.4	3.9	4.1	2.0
CACM	33	299	653	1141	840	10.0	29.6	29.2	30.8	30.8	7.5	26.8	21.6	22.0	21.8
CARICOM[c]	27	73	212	354	360	12.2	16.6	17.6	20.0	22.5	4.5	7.3	6.7	6.4	9.3
LAIA	564	1290	4434	1027	1200	19.4	21.2	26.9	28.1	27.5	7.7	10.2	12.8	13.5	10.2
of which:															
Andean Group	25	109	594	955	1037	28.8	29.3	36.2	31.6	37.1	0.7	2.3	4.2	3.5	4.3
CEAO	6	73	177	296	406	14.8	15.1	13.6	15.9	20.7	2.0	9.1	6.7	6.9	11.6
ECOWAS	17	61	478	1056	860	6.7	8.6	20.5	6.2	21.3	1.2	2.1	3.1	3.9	4.1
CEPGL	—	2	3	5	5	0.0	6.5	31.4	49.7	30.0	0.0	0.2	0.1	0.2	0.2
MRU	—	—	2	2	7	0.6	4.4	1.8	8.7	20.0	0.0	0.1	0.2	0.1	0.1

[a] based on export (f.o.b.) data.
[b] figures adjusted to exclude *entrepôt* trade.
[c] excluding Eastern Caribbean Common Market.
[d] The full names of the groupings are as follows (the dates indicate year of establishment):

ASEAN   Association of South-East Asian Nations, 1967
UDEAC   Customs and Economic Union of Central Africa, 1964
CACM   Central American Common Market, 1960
CARICOM   Caribbean Community, 1973 (based on Caribbean Free Trade Association (CARIFTA) 1968)
LAIA   Latin American Integration Association, 1980 (formerly LAFTA, 1960)
CEAO   West African Economic Community, 1974 (initially West African Customs Union, 1959)
ECOWAS   Economic Community of West African States, 1975
CEPGL   Economic Community of the Great Lakes Countries, 1976
MRU   Mano River Union, 1973

Source: UNCTAD (1985) p. 37.

level of economic interdependence among the member countries of a grouping, but as an indicator of the degree or progress of integration they are, for several reasons, of limited value. In the first place, the degree of integration is a relative concept that refers implicitly to the extent to which the potential for profitable integration is actually exploited. Actual trade and capital flows can throw little light on the opportunities that remain to be exploited in a group, nor do recorded intra-bloc trade flows invariably reflect only mutually profitable trade. Furthermore, trade ratios do not reveal the degree to which the trade flows have been affected by integration rather than reflecting an economic interdependence that would exist anyway. To throw light on such questions requires an empirical analysis of integration in terms of the concepts and effects considered in customs union theory – a matter to which we now turn.

MEASURING THE EFFECTS OF INTEGRATION

In Chapter 2 seven different aspects of the impact of a customs union were distinguished. Up to the present time the bulk of the systematic quantitative work that has been undertaken on customs unions and integration has been concerned with the first of the aspects there distinguished, namely with their impact on trade flows and international specialization and, to a lesser extent, with the implications of the trade changes for income and welfare. A limited amount of quantitative work has also been undertaken on the trade and welfare effects of scale economics (though not on an aggregative basis), and on the impact of integration on the terms of trade. The impact of integration on growth has been almost completely neglected. Virtually the only other aspect of integration to have been systematically appraised in aggregative terms is its effects on foreign direct investment.

Attempts to estimate the impact of these various aspects of customs unions or other forms of integration on trade may be characterized in the first place according to the time perspective from which they are undertaken and secondly according to the methodology employed.

The most general distinction that can be made amongst alternative empirical studies rests on the dichotomy between *ex ante* and *ex post* studies. *Ex ante* studies are undertaken prospectively for some proposed group or for the enlargement of an existing group. Data will be available for the recent experience and the actual position of the countries concerned in the pre-integration situation and the problem is to estimate the outcome with integration. *Ex post* studies, on the other hand, are undertaken when the group has been in existence for some time. The experience of the economies under integration as expressed in their recorded economic performance over a period is known and the problem is to estimate the development that would have taken place in its absence.

The second principal criterion for classifying empirical studies of integration rests on the methodology primarily employed for estimating the effects. From this standpoint a three-fold distinction may be made, although the distinctions are not always clear cut since more than one method may be used.

One approach attempts to estimate the effects of integration directly by relying on a specified analytical model, the parameters of which are estimated from available empirical data using standard statistical techniques. The *analytical* approach as it may be termed, can be employed both for *ex ante* and *ex post* evaluation, but severe data limitations have restricted its application.

A second approach, which is more popular but which can be used only for *ex post* studies, attempts to assess the effects of integration indirectly by means of residual imputation procedures. *Residual* models have the characteristics that they seek to quantify, by reference to a variety of explanatory factors, the development that the economies in question could be expected to have experienced in the absence of integration. The impact of integration is then taken to be the unexplained residual that is obtained by subtracting the projections so arrived at for the past period from the actually recorded magnitudes for the same period. On this approach, the relationships through which integration exercises its impact are not directly specified. The plausibility of any estimate that is made on this basis is essentially a matter of judgement, which must be based on the factors that have been taken into account in estimating the unknowable *anti-monde*. The performance of analytical models, on the other hand, can in due course be tested against experience after integration has taken place.

A third approach to quantifying the effects of integration is less formal, and in practice less aggregative. This is the *survey* method. It rests on surveys of the views of entrepreneurs and other experts on the conditions of particular sectors and industries and the extent to which they consider that specified changes brought about by integration that has been experienced, or by integration that is in prospect, have affected, or can be expected to affect, relevant market-determined variables such as sales in domestic and partner markets. Alternatively (in the case of entrepreneurs), their behaviour and strategy can be surveyed in relation to matters that may be under their direct control, such as investment and divestment and plant specialization and the choice between serving markets in the union by export or by the establishment of subsidiary plants. The survey of opinion or behaviour in relation to these matters shades over into the case-study approach, which may generate verifiable statistical data to which 'analytical' or other methods may then be applied.

Running across the three-fold methodological distinction made here there is the further distinction between aggregative or economy-wide studies, sectoral studies and studies of particular industries or even enterprises. In practice, the survey method must rest on a sample. Surveys, backed up by case studies to generate quantitative statistical data, are an essential foundation to empirical appraisals of many key aspects of integration.

THE EFFECTS OF INTEGRATION ON TRADE FLOWS, INCOME AND WELFARE: THE CASE OF THE EC

Most of the empirical work relating to the effects of integration is concerned primarily with the crucial question of its impact on trade flows and in the European context inevitably much of it has focused on the EC. This work has been the subject of valuable surveys by Verdoorn and Schwartz (1972), Sellekaerts (1973), Corden (1975), Balassa (1975b), Mayes (1978) and Winters (1987). The particular question of its correspondence to the concepts of theoretical analysis is considered in Pelkmans and Gremmen (1983).

Ex ante analyses of the effects on trade flows of the initial formation of a customs union in Western Europe have mainly followed the pioneering analytical approach developed by Verdoorn (1952), in the course of which he examined within a general equilibrium framework the effects of such a union on trade flows, the terms of trade and the balance of payments. Verdoorn's study has never been translated, but a simplified version of his model can be found in Johnson (1964) and in Krause (1968). This method was later applied by Krause (1968) at a time when the EC had been in existence for some years, in order to predict the effects of its formation on the United States.

In a full *ex ante* analysis it would be necessary to forecast trade in the post-integration period assuming (1) that the EC would not be established, and (2) that the EC would be established. Most of the *ex ante* analyses largely sidestep the question of the future values of variables that are exogenously determined independently of the integration process. Verdoorn himself, for instance, estimated the changes that a customs union could be expected to bring about relative to the trade matrix of a current year, namely 1951. The analysis is of necessity highly stylized. He assumed a price elasticity of demand for imports from all sources of $-\frac{1}{2}$ and a share elasticity of imports from non member countries of -2.[1] The elasticities were assumed to be the same for all products. These values were based on statistical analysis and corresponded to average experience in Benelux prior to integration. An infinitely elastic supply curve for exports was assumed, implying that the whole of any tariff change was passed on to prices.

Ideally, import demand functions should be estimated separately for individual commodity categories, or at least for major sectors. It is particularly important to distinguish the agricultural sector separately since it is often protected by quantitative restrictions and does not respond freely to market forces. In practice, the limited availability of price data normally precludes any significant disaggregation, and estimates have to be based on a country's total imports. Such results may be biased by the operation of trade restrictions and may mask shifts between commodity categories, which can be revealed only by disaggregation.

The more recent examples of *ex ante* estimation of integration effects have been concerned with the impact of the enlargement of the EC. Notable studies of this kind are those of Williamson (1971) and of Miller and Spencer (1977), both of which were concerned with estimating the impact on Britain of accession to the EC, the former in a partial, the latter in a general, equilibrium framework. The survey method distinguished above, but rarely applied to aggregative studies, formed the basis of an estimate made in 1966–7 by the Confederation of British Industry of the effects on British industry of Britain's prospective accession. Kreinin (1973) attempted a more general study of the effects of enlargement on trade flows, utilizing estimates of price and substitution elasticities. A number of still more recent *ex ante* studies, some of them of a partial equilibrium and informal character, have been undertaken in connection with the second enlargement of the European Community, which began with the accession of Greece in 1980 and was concluded with the accession of Portugal and Spain in 1986 (Donges, 1982; Yannopoulos, 1979, 1986; Sawyer, 1984). A later example of *ex ante* analysis in a different analytical vein is that of Baysan (1984) who attempts to estimate the impact of Turkey's possible accession to the EC (really simulating free trade) on the basis of an input–output model, the use of which for trade policy appraisals has become popular in the current decade.

Most quantitative studies of the trade effects of the EC have been undertaken from an *ex post* standpoint and they have relied mainly on the method of residual imputation, though sometimes embodying significant analytical elements. The earliest *ex post* analyses of trade impacts relied solely on trade flow data and simply calculated changes in the shares of the recorded imports of different commodity groups and aggregate trade for partner countries and the rest of the world in pre- and post-integration years or periods. Assuming that the shares would have remained constant in the absence of integration, changes in the share of intra-bloc trade in total trade such as are shown in Tables 13.1 and 13.2 are then taken to indicate the integration effect.

This procedure has serious shortcomings. First, to assume that, in the absence of integration, market shares would have remained constant attributes the whole of the change in shares to integration. This is unlikely to be so if over the period there have been significant changes in tastes, technology, costs and competitiveness, in commercial policy other than tariffs, or in exchange controls. Secondly, comparison of import shares alone is incapable of measuring trade expansion, trade creation or trade diversion, since the behaviour of domestic output is not indicated. No matter whether an increase in a member's share of imports from partners reflects the replacement of higher-cost domestic production or the displacement of lower-cost imports from non-members, it will in either case raise the share of intra-bloc trade while reducing that of the rest of the world to exactly the same extent. Calculations of this kind are consequently useful only in showing what changes in trade flows did occur and in measuring their extent in general terms.

To overcome the first difficulty it is necessary to construct an appropriate *anti-monde* with which recorded trade flows can be compared for the purpose of arriving at the effect of integration. No wholly satisfactory way exists of making allowance for the changes in shares that would in any case have occurred independently of integration, but a number of approaches have been employed. A crucial distinction to make amongst *ex post* studies concerns the methods used to construct the *anti-monde*. To overcome the second difficulty, namely to measure and separate trade creation and trade diversion, which is vital for analytical purposes, several approaches may be followed. Two early and influential approaches to the treatment of both issues are to be found in the work of Balassa (1967, 1975b) and Truman (1969, 1972, 1975).

Balassa (1967, 1975b) applies the residual imputation method to *anti-mondes* calculated solely from pre-integration time series in the importing countries. His approach rests on what he calls the *ex post* income elasticity of import demand, defined as the ratio of the average annual rate of change of imports to that of gross national product at constant prices. He assumes that these elasticities would remain unchanged in the absence of integration. Observed changes in the post-integration elasticities are then attributed to the effects of integration. By distinguishing between the income elasticities for total trade, intra-area trade and trade with non-members, he seeks to derive estimates for both trade creation and trade diversion. The argument, not wholly transparent, is that

> . . . a rise in the income elasticity of demand for intra-area imports would indicate gross trade creation, while an increase in the income elasticity of demand for imports from all sources of supply would give expression to trade creation proper. In turn, a fall in the income elasticity of demand for extra-area imports would provide evidence of the trade-diverting effects of the union. (Balassa, 1967, pp. 1–21)

By relating imports to gross national product, Balassa's method attempts to take account of one important source of changes in the shares of imports in consumption that could be expected to operate independently of integration. Given greater than unity income elasticities of demand for imports in the pre-integration period, the share of imports in consumption would increase over time even in the absence of integration. A disadvantage of the method, however, is that it does not allow trade creation to be separated from trade diversion in intra-partner trade (or to distinguish certain other important trade effects) because it fails to treat the level of home production explicitly. This shortcoming is not present in Truman's analysis to which we next turn.

Truman's method (1969, 1972, 1975) of dealing with the identification of trade diversion and trade creation is the one that has the most explicit links with customs union theory. It has already been pointed out that an examination of import *shares* alone cannot discriminate between trade creation and trade diversion. Essentially this is because it cannot establish the size and direction of the domestic production effect, on which the estimation of trade creation turns. In order to determine the domestic production effect, Truman has analysed shares of expenditure in apparent consumption. Expenditure on apparent consumption (C) is defined as gross domestic production (V) less exports (B) plus imports from partners (M_P) and imports from non-members (M_W); that is,

$$C = V - B + M_\mathrm{p} + M_\mathrm{w}.$$

Then, if D (= $(V/C - B/C)$ denotes the domestic share, and P (= M_p/C) and W (= M_w/C) respectively denote the corresponding shares represented by imports from the partner countries and the rest of the world,

$\Delta D < 0$ indicates gross trade creation

$\Delta P > 0$ indicates net trade creation

$\Delta W < 0$ indicates trade diversion.

One problem that is often neglected in conventional customs union theory is that the process of tariff alignment involved in the establishment of a common external tariff may result in a net expansion of trade with the non-members as a result of a reduction in the tariffs of member countries with initially high tariffs. This may be termed 'external' trade creation, as contrasted with 'internal' trade creation, which arises within the group. Similarly, tariff alignment may give rise to a contraction of trade if there is an increase in the average level of tariffs faced by non-members. This may be termed 'trade erosion', and like trade creation it may be internal or external. One of the merits of Truman's analysis is that, unlike that of Balassa, it makes it possible to identify these various outcomes.

With respect to the crucial question of the *anti-monde* itself, Truman initially made the assumption that the shares in apparent consumption attributable to the three sources – namely the home country (D), and imports from partners (P) and the rest of the world (W) – would have remained at their pre-integration levels in the absence of integration despite the fact that a rising trend in P and W was previously apparent (partly no doubt due to previous trade liberalization of a kind that could not be repeated). In a later modification of his work (1975) Truman provided revised estimates on an adjusted basis. This allows *anti-monde* shares to evolve through time in response to income trends and cyclical factors and attempts to remove a possible source of bias that could result in an overstatement of trade creation and an understatement of trade diversion.

The two approaches just outlined only consider variables affecting *anti-monde* trade that operate within the importing country alone and they are largely demand determined. The operation of other factors that might *a priori* be expected to be of significance, such as the character of the trade, prices and economic variables in the exporting countries and the rest of the world and information bearing on them, is neglected. For instance, import shares might be expected to expand as a result of the operation of factors known to impart a pro-trade bias to income growth, notably intra-industry trade. Equally, shares may also be significantly affected by a secular loss of competitiveness on the part of European industries.

No wholly satisfactory way exists of making allowance for the operation of these other factors, and data limitations are in any case often severe, but a number of plausible approaches have been employed. One of the most important involves the use of cross-section data in combination with time series information. One such approach involves the use of the changing shares that various bloc suppliers have experienced in third markets where no preferences have been enjoyed, it being assumed that in the absence of integration these changing shares would also have applied to intra-bloc trade. Thus, if the share of West German exports in the imports of countries outside the EC has risen over the relevant period of integration, it would be assumed that, even in the absence of integration, the West German shares with its other EC partners would have gone up similarly. This approach, pioneered by Lamfalussy (1963), has been refined by Williamson and Bottrill (1971) in their study of the effects of the EC on trade flows in manufactures. It has two principal disadvantages. First, it takes no account of information relating to the importing country, and secondly, like the import share approach of which it represents a modification, it is incapable of distinguishing between trade creation and trade diversion. Kreinin (1972) while focusing on import consumption ratios for the determination of his *anti-monde*, uses the experience of third countries (UK, USA and Japan) as a control group or normalizer – a suspect procedure with a group as significant as the EC because of interdependence.

An entirely different approach is that of Aitken (1973). He makes use of a cross-sectional gravity trade model of the kind originally developed by Linneman (1966) to relate exports from one country to another to their levels of income, population and distance from each other. This is used to define what trade would have been between preferred partners in the absence of integration. The study is limited to aggregative trade flows and no commodity breakdown is provided. The procedure only provides a measure of gross trade creation and does not identify trade diversion.

The share approach has also been further developed by Prewo (1974), who also makes use of the gravity approach in his attempt to estimate trade creation and trade diversion within an input–output framework. This offers a possibility of throwing light on the impact on trade creation and trade diversion of trade in intermediate products, which is a neglected aspect of other EC(6) estimates.

Table 13.3 summarizes the estimates of the trade flow effects of the Six, which are the outcome of the *ex post* analyses to which reference has been made in this chapter. The terms 'trade created' and 'trade diverted' are used here to denote the trade value measures that are the primary concern of these estimates – to distinguish them from the welfare measures of trade creation and trade diversion, which are discussed in the next section. The variety of these estimates reflects the difficulty that there is no wholly satisfactory way of estimating the effect of integration on trade flows. All attempts to isolate these effects are affected by the specific assumptions employed, by the choice of period, by the methods used to compute income elasticities or relative shares, and by the allowance, if any, that is made for structural changes not attributable to the EC, such as trade liberalization and changes in competitiveness for which only approximate allowance can be made. These considerations suggest that no single estimate should be given too much weight. Nevertheless, although there must inevitably be a wide range of uncertainty, collectively the studies suggest certain general conclusions and perhaps also enable the relative orders of magnitude to be established with reasonable confidence.

Two important general conclusions can be derived from these trade studies. First, most estimates suggest that for manufactured products (to which most of the studies are limited) the value of trade created was considerable and far outweighed the value of trade diverted. There has certainly been some offset to this from the trade that has without question been diverted in agriculture, which Balassa (1975b) has estimated at $1,300 million (p. 115). Secondly, several of the studies suggest that the formation of the EC has resulted in a good deal of external trade creation. From both points of view it may be concluded that the effects of the EC have been favourable to allocative efficiency at a global level.

The Income and Welfare Effects of the EC

Estimates of integration-induced trade flows provide no direct indication of the income and welfare effects that result from trade creation and trade diversion. However, on their basis, welfare effects may be approximately estimated. The conventional and very crude way of doing this is to multiply the volume of trade created or diverted by half of the tariff. This can be justified in terms of the analysis presented in Chapter 2, assuming that the supply and

Table 13.3 Estimates of trade created and trade diverted in the EC (*ex post*, residual imputation)

Author	Period studied	Trade created				Trade diverted[b]			
		All goods US$ bn	%[a]	Manufactures US$ bn	%[a]	All Goods US$ bn	%[a]	Manufactures US$ bn	%[a]
Prewo	1970	19.8	23	18.0	34	-2.5	6	-3.1	15
Truman	1968								
(unadjusted)		—	—	9.2	26	—	—	-1.0	7
(adjusted)		—	—	2.5	7	—	—	0.5	4
Balassa	1970	11.3	13	11.4	21	0.3	1	0.1	0
Kreinin	1969–70	—	—	8.4	—	—	—	1.1	—
(unweighted average of 3 estimates)									
Williamson and Bottrill	1969	—	—	11.2[c]	25	—	—	0	0
Aitken	1967	9.2	14	—	—	0.6	2	—	—

[a] Percentages relate to total and extra-area imports of all goods and of manufactured products.
[b] Numbers with negative signs represent external trade creation.
[c] Unweighted average of alternative estimates.

Sources: Prewo (1974), Truman (1969), Balassa (1975b), Kreinin (1972), Williamson and Bottrill (1971), Aitkin (1973)

demand functions are linear and that production is carried on under conditions of increasing cost.

Estimates of the welfare effects of integration arrived at on this basis uniformly point to the conclusion that, although there are certainly gains to be derived from trade creation, they appear to be small. For instance, Scitovsky (1958) cites the estimates by Verdoorn, which suggest that *ex ante* the trade creation gains for the members of a Western European customs union would for 1951 have amounted to only some 0.05 per cent of the aggregate annual national income of the members. Verdoorn also reckoned that the gain from the integration effect on the terms of trade might be seven times as large as this (0.35 per cent). Scitovsky (1958) himself has considered Verdoorn's estimates of trade creation gains to be probably too low, in part because the elasticities used were those criticized in the trade literature as being too low; but, as he has pointed out, the gains would still be insignificant even if, by way of correction, those estimates were raised five or even twenty-five fold. A later study by Petith (1977) also gives emphasis to the relative importance of gains from improvements in the terms of trade, suggesting in his case that they may have been from two to six times as large (0.3–1.0 per cent of GNP) as the 'static' gains.

Balassa has also presented estimates of the income gains that would result from his own *ex post* estimates of trade created and trade diverted, reported in Table 13.3. Assuming an average tariff of 12 per cent, the gain from the $11,400 million of trade created in 1970 in manufactured goods would amount to $700 million, which is roughly 0.15 per cent of the combined gross national product of the member countries. Taking the value of trade diverted in agriculture at $1,300 million and applying an average rate of protection of 47 per cent yields an estimated $300–400 million as the static cost of trade diversion in agriculture (Balassa, 1975b). These calculations disregard the welfare effects of any induced changes in exchange rates required to maintain equilibrium.

Both of the foregoing estimates refer to the gains from specialization, but they neglect scale economies. On the face of it, this seems to be a serious deficiency, since, as has been noted in Chapter 3, much of the expansion that has occurred in intra-EC trade appears to have taken the form of increased specialization within particular industries, rather than of a movement of resources from import-competing to exporting industries. Intra-industry specialization and trade yield benefits, partly from a better satisfaction of consumer demand for variety and partly from the exploitation of scale economies.

Many technical difficulties confront attempts to estimate the effects of scale economies in the EC, and there are few aggregative studies of their magnitude. Balassa himself has relied on estimates made by Walters (1963) for the USA, which suggest that, during the first half of the present century, a doubling of inputs in the US non-agricultural sector was accompanied by an increase of approximately 130 per cent in output. This relationship presumably reflects the effects not only of scale economies but also of dynamic factors. If a relationship of this order were nevertheless applied to the trade created in the EC, the resulting gain in gross national product would be slightly over 0.5 per cent, which is equal to about one-tenth of the overall annual rate of growth of income of the member countries for 1970. On this basis, these gains, which are sometimes misleadingly termed 'dynamic', would be substantially larger than the so-called 'static' gains. These calculations, however, are clearly highly tenuous. To say this is not, of course, to deny the role of scale economies. Important evidence for believing them to be significant in the EC and estimates of their magnitude are to be found in a quantitative study by Owen (1983).

Owen's approach starts from the level of the enterprise and the industry and is rooted in detailed surveys of the cost structures, technologies and trade patterns of three important industries in major EC countries, namely white goods (washing machines and refrigerators), trucks and cars. For these three industries he has calculated the scale-related cost reductions that have resulted from intra-Community trade creation. These gains are put at 54 per cent of the observed trade flows for washing machines, 135 per cent for refrigerators, 53 per cent for cars and 4 per cent for trucks. These estimates include the savings that result from the displacement of high-cost marginal producers in the importing countries, and, in the case of refrigerators only, the savings from the substantial favourable indirect effect on the efficiency of the surviving capacity in the importing country that was observed. Disregarding that quasi-dynamic element of gain, the ratios of static resource benefits to trade (which may approximately be identified with the cost reduction effect discussed in Chapter 3) clustered around 50 per cent. That level is accordingly adopted as an indicator of the potential aggregated gains from scale in manufacturing for the EC economies as a whole. Applying that cost reduction ratio to the share of the Community-induced trade in manufactures (taken to be 75 per cent) that originates in scale-related cost differences, as opposed to the demand for variety, leads Owen to suggest that the aggregated scale benefits from intra-Community trade in manufactures could have amounted to some 3–6 per cent of the combined GDP of the Six for 1980.

The attribution of such high scale and cost reduction effects to industries in the EC across-the-board on the basis of only four case studies is necessarily a wholly speculative exercise. But it is hardly open to dispute that an extension of the industry-based case study approach appears to offer a better prospect of providing a solid foundation for a study of the impact of intra-Community specialization on scale economies than any alternative that has so far been put forward.

Estimating the Distributional Impact of Integration

The *ex post* estimates so far discussed relate to the impact of integration on trade and income from the standpoint of the bloc as a whole and do not specifically consider the intra-bloc impact. In practice the distributional impact of integration on the separate members of a group is vitally important; and, not surprisingly, much effort has been devoted to trying to estimate it for various blocs.

In order to estimate this impact it is first necessary to disaggregate the trade flow effects by country. The amount of created and diverted trade that arises in respect of a particular country's imports from the rest of the group must then be estimated. For this purpose (if an *ex post* evaluation is in question) Truman's approach is the most useful. It is then necessary to estimate trade creation and trade diversion in the income or welfare sense, country by country, utilizing the techniques already discussed. In principle such an exercise could also be undertaken from an *ex ante* standpoint by utilizing the various techniques already considered or other more sophisticated methods.

Secondly, it is necessary to take account of the export expansion that a country enjoys with its partners, irrespective of whether from their point of view it represents trade creation or trade diversion since this distinction is irrelevant to the exporting country's gain. The latter arises from the opportunity to export on better terms than would otherwise be possible and will be equivalent to the loss of income that would be suffered if the produce in question had instead to be sold either in the domestic markets of the exporting country or in the markets of the rest of the world.

In estimating the income or welfare effects of integration-induced trade flow changes, the conventional method bases itself on a partial equilibrium methodology such as that set out in Chapter 2 and it involves measuring changes in consumers' and producers' surplus. Thus, for trade creation, a conventional measure (Krauss, 1972) multiplies the amount of trade created by half the relevant tariff rate. This approach implicitly assumes that the supply price of the product from the rest of the world is given (the 'small' customs union case), that the country's pre-union tariff is equal to the common external tariff, and that union supply price is increasing. A similar approach could be employed for measuring the gains from trade expansion. The gains from increased exports would then be equated to the amount of trade expansion multiplied by half the tariff. The cost of trade diversion on the other hand, would be represented by the amount of trade diverted multiplied by the full amount of the relevant tariff. Thus for the simplest possible case involving a single country, the static gains in this strictly orthodox formulation would be measured by the following:

for an importable:

$$t \cdot \frac{TC}{2} - t \cdot TD$$

for an exportable:

$$t \cdot \frac{TE}{2}$$

where TC is trade created on imports, TD is trade diverted on imports, and TE is trade expansion to partners (which may be either trade creation or trade diversion from their points of view), and t is the 'relevant' tariff. This formulation assumes that the union products in question are being produced under conditions of increasing cost. If there are returns to scale, the expression would require modification. Also, for cases such as those discussed in Chapter 2, where tariff harmonization is involved, the relevant tariff for measuring the gain from trade created and trade expansion would not be the common external tariff but the difference between it and the previous national tariff.

The approach just outlined rests partly on the conventional method for measuring changes in consumers' surplus to which there are many valid objections even when trade liberalization affects only a single market, or a few. Where a large number of related markets are affected, as would be in the case for the formation of a customs union, so that costs, demands and prices in different markets would not be independent, then, as noted in Chapter 2, such a procedure cannot be justified although its practicality has retained adherents for it. A more convincing measure is unlikely to be forthcoming other than in a more general formulation. The further development of approaches such as those utilized in the studies reported in the rest of this chapter point the way to promising improvements that are relevant to the estimation of the distributional impact of customs unions and wider forms of integration and to their overall impact.

These qualifications should be particularly borne in mind in considering the merits of the very popular approach that seeks to infer the distribution of gains and losses in a regional grouping from the intra-bloc trade balances. Even in the context of the orthodox approach these are apt to be extremely misleading for several reasons, of which the following are the more important. In the first place, some part of the trade flows will be independent of the customs union or common market. Only the trade that is created or diverted can properly be attributed to the common market. Secondly, there will be a gain on some component of imports (from trade created) and a loss on the remainder (from trade diverted). Thirdly, increased exports to the group will also generate a gain to the exporting country, irrespective of its character. Finally, since rates of tariff vary on different elements of the trade flows, any direct connection between intra-bloc trade balances and gains and losses disappears even on the part of trade that can be regarded as integration-induced. The distributional studies discussed in the following two sections rest on a much more comprehensive basis.

The Impact of Integration: The Case (ex-ante) of British Entry into the EC

Several *ex ante* studies of the impact of integration were produced in connection with Britain's entry into the EC in 1973. These studies have been illuminatingly compared by Miller (1971). Most of these estimates concentrated on the balance of payments effects. Miller has attempted to present these on a uniform basis, bringing out their underlying assumptions and adding estimates of resource (welfare) costs. The effects estimated are the static effects, measured at the end of the transitional period (1980).

The welfare effects of entry can be considered under a number of heads:

(1) The gains from trade creation and the losses from trade diversion, assuming balanced trade. These are the gains and losses in the efficiency of production and consumption resulting from the tariff effects.

(2) The resource cost or welfare effects resulting from the various

balance of payments effects associated with entry. Conceptually, these may be divided into two:

(a) the effects associated with the tariff changes; and
(b) the effects associated with transfers of various kinds, including the cost of the rise in the price of imported food and the unrequited transfer payments of an official nature, such as the transfers of various taxes and levies to the EC budget.

For (a), the resource costs are measured by the size of the change in domestic absorption of resources needed to change the trade balance by the appropriate amount, assuming that output is maintained constant by demand management policy. This is arrived at by dividing the balance of payments deficit associated with the tariff changes by the sum of the import elasticities minus 1. The justification for this procedure is that a deficit involves a relative overpricing of UK goods; its rectification involves a worsening of the terms of trade. It is this that generates the resource cost of the tariff-induced changes.

For (b), the transfer effects, the calculation is different, for the transfer itself involves a direct loss of welfare. To arrive roughly at the resource cost in this case one might take the amount transferred and add to it the extra cost of improving the balance of payments by that amount, using the formula mentioned above for the previous calculation. An adjustment would be necessary, however, to take account of the fact that the raising of taxes in the paying country and their reduction in the recipient countries will have income effects, which should reduce the need for price adjustment through depreciation.

Table 13.4, adapted from Miller (1971), shows in abbreviated form the outcome of the welfare estimates considered. It should be noted that only the Miller–Spencer and Josling–Williamson calculations provide estimates for trade creation. The upper part of the table ((1)–(5)) shows the cost of entry before official transfers. This relates to the costs and benefits of trade creation in manufactures and of trade diversion in food and the loss on the terms of trade. Taking a figure of £500 million as equivalent to 1 per cent of gross national product and disregarding certain index-number problems (Miller, 1971), it can be seen that the resource cost estimates before official transfers range from negligible dimensions in the cases of Josling–Williamson and Miller–Spencer, to as much as 0.6 per cent of GNP for Kaldor and the inelastic estimate of the 1970 White Paper. The greater part of the costs of entry arise from the official

Table 13.4 Alternative estimates of static gains and losses for the United Kingdom in 1980 arising from entry into the EC (£ million at 1969 prices)

Source of gains/losses	Kaldor High	Kaldor Low	Miller and Spencer	Josling and Williamson	1970 White Paper Inelastic	1970 White Paper Elastic	1971 White Paper
(1) Gains from trade creation (manufactures)	—	—	56	75	—	—	—
(2) Loss from rise in price of food (trade diversion)	-267	-267	-206	-131	-485	-294	-238
(3) Terms-of-trade loss from deficit on manufactures	-50	-20	—	-25	-70	-12	—
(4) Terms-of-trade gain from import saving on food	—	—	118	75	240	107	47
(5) Cost of entry before official transfers to Community budget	-317	-287	-32	-6	-315	-199	-191
(6) Transfer cost of entry	-827	-453	-625	-447	-790	-509	-369
(7) Total cost	-1,144	-740	-657	-453	-1,105	-708	-560

Note: Positive signs denote gains and negative signs losses.
Source: Adapted from Miller (1971), p. 70

transfers. Taking these into account as well, the estimates of total costs range from just below 1 per cent to just over 2 per cent of gross national product. An estimate of total resource costs of 1¼ per cent of gross national product seems, on the basis of the assumptions then made, the right order of magnitude.

It should be emphasized that these estimates relate to the static welfare costs and benefits and take no account of any possible dynamic gains from entry, or gains from an increase in technical efficiency or from the exploitation of scale economies.

Ex Post *Studies of the Effects on the UK of Accession to the EC*

Before the UK joined the EC, domestic assessments generally accepted that there would be substantial short-term costs for the country, both as a result of the operation of the CAP and because of the budgetary transfer costs that would be involved – although, as shown in Table 13.4, estimates of the precise magnitudes of these elements varied. Proponents of entry argued, however, that these costs would be more than offset by the so-called dynamic gains arising from the impact of increased competition and the operation of economies of scale. These were expected to bring about an improvement in the net export performance of manufactures. Since Britain entered the EC in 1973, dramatic changes have occurred in its position vis-à-vis its European partners, although not all in the direction that supporters of entry had envisaged.

Several attempts have been made to quantify the changes that have occurred, to examine the extent to which they are actually attributable to membership of the EC, and to provide some indication of the trade, balance of payments and welfare effects involved. The turbulent period through which the international economy has been passing since 1973 makes such assessments particularly difficult. Trade effects are nevertheless basic to any systematic evaluation of the EC impact on the UK.

One notable study of these trade effects, which partly rests on an extensive survey of the opinions of manufacturers, has been carried out by the Select Committee on the European Communities of the House of Lords (House of Lords, 1983). Its conclusions, arrived at after taking into account the results of certain aggregative studies undertaken on its behalf, are essentially qualitative although not the less interesting and important on that account. It is claimed that most of the evidence points to the conclusion that membership had been beneficial, but it was rarely considered to be a major influence on exports or imports. This perception is not, however, supported by the results of the principal aggregative trade assessments that have been made which are summarized together with the results of certain other studies that are also of interest in Table 13.5.

Of the major aggregative studies of British post-accession trade experience (Daly, 1978; Morgan, 1980; Mayes, 1983; Fetherston, Moore and Rhodes, 1979; Winters, 1984, 1987), only those of Fetherston *et al.* (col. 1) and Winters (col. 4) can be directly related to trade creation and trade diversion. The former arrive at the *anti-monde* by adjusting time series of actual import and export shares by reference to changes in aggregate demand, time, and relative unit labour costs (to capture the competitiveness factor), using alternative sets of assumed elasticities to generate a range of results. Winters' analysis, the most sophisticated and exhaustive to date, allows for demand, costs and relative price effects in an innovative way in a technique that is as much analytical as residual. His estimates have a strong theoretical basis, and they are probably the most reliable available.

The message of both studies in relation to the trade effects is in fact similar, although the estimates differ. Accession did stimulate Britain's manufactured exports to her new partners, but her imports of manufactures from the same sources increased even more rapidly, so that the outcome was a massive deficit in trade in manufactures with her partners. A trend towards importation from Europe had in fact already been evident before accession and perhaps reflects 'natural' integration as well as the impact of the rapidly rising productive capacity of the Six, but it seems clear that the trend accelerated markedly after 1973. Accession also reduced the UK's exports to other markets. It did not, however, reduce imports from other sources, which implies that no trade was diverted in the course of the rapid and substantial trade switch towards Europe. According to Winters, as much as 70 per cent of the change in Britain's manufactured imports from her partners is attributable to the EC effect. In combination, the EC-induced changes reduced the gross output of manufactures through reduced domestic sales by at least £3 billion or about 1.5 per cent of GNP, and worsened the trade balance to a similar extent, and the effect could easily have been twice as great.

It must not be assumed that this trade impact was necessarily harmful. Fetherston, Moore and Rhodes do take that view, essentially because of their claim that the associated trade deficit had a depressing effect on the level of economic activity, which they put at a cost of 6 per cent of GDP for 1977. Such a Keynesian interpretation would be inappropriate in the context of a freely floating exchange rate regime. Nevertheless, to the extent that the trade

Table 13.5 *Ex post* estimates of trade effects and gains and losses for the UK arising from membership of the EC (£ million)

Effects	1977 (1)	1978 (2)	Year studied 1980 (3)	1979 (4)	1973-9 (5)	1980 (6)
Trade effects						
Imports of manufactures from the EC	+2,549			+8,000		
Imports of manufactures from the rest of the world	+ 494			0		
Exports of manufactures to the EC	+ 507			+4,450		
Exports of manufactures to the rest of the world	− 396			−1,660		
Gains and losses[a]						
Transfer costs via budget:						
Total, incl. agriculture (EAGGF)	−1,046		−1,203			
EAGGF costs only		−673				
Costs of trade diversion						
Manufactured products (net loss from rise in price of manufactures)			−100 to −200[b]			
Agricultural products (loss from rise in price of food)		−110 to −145	−127[c]			
Welfare cost (−) or benefit (+) as % of GDP	−6[d]				−2 to −3	+0.35

[a] Positive signs denote gains and negative signs losses.
[b] Calculated by applying average tariff rate to intra EC trade deficit in manufactures.
[c] The mean estimate of Rollo and Warwick.
[d] National income forgone, in relative terms, from the depressing effect of the trade deficit on domestic activity.

Sources: (1) Fetherston, Moore and Rhodes (1979); (2) Rollo and Warwick (1979); (3) Godley (1980); (4) Winters (1987); (5) & (6) Grinols (1984). See also *Cambridge Economic Policy Review*, April 1979, for estimates of budgetary and CAP-induced trade transfers.

deficit did result in a lower exchange rate than would otherwise have been experienced, then the implied terms-of-trade effect must be taken into account as a 'resource cost' in any evaluation of costs and benefits.

The two studies referred to primarily generate estimates of trade created and trade diverted in manufactures. If the orthodox approach to the estimation of welfare effects that is set out on pages 249–50 were to be applied to the results of these calculations, then the trade effects of accession in this sector *per se* would presumably have to be judged to be beneficial, since the studies in question suggest that a substantial volume of trade has been created whereas no trade diversion has occurred. At the same time, since the average EC tariff level was only of the order of 7 per cent, the gains could hardly have been considerable. Conventional methods, however, almost certainly underestimate the static welfare gains from trade creation in the EC for a variety of reasons already discussed, including their disregard of variety and the implications of economies of scale.

A more important qualification to such orthodox welfare calculations based on trade effects (a partially offsetting detrimental effect derives from trade diversion in agricultural products) arises from the need in any overall impact study to take account of the *ex post* transfer costs or benefits that are produced by the methods of financing the EC budget. Although there are difficulties in estimating these magnitudes, for reasons that have been noted in Chapter 7, the problems are mainly statistical and the likely margins of error are modest. These transfer costs have indisputably been substantial in Britain's case. They represent an equivalent national income cost, and an approximately equivalent balance of payments cost. Their weight must dominate any welfare calculation for the United Kingdom for most of the post-accession period up to the beginning of the 1980s.

Welfare effects are not in fact the main focus of either of the *ex post* studies for Britain that have been cited up to this point. They are, however, central to another study, namely that of Grinols (1984). This represents an ambitious attempt to measure the total welfare effects of British accession for the period 1973–80, taking into account both trade and price effects as well as the transfer costs that arise from the EC budget. This novel approach is grounded in the theory of revealed preference. This is employed to estimate the additional income that would be needed by Britain after accession to permit it to consume its pre-accession bundle of goods. The estimate so arrived at is then corrected to allow for the favourable production and consumption effects that would follow the price changes, partly offsetting the adverse effect of trade diversion. The whole is then adjusted to take account of transfers through the budget. On this basis, an estimate of a net accession cost to Britain of some 2–3 per cent of GDP over the period 1973–79 is arrived at. It is of note that the net cost falls progressively over that period, and that for 1980 a small positive welfare benefit emerges for the first time. Grinol's study represents an original and interesting approach to the problem, but the confidence that is attached to his results must be weakened by the fact that it is grounded in a very crude method of estimating the price effects of accession, which, for example, effectively attributes the terms-of-trade costs of the commodity boom of 1974 and the depreciation of the pound in 1978 entirely to accession (Winters, 1987).

It is fair to say that no wholly convincing and comprehensive *ex post* studies of the welfare aspects of accession for the UK have yet been published. At the same time there are signs that the factors that in the past have given rise to major negative welfare effects for Britain – and in particular the substantial net budget transfers – are no longer of such significance. For this and other reasons, the 1980s may have at last ushered in a period when the effects of the UK's accession on national welfare will be demonstrated to be unequivocally positive.

CONCLUSION

This chapter has outlined approaches that have been employed to quantify the effects of economic integration on trade, income and welfare and has reviewed the results of some of the estimates of such effects in relation to the EC. The difficulties in the way of arriving at dependable estimates on static assumptions have been discussed at length and need not be repeated here. In conclusion, it should also be stressed that estimates of static effects, however dependable, do not present the whole picture. Integration also gives rise to the operation of dynamic forces, which in principle may either reinforce or offset the changes to be expected from the static analysis. Virtually without exception, all theoretical analyses suggest that any production and trade repercussions of the dynamic effects would be favourable for the group, although it is recognized that intra-regional effects might be damaging for some member states. This distributional consideration primarily raises issues of regional policy in an economic community, discussed in Chapter 10. The quantification of dynamic effects, is, however, a task that has scarcely begun.

Finally, it should be pointed out that welfare is affected by variables other than levels of income and employment and their rates of growth. The stability of income is a material dimension of welfare, and there are others that may be just as important. So far, relatively few empirical studies have been made of how other aspects of welfare may be affected by integration, but they are beginning to accumulate (Balassa, 1975a) and should not be overlooked.

NOTE

1 The price elasticity of demand for imports of product i from all sources is given by $\eta_i = (\Delta Q_m \cdot P_m)/(\Delta P_m \cdot Q_m)$ where P_m = import price and Q_m = quantity of imports for product i.

2 The share elasticity of imports of product i by country j is given by

$$ES_{ij} = \frac{\Delta(M_f/M_j) \cdot P_m}{\Delta P_m \cdot (M_f/M_j)}$$

where M_f = value of imports from non-member countries and
M_j = value of imports from all sources for product i.

BIBLIOGRAPHY

Aitken, N. D. (1973), 'The effects of the EEC and EFTA on European trade: a temporal cross-section analysis', *American Economic Review*, vol. 63, pp. 881–92.

Allen, P. R. (1975), *Organization and Administration of a Monetary Union*, Princeton Studies in International Finance (Princeton, NJ: International Finance Section, Department of Economics, Princeton University).

Allen, P. R. (1982), 'Increased wage or productivity differentials in a monetary union', in M. T. Sumner and G. Zis (eds.) *European Monetary Union: Progress and Prospects* (London: Macmillan), pp. 195–215.

Allen, P. R. (1983), 'Cyclical imbalance in a monetary union', *Journal of Common Market Studies*, vol. XXI, no. 3, pp. 313–27.

Allen, P. R. (1986), *The ECU: Birth of a New Currency* (New York: Group of Thirty).

Allen, P. R. and Kenen, P. (1980), *Asset Markets, Exchange Rates and Economic Integration* (Cambridge: Cambridge UP).

Aquino, T. (1978), 'Intra-industry trade and intra-industry specialisation as concurrent sources of international trade in manufactures', *Weltwirtschaftliches Archiv*, vol. 114, pp. 275–95.

Arndt, S. W. (1968), 'On discriminatory versus non-preferential tariff policies', *Economic Journal*, vol. 78, pp. 971–9.

Arndt, S. W. (1969), 'Customs union and the theory of tariffs', *American Economic Review*, vol. 59, pp. 108–18.

Artis, M. and Miller, M. H. (1986), 'On joining the EMS', *Midland Bank Review*, Winter, pp, 11–20.

Artis, M. and Ostry, S. (1986), *International Economic Policy Coordination*, Chatham House Papers, Fifth Series, no. 30 (London: RIIA).

Bacon, R., Godley, W. and McFarquhar, A. (1978), 'The direct costs to Britain of belonging to the EEC', *Economic Policy Review*, no. 4, pp. 44–49.

Balassa, B. (1962), *The Theory of Economic Integration* (London: Allen & Unwin).

Balassa, B. (1965), 'Trade liberalization and "revealed" comparative advantage', *The Manchester School*, vol. 33, pp. 99–123.

Balassa, B. (1966), 'Tariff reductions and trade in manufactures among industrial countries', *American Economic Review*, vol. 56, pp. 466–73.

Balassa, B. (1967), 'Trade creation and trade diversion in the European Common Market', *Economic Journal*, vol. 77, pp. 1–21.

Balassa, B. (1975a), 'Structural policies in the European Common Market', in B. Balassa (ed.), *European Economic Integration* (Amsterdam: North-Holland; New York: American Elsevier), pp. 225–74.

Balassa, B. (1975b), 'Trade creation and diversion in the European Common Market: an appraisal of the evidence', in B. Balassa (ed.), *European Economic Integration* (Amsterdam: North-Holland; New York: American Elsevier), pp. 79–118.

Balassa, B. (1977), 'Effects of commercial policy on international trade, the location of production, and factor movements', in B. Ohlin *et al.* (eds) (1977), pp. 230–58.

Balassa, B. (1979), 'Intra-industry trade and the integration of the developing countries in the world economy', in H. Giersch (ed.), *On the Economics of Intra-Industry Trade* (Tübingen: J. C. B. Mohr), pp. 245–270.

Baldwin, R. E. (1970), *Non-tariff Distortions of Trade* (Washington, DC: Brookings Institution; London: Allen & Unwin).

Baysan, T. (1984), 'Some economic aspects of Turkey's accession to the EC: resource shifts, comparative advantage and static gains', *Journal of Common Market Studies*, vol. XXIII, pp. 15–34.

de Beers, J. S. (1941), 'Tariff aspects of a federal union', *Quarterly Journal of Economics*, vol. 56, pp. 49–92.

Berglas, E. (1979), 'Preferential trading theory: the *n* commodity case', *Journal of Political Economy*, vol. 87, pp. 315–31.

Berglas, E. (1981), 'Harmonisation of commodity taxes; destination, origin and restricted origin principles', *Journal of Public Economics*, vol. 16, no. 3, pp. 377–87.

Berglas, E. (1983), 'The case for unilateral tariff reductions; foreign tariffs rediscovered', *American Economic Review*, vol. 73, pp. 1141–2.

Blanchard, O. (ed.) (1986), *Restoring Europe's Prosperity* (Cambridge, Mass: MIT Press).

Bogomolov, O. T. (1976), 'Integration by market forces and through planning', in F. Machlup (ed.), *Economic Integration: Worldwide, Regional, Sectoral* (London: Macmillan), pp. 305–17.

van Brabant, J. (1980), *Socialist Economic Integration* (Cambridge: Cambridge UP).

van Brabant, J. (1984), 'The USSR and socialist economic integration', *Soviet Studies*, vol. 36, no. 1, pp. 127–38.

Brada, J. C. and Mendez, Jose A. (1985), 'Economic integration among developed, developing and centrally planned economies: a comparative analysis', *Review of Economics and Statistics*, vol. LXVII, no. 4, pp. 549–56.

Broner, A. (1976), 'The degree of autarky in centrally planned economies', *Kyklos*, vol. 29, no. 3, pp. 478–94.

Brown, A. J. (1985), 'The general Budget', in A. El-Agraa (ed.), *The Economics of the European Community* (Oxford: Philip Allan), pp. 301–13.

Brown, J. F. (1963), *Survey: a journal of East–West studies*, October, pp. 22–4.

Buck, T. W. and Harper, J. (1978), 'Regional income inequality in the

European Economic Community', *Tijdschrift voor Economie en Management*, vol. 23, pp. 337–49.

Buckley, P. J. and Artisien, P. (1987), 'Policy issues of intra-EC direct investment: British, French and German multinationals in Greece, Portugal and Spain, with special reference to employment effects', *Journal of Common Market Studies*, forthcoming.

Buckley, P. J. and Casson, M. (1976), *The Future of the Multinational Enterprise* (London: Macmillan).

Buckley, P. J. and Pearce, R. I. (1977), 'Overseas production and exporting by the world's largest enterprises – a study in sourcing policy', *University of Reading Discussion Paper in International Investment*, no. 39, 1977.

Buckley, P. J. and Pearce, R. (1981), 'Market servicing by multinational manufacturing firms: exporting versus foreign production', *Managerial and Decision Economics*, vol. 2, pp. 229–46.

Buckwell, A. E., Harvey, D. R., Thomson, K. J. and Parton, K. A. (1982), *The Costs of the Common Agricultural Policy* (London: Croom Helm).

Buiter, W. H. and Marston, R. C. (eds.) (1985), *International Economic Policy Co-ordination* (Cambridge: Cambridge UP).

van den Bulcke, D. *et al.* (1979), *Investment and Divestment Policies of Multinational Corporations in Europe* (Farnborough: Saxon House/ECSIM).

Bulletin of the European Communities (monthly) (Luxemburg: European Communities).

Byé, M. (1950), 'Unions douanières et données nationales', *Economie appliquée*, vol. 3, pp. 121–57; reprinted in translation as 'Customs unions and national interests', *International Economic Papers*, no. 3 (1953).

Calmfors, L. (ed.) (1983), *Long Run Effects of Short-Run Stabilisation Policy* (London: Macmillan).

Cantwell, J. (1987), 'The reorganisation of European industries after integration: selected evidence on the role of transnational enterprise activities', *Journal of Common Market Studies*, forthcoming.

Carnoy, M. (1972), *Industrialization in a Latin American Common Market* (Washington, DC: Brookings Institution).

Carter, M. and Maddock, R. (1984), *Rational Expectations: Macroeconomics for the 1980s?* (London: Macmillan).

Casson, M. (ed.) (1985), *Multinationals and World Trade* (London: Allen and Unwin).

Caves, R. (1980), 'Investment and location policies of multinational companies', *Schweizerische Zeitschrift für Volkswirtschaft und Statistik*, vol. 116, pp. 321–338.

Caves, R. (1982), *Multinational Enterprise and Economic Analysis* (Cambridge: Cambridge UP).

Cnossen, S. and Shoup, C. S. (1986), 'Co-ordination of value-added taxes', in S. Cnossen (ed.), *Tax Co-ordination in the EC* (Deventer: Kluwer).

Cobham, D. (1984), 'Convergence, divergence and realignment in British macroeconomics', *Banca Nazionale del Lavoro Quarterly Review*, no. 146, pp. 159–76.

Collier, P. (1979), 'The welfare effects of customs unions: an anatomy', *Economic Journal*, vol. 89, pp. 84–95.

Commission of the European Communities (Annual), *General Report on the Activities of the European Communities* (Brussels: the Commission).

Commission of the European Communities (1972), *First Report on Competition Policy* (Brussels: the Commission).

Commission of the European Communities (1973a), *Report on the Regional Problems in the Enlarged Community* (Thomson Report) (Brussels: the Commission).

Commission of the European Communities (1973b), *Multinational Undertakings Policy Statement* (Brussels: the Commission).

Commission of the European Communities (1975), *Action Programme for Taxation* (Communication from the Commission to the Council).

Commission of the European Communities (1976), *Fifth Report on Competition Policy* (Brussels: the Commission).

Commission of the European Communities (1977a), *Report of the Study Group on the Role of Public Finance in European Integration*, vols 1 and 2 (Brussels: the Commission).

Commission of the European Communities (1977b), *Sixth Report on Competition Policy* (Brussels: the Commission).

Commission of the European Communities (1977c), *Seventh Directive on VAT* (Brussels: the Commission).

Commission of the European Communities (1979), *Twelfth General Report (1978) on the Activities of the European Communities* (Brussels: the Commission).

Commission of the European Communities (1981), *First Periodic Report on the Social and Economic Situation of the Regions of Europe* (Brussels: the Commission).

Commission of the European Communities (1981), *Study of the Regional Impact of the Common Agricultural Policy*, Regional Policy Series no. 21 (Luxemburg: European Communities).

Commission of the European Communities (1982), *European Regional Development Fund: Seventh Annual Report (1981)* (Brussels: the Commission).

Commission of the European Communities (1984a), *Study of the Regional Impact of the Community's External Trade Policy*, Regional Policy, Series No. 22 (Luxemburg: European Communities).

Commission of the European Communities (1984b), *The Regions of Europe (Second Periodic Report on the Social and Economic Situation of the Regions of the Community)* (Luxemburg: the Commission).

Commission of the European Communities (1985), *Completing the Internal Market* (Luxemburg: European Communities).

Commission of the European Communities (1987), *Report by the Commission to the Council and Parliament on the Financing of the Community Budget*, COM (87) 101 (Brussels: the Commission).

Commission of the European Economic Community (1963), *Report of the*

Fiscal and Financial Committee on Tax Harmonization in the Common Market (Neumark Report) (Brussels: the Commission); reprinted in translation as *Tax Harmonisation in the Common Market* (Chicago: Commerce Clearing House).

Commission of the European Economic Community (1966), *The Development of a European Capital Market* (Segré Report) (Brussels: the Commission).

Cooper, C. A. and Massell, B. F. (1965), 'Towards a general theory of customs unions for developing countries', *Journal of Political Economy*, vol. 73, pp. 461–76.

Cooper, R. N. (1976), 'Worldwide versus regional integration: is there an optimum size of the integrated area?', in F. Machlup (ed.), *Economic Integration: Worldwide, Regional, Sectoral* (London: Macmillan), pp. 41–53.

Cooper, R. N. (1985), 'Economic interdependence and co-ordination of economic policies', in R. W. Jones and P. B. Kenen, *Handbook of International Economics*, vol. 2 (Amsterdam: North-Holland), pp. 1195–234.

Corden, W. M. (1970), 'The efficiency effects of trade and protection', in I. A. Mcdougall and R. H. Snape (eds), *Studies in International Economics* (Amsterdam: North-Holland), pp. 1–17.

Corden, W. M. (1971), *The Theory of Protection* (Oxford: Clarendon).

Corden, W. M. (1972a), *Monetary Integration*, Essays in International Finance, no. 93 (Princeton, NJ: International Finance Section, Princeton University).

Corden, W. M. (1972b), 'Economies of scale and customs union theory', *Journal of Political Economy*, vol. 80, pp. 465–75.

Corden, W. M. (1974), *Trade Policy and Economic Welfare* (Oxford: Clarendon).

Corden, W. M. (1975), 'The costs and consequences of protection: a survey of empirical work', in P. B. Kenen (ed.), *International Trade and Finance: Frontiers for Research* (Cambridge: Cambridge UP), pp. 51–91.

Corden, W. M. (1976), 'Customs union theory and the non-uniformity of tariffs', *Journal of International Economics*, vol. 6, pp. 99–106.

Corden, W. M. (1985a), 'International trade theory and the multinational enterprise', in W. M. Corden, *Protection, Growth and Trade* (Oxford: Blackwell), pp. 157–77.

Corden, W. M. (1985b), *Inflation, Exchange Rates and the World Economy*, 3rd edn (Oxford: Clarendon).

Council for Mutual Economic Assistance (1980), *The Evening Out of Levels of National Economic Development and the International Economic Relations* (Moscow: CMEA).

Council for Mutual Economic Assistance, *Basic Documents of the Council for Mutual Economic Assistance* (Moscow: CMEA).

Cross, R. (ed.) (1987), *Unemployment, Hysteresis and the Natural Rate Hypothesis* (Oxford: Basil Blackwell).

Csikós-Nagy, B. (1976), 'Report on group discussion', in F. Machlup (ed.)

Economic Integration: Worldwide, Regional, Sectoral (London: Macmillan), pp. 335–8.

Curzon, V. (1974), *The Essentials of Economic Integration* (London: Macmillan).

Cushman, J. (1983), 'The effects of real exchange rate risk on international trade', *Journal of International Economics*, vol. 18, pp. 45–63.

Daly, A. E. (1978), 'Visible trade and the Common Market', *National Institute Economic Review* (November), pp. 42–54.

Denton, G. (1984), 'Re-structuring the EC Budget: implications of the Fontainebleau Agreement', *Journal of Common Market Studies*, vol. XXIII, pp. 117–40.

Dixon, R. J. and Thirlwall, A. P. (1975), *Regional Growth and Unemployment in the United Kingdom* (London: Macmillan).

Donges, J. B. *et al.* (1982), *The Second Enlargement of the European Community: Adjustment Requirement and Challenges for Policy Reform* (Tübingen: J. C. B. Mohr).

Dosser, D. (1967), 'Economic analysis of tax harmonisation', in C. S. Shoup (ed.) (1967), vol. 1, pp. 1–144.

Dosser, D. (1972), 'Customs unions, tax unions, and development unions', in R. M. Bird and J. G. Head (eds), *Modern Fiscal Issues: Essays in Honor of Carl S. Shoup* (Toronto: Toronto UP), pp. 86–103.

Dosser, D. (1973), 'Tax harmonisation in the European Community', *Three Banks Review*, no. 98, pp. 49–64.

Drabek, Z. and Greenaway, D. (1984), 'Economic integration and intra-industry trade: the CMEA and EEC compared', *Kyklos*, vol. 37, pp. 444–69.

Dunning, J. H. (1977), 'Trade, location of economic activity and the MNE: a search for an eclectic approach', in B. Ohlin *et al.* (eds), (1977), pp. 395–418.

Dunning, J. H. (1981), *International Production and the Multinational Enterprise* (London: Allen & Unwin).

Dunning, J. H. (1983), 'Changes in the level and structure of international production: the last one hundred years', in M. Casson (ed.), *The Growth of International Business* (London: Allen & Unwin).

Dunning, J. H. (ed.) (1985), *Multinational Enterprises, Economic Structure and International Competitiveness* (Chichester: John Wiley).

Economist Intelligence Unit (1957), *Britain and Europe* (London: EIU).

El-Agraa, A. and Jones, A. J. (1980), *The Theory of Customs Unions* (Oxford: Philip Allan).

European Coal and Steel Community (1953), *Report on the Problems Raised by the Different Turnover Tax Systems Applied within the Common Market* (Tinbergen Report) (Luxemburg: High Authority, ECSC).

European Free Trade Association (1969), *The Effects of EFTA on the Member Countries* (Geneva: EFTA).

Fallenbuchl, Z. (1974), 'East European integration: Comecon', in Joint

Economic Committee, Congress of the US, *Reorientation and Commercial Relations of the Economies of Eastern Europe* (Washington, DC: Government Printing Office).

Fetherston, M., Moore, B. and Rhodes, J. (1979), 'EEC membership and UK trade in manufactures', *Cambridge Journal of Economics*, vol. 3, pp. 399–407.

Fleet, K. (1982), 'Investment into the United Kingdom by third countries', mimeo (London: European League for Economic Co-operation).

Fleming, M. (1962), 'Domestic financial policies under fixed and under floating exchange rates', *International Monetary Fund Staff Papers*, vol. 9, pp. 369–79.

Fleming, M. (1971), 'On exchange rate unification', *Economic Journal*, vol. 81, pp. 467–88.

Forte, F. (1977), 'Principles for the assignment of public economic functions in a setting of multilayer government', in Commission of the European Communities (1977a), vol. 2, pp. 321–58.

Franko, L. G. (1976), *The European Multinationals: A Renewed Challenge to American and British Big Business* (London: Harper & Row).

Friedman, M. (1953), 'The case for flexible exchange rates', in M. Friedman, *Essays in Positive Economics* (Chicago: University of Chicago Press) pp. 157–203; reprinted in R. E. Caves and H. G. Johnson (1968), *Readings in International Economics* (Homewood, Ill: Irwin).

Friedman, M. (1968), 'The role of monetary policy', *American Economic Review*, vol. 58, pp. 1–17.

Friedman, M. (1975), *Unemployment versus Inflation?: An Evaluation of the Phillips Curve* (London: Institute of Economic Affairs).

Georgakopoulos, T. (1974), 'Trade creation and trade diversion in tax unions and customs unions', *Public Finance Quarterly*, vol. 2, pp. 411–31.

Godley, Wynne (1980), 'The United Kingdom and the Community Budget', in W. Wallace (ed.) (1980), pp. 72–90.

Gotur, P. (1985), 'Effects of exchange rate volatility on trade: some further evidence', *IMF Staff Papers*, vol. 32, no. 3, pp. 475–512.

de Grauwe, P. (1975), 'Conditions for monetary integration: a geometric interpretation', *Weltwirtschaftliches Archiv*, vol. 111, pp. 634–44.

Greenaway, D. and Milner, C. (1986), *The Economics of Intra-Industry Trade* (Oxford: Basil Blackwell).

Gregory, T. E. (1921), *Tariffs: A Study in Method* (London: Griffin).

Grinols, E. L. (1984), 'A thorn in the lion's paw. Has Britain paid too much for Common Market membership?', *Journal of International Economics*, vol. 16, pp. 271–93.

Grubel, H. (1967), 'Intra-industry specialization and the pattern of trade', *Canadian Journal of Economics and Political Science*, vol. 22, pp. 374–88.

Grubel, H. (1982), 'The theory of international capital movements', in J. Black and J. H. Dunning (eds) *International Capital Movements* (London: Macmillan) pp. 1–21.

Haberler, G. von (1936), *The Theory of International Trade*, trans. A. W. Stonier and F. Benham (London: Hodge).

Haberler, G. (1964), 'Integration and growth in the world economy in historical perspective', *American Economic Review*, vol. 54, pp. 1–22.

Hamada, K. (1985), 'The political economy of monetary integration: a public economics approach', in *The Political Economy of International Monetary Interdependence* (Cambridge, Mass: MIT Press), pp. 27–44.

Hamilton, B. and Whalley, J. (1985), 'Geographically discriminatory trade arrangements', *Review of Economics and Statistics*, vol. 67, pp. 446–55.

Han, S. S. and Liesner, H. H. (1971), *Britain and the Common Market: The Effect of Entry on the Pattern of Manufacturing Production*, University of Cambridge Department of Applied Economics, Occasional Paper 27 (Cambridge: Cambridge UP).

Heiss, H. W. (1970), 'The Council of Mutual Economic Assistance: developments since the mid-1960s', in *Economic Development in Countries of Eastern Europe*, Joint Economic Committee Print (Washington, DC: Government Printing Office).

Helliwell, J. F. and Padmore, T. (1985), 'Empirical studies of macro-economic interdependence', in R. W. Jones and P. B. Kenen (eds), *Handbook of International Economics*, vol. 2 (Amsterdam: North-Holland), pp. 1107–51.

Helpman, E. (1984), 'A simple theory of international trade with multinational corporations', *Journal of Political Economy*, vol. 79, pp. 1059–72.

Her Majesty's Government (1970), *Britain and the European Communities: An Economic Assessment*, Cmnd 4289 (London: HMSO).

Her Majesty's Government (1971), *The United Kingdom and the European Communities*, Cmnd 4715 (London: HMSO).

Her Majesty's Government (1978a), *The European Monetary System*, Cmnd 7405 (London: HMSO).

Her Majesty's Government (1978b), *The European Monetary System: Resolution of the European Council*, Cmnd 7419 (London: HMSO).

Hewett, E. A. (1974), *Foreign Trade Prices in the Council for Mutual Economic Assistance* (London and New York: Cambridge UP).

Hewett, E. A. (1977), 'Prices and resource allocation in intra-CMEA trade', in A. Abouchar (ed.), *The Socialist Price Mechanism* (Durham, NC: Duke UP), pp. 95–128.

Hewett, E. A. (1984), 'Soviet economic relations with the CMEA countries', in P. Joseph (ed.), *The Soviet Economy after Brezhnev* (Brussels: NATO), pp. 241–53.

Hirschman, A. O. (1958), *The Strategy of Economic Development* (New Haven, Conn: Yale UP).

Hodges, M. and Wallace, W. (eds) (1981), *Economic Divergence in the European Community* (London: Allen & Unwin).

Holland, S. (1980), *Uncommon Market* (London: Macmillan).

Holzman, F. D. (1974), *Foreign Trade under Central Planning* (Cambridge, Mass: Harvard UP).

Holzman, F. D. (1976), *International Trade under Communism: Politics and Economics* (London: Macmillan).
Holzman, F. D. (1985), 'Comecon: a trade-destroying customs union?' *Journal of Comparative Economics*, vol. 9, pp. 410–23.
Hood, N. and Young, S. (1980), *European Development Strategies of U.S. Owned Manufacturing Companies Located in Scotland* (Edinburgh: HMSO).
Hood, N. and Young, S. (1983), *Multinational Enterprises in the British Isles* (London: HMSO).
Horst, T. (1973), 'The simple analytics of multi-national firm behaviour', in M. B. Connolly and A. K. Swoboda (eds), *International Trade and Money* (London: Allen & Unwin), pp. 72–84.
House of Commons (1984), Select Committee on Trade and Industry, *The Growth in the Imbalance of Trade in Manufactured Goods between the UK and Existing and Prospective Members of the EEC*, H. C. 461/329 (London: HMSO).
House of Commons (1985a), Treasury and Civil Service Committee Session 1984–85, *Memoranda on the European Monetary System* (London: HMSO).
House of Commons (1985b), Treasury and Civil Service Committee Session 1984–85, *The European Monetary System, vol. 1* (London: HMSO).
House of Lords (1983), Select Committee on the European Communities Session 1983/84), *The United Kingdom's Changing Trade Patterns subsequent to Membership of the European Community* (London: HMSO).
House of Lords (1985), Select Committee on Overseas Trade, *The Causes and Implications of the Deficit in the UK's Balance of Trade in Manufactures*, H. L. 238 (London: HMSO).
Hufbauer, G. C. and Adler, F. (1968), *U.S. Manufacturing Investment and the Balance of Payments* (Washington, DC: US Treasury Dept).

Ingram, J. C. (1973), *The Case for European Monetary Integration*, Essays in International Finance, no. 98 (Princeton, NJ: International Finance Section, Princeton University).
Institute for Latin American Integration (1984), *The Latin American Integration Process in 1984* (Buenos Aires: Inter-American Development Bank).
International Monetary Fund (1984), *Exchange Rate Volatility and World Trade*, Occasional Paper no. 28 (Washington, DC: IMF).
International Monetary Fund (1986), *The European Monetary System: Recent Developments*, Occasional Paper no. 48 (Washington, DC: IMF).
Ishiyama, Y. (1975), 'The theory of optimum currency areas: a survey', *International Monetary Fund Staff Papers*, vol. 22, pp. 344–83.

Jacquemin, A. (ed.) (1984), *European Industry: Public Policy and Corporate Strategy* (Oxford: Oxford UP).
Jenkins, R. (1978), 'European monetary union', *Lloyds Bank Review*, no. 127, pp. 1–14.

Johnson, H. G. (1960), 'The cost of protection and the scientific tariff', *Journal of Political Economy*, vol. 68, pp. 327–45.

Johnson, H. G. (1961), 'Towards a general theory of the balance of payments', in *International Trade and Economic Growth: Studies in Pure Theory* (Cambridge, Mass.: Harvard UP), pp. 153–68.

Johnson, H. G. (1962), 'The economic theory of customs unions', *Pakistan Economic Journal*, vol. 10, pp. 14–32; reprinted in H. G. Johnson, *Money, Trade and Economic Growth* (London: Allen & Unwin).

Johnson, H. G. (1964), 'The international competitive position of the United States and the balance of payments for 1968: a review article', *Review of Economics and Statistics*, vol. 46, pp. 14–32.

Johnson, H. G. (1965), 'An economic theory of protectionism, tariff bargaining and the formation of customs unions', *Journal of Political Economy*, vol. 73, pp. 256–83.

Johnson, H. G. and Krauss, M. (1970), 'Border taxes, border tax adjustments, comparative advantage, and the balance of payments', *Canadian Journal of Economics*, vol. 3, pp. 595–602.

Josling, T. E. (1971), 'The effects of adopting the Common Agricultural Policy', in S. Holland (ed.), *The Price of Europe: a Reassessment* (London: Federal Trust), pp. 5–6.

Kaldor, N. (1970), 'The case for regional policies', *Scottish Journal of Political Economy*, vol. 17, pp. 337–48.

Kaldor, N. (1971), 'The dynamic effects of the Common Market', in D. Evans (ed.), *Destiny or Delusion: Britain and the Common Market* (London: Gollancz), pp. 59–91.

Kaser, M. (1967), *Comecon: Integration Problems of the Planned Economies*, 2nd edn (London: Oxford UP).

Kemp, M. C. (1969), *A Contribution to the General Equilibrium Theory of Preferential Trading* (Amsterdam: North-Holland).

Kenen, P. (1969), 'The theory of optimum currency areas: an eclectic view', in R. A. Mundell and A. K. Swoboda (eds), *Monetary Problems of the International Economy* (Chicago, Ill: Chicago UP), pp. 41–60.

Kenen, P. (1976), *Capital Mobility and Financial Integration: A Survey*, Princeton Studies in International Finance (Princeton, NJ: International Finance Section, Department of Economics, Princeton University).

Knickerbocker, F. T. (1973), 'Multinational enterprise and oligopolistic reaction', mimeo. (Boston, Mass: Harvard Business School).

Kohn, M. J. (1976), 'Developments in Soviet–Eastern European terms of trade, 1971–75', in Joint Economic Committee, Congress of the US, *Soviet Economy in a New Perspective* (Washington, DC: Government Printing Office).

Kojima, K. (1971), *Japan and a Pacific Free Trade Area* (London: Macmillan).

Krause, L. B. (1968), *European Economic Integration and the United States* (Washington, DC: Brookings Institution).

Krauss, M. B. (1972), 'Recent developments in customs union theory: an interpretative survey', *Journal of Economic Literature*, vol. 10, pp. 413–36.

Kreinin, M. E. (1969), 'Trade creation and diversion by the EEC and EFTA', *Economia Internazionale*, vol. 22, pp. 273–80.

Kreinin, M. E. (1972), 'Effects of the EEC on imports of manufactures', *Economic Journal*, vol. 82, pp. 897–920.

Kreinin, M. E. (1973), 'The static effects of EEC enlargement on trade flows', *Southern Economic Journal*, vol. 39, pp. 559–68.

Krueger, A. (1983), *Exchange Rate Determination* (Cambridge: Cambridge UP).

Krugman, P. R. (1983), 'The "new" theories of international trade and the multinational enterprise', in C. P. Kindleberger and D. B. Andretsch (eds), *The Multinational Corporation in the 1980s* (Cambridge, Mass: MIT Press), pp. 57–73.

Laidler, D. (1986), 'The new classical contribution to economics', *Banca Nazionale del Lavoro Quarterly Review*, no. 156, pp. 27–55.

Lamfalussy, A. (1963), 'Intra-European trade and the competitive position of the EEC', *Transactions of the Manchester Statistical Society*, session 1962–63, pp. 1–19.

Lavigne, M. (1983), 'The Soviet Union inside COMECON', *Soviet Studies*, vol. 35, no. 2, pp. 135–53.

Leibenstein, H. (1966), 'Allocative efficiency versus "X-efficiency"', *American Economic Review*, vol. 56, pp. 392–415.

Lemaitre, P. and Goybet, C. (1984), 'Multinational companies in the EEC', I. R. M. Multinational Report, no. 1, parts A and B (Chichester: John Wiley).

Linneman, H. (1966), *An Econometric Study of International Trade Flows* (Amsterdam: North-Holland).

Lipsey, R. G. (1960), 'The theory of customs unions: a general survey', *Economic Journal*, vol. 70, pp. 496–513.

Lipsey, R. G. (1970), *The Theory of Customs Unions: A General Equilibrium Analysis* (London: Weidenfeld & Nicolson).

Lipsey, R. G. and Smith, M. G. (1985), *Taking the Initiative: Canada's Trade Options in a Turbulent World* (Toronto: C. D. Howe Institute).

List, F. (1885), *The National System of Political Economy* (London: Longman Green).

Llewellyn, D. T. (1980), *International Financial Integration: The Limits of Sovereignty* (London: Macmillan).

Lloyd, P. J. (1982), 'A 3x3 theory of customs unions', *Journal of International Economics*, vol. 12, pp. 41–63.

Lodge, J. (1986), 'The Single European Act: towards a new Euro-dynamism?', *Journal of Common Market Studies*, vol. XXIV, pp. 203–23.

Lunn, J. (1980), 'Determinants of US direct investment in the EEC: further evidence', *European Economic Review*, vol. 13, pp. 93–101.

McCulloch, J. R. (1832), *A Dictionary of Commerce* (London: Longman, Rees, Orme, Brown, Green and Longman).

MacDougall, G. D. A. (1960), 'The benefits and costs of private investment from abroad: a theoretical approach', *Economic Record*, vol. 36, pp. 13–35.

MacDougall, G. D. A. (1975), 'Discussion Paper', in *Report of the Study Group on Economic and Monetary Union in 1980*, Annex II (Brussels: the Commission), pp. 97–103.

MacDougall Report (1977), see Commission of the European Communities (1977a).

Machlup, F. (1977), *A History of Thought on Economic Integration* (London: Macmillan).

McKinnon, R. I. (1963), 'Optimum currency areas', *American Economic Review*, vol. 53, pp. 717–24.

McKinnon, R. I. (1981), 'The exchange rate and macroeconomic policy. Changing post-war perceptions', *Journal of Economic Literature*, vol. 19, pp. 531–57.

McManus, J. G. (1972), 'The theory of the international firm', in G. Paquet (ed.), *The Multinational Firm and the Nation State* (Ontario: Collier Macmillan), pp. 66–93.

McMillan, C. H. (1973), 'Factor proportions and the structure of Soviet foreign trade', *Association for Comparative Economic Studies Bulletin*, vol. 15, pp. 57–81.

McMillan, J. and McCann, E. (1981), 'Welfare effects in customs unions', *Economic Journal*, vol. 91, pp. 697–703.

Magnifico, G. and Williamson, J. (1972), *European Monetary Integration* (London: Federal Trust).

Makower, H. and Morton, G. (1953), 'A contribution towards a theory of customs unions', *Economic Journal*, vol. 63, pp. 33–49.

Marer, P. (1985), *Dollar GNPs of the USSR and Eastern Europe* (Washington, DC: The World Bank).

Marques Mendes, A. J. (1986), 'The contribution of the European Community to economic growth', *Journal of Common Market Studies*, vol. XXIV, pp. 261–77.

Marrese, M. and Vanous, J. (1983), *Soviet Subsidization of Trade with Eastern Europe: A Soviet Perspective* (Berkeley, Calif: Institute of International Studies).

Mayes, D. (1978), 'The effects of economic integration on trade', *Journal of Common Market Studies*, vol. XVII, pp. 1–25.

Mayes, D. (1983), Memorandum, in House of Lords (1983), pp. 66–86.

Meade, J. E. (1953), *Problems of Economic Union* (London: Allen & Unwin).

Meade, J. E. (1955a), *The Theory of Customs Unions* (Amsterdam: North-Holland).

Meade, J. E. (1955b), *Trade and Welfare* (London: Oxford UP).

Meade, J. E. (1957), 'The balance of payments problems of a European free trade area', *Economic Journal*, vol. 67, pp. 379–96.

Meade, J. E. (1974), 'A note on border-tax adjustments', *Journal of Political Economy*, vol. 82, pp. 1013–15.

Mendershausen, H. (1959), 'Terms of trade between the Soviet Union and smaller Communist countries, 1955–57', *Review of Economics and Statistics*, vol. 41, pp. 106–18.

Mendershausen, H. (1960), 'The terms of Soviet–Satellite trade: a broadened analysis', *Review of Economics and Statistics*, vol. 42, pp. 152–63.

Mennes, L. B. M. (1973), *Planning Economic Integration among Developing Countries* (Rotterdam: Rotterdam UP).

Mennes, L. B. M. and Stoutjesdijk, A. (1985), *Multicountry Investment Analysis* (Baltimore, Md: Johns Hopkins UP).

Michaely, M. (1976), 'The assumptions of Jacob Viner's theory of customs unions', *Journal of International Economics*, vol. 6, pp. 75–93.

Miller, M. H. (1971), 'Estimates of the static balance of payments and welfare costs of United Kingdom entry into the Common Market', *National Institute Economic Review*, no. 57, pp. 69–83.

Miller, M. H. and Spencer, J. E. (1977), 'The static economic effects of the UK joining the EEC: a general equilibrium approach', *Review of Economic Studies*, vol. 44, pp. 71–93.

Montias, J. M. (1967), *Economic Development in Communist Rumania* (Cambridge, Mass: MIT Press).

Morgan, A. D. (1980), 'The balance of payments and British membership of the European Community', in W. Wallace (ed.) (1980), pp. 57–71.

Mundell, R. A. (1961), 'A theory of optimum currency areas', *American Economic Review*, vol. 53, pp. 657–64.

Mundell, R. A. (1962), 'The appropriate use of monetary and fiscal policy for internal and external stability', *International Monetary Fund Staff Papers*, vol. 9, pp. 70–7.

Mundell, R. A. (1964), 'Tariff preferences and the terms of trade', *The Manchester School of Economic and Social Studies*, vol. 32, pp. 1–13.

Mundell, R. A. (1973), 'Uncommon arguments for common currencies', in H. G. Johnson and A. K. Swoboda (eds), *The Economics of Common Currencies* (London: Allen & Unwin), pp. 114–32.

Musgrave, P. (1967), 'Harmonization of direct business taxes: a case study', in C. S. Shoup (ed.) (1967), vol. 2, pp. 207–343.

Musgrave, R. A. (1969), *Fiscal Systems* (New Haven, Conn. and London: Yale UP).

Mycielski, J. (1967), 'A model of regional harmonization of national development plans', *Economic Bulletin for Asia and the Far East*, vol. 18, pp. 44–71.

Mycielski, J. and Piasczynski, W. (1965), 'A mathematical model of international economic co-operation', in *Proceedings of the First Scandinavian–Polish Regional Science Seminar*.

Myrdal, G. (1957), *Economic Theory and Underdeveloped Regions* (London: Duckworth; reprinted London: Methuen, 1963).

Negishi, T. (1969), 'The customs union and the theory of second best', *International Economic Review*, vol. 10, pp. 391–7.

Neumark Report (1963), see Commission of the European Economic Community (1963).

Norman, G. and Dunning, J. H. (1984), 'Intra-industry foreign direct investment: its rationale and trade effects', *Weltwirtschaftliches Archiv*, vol. 120, pp. 522–40.

North Atlantic Treaty Organisation (1977), *COMECON: Progress and Prospects* (Brussels: NATO).

North Atlantic Treaty Organisation (1983), *External Economic Relations of CMEA Countries: Their Significance and Impact in a Global Perspective* (Brussels: NATO).

North Atlantic Treaty Organisation (1987), *The Economies of Eastern Europe and their Foreign Economic Relations* (Brussels: NATO).

Oates, W. (1972), *Fiscal Federalism* (New York: Harcourt Brace Jovanovich).

Oates, W. (1977), 'Fiscal federalism in theory and practice: applications to the European Community', in Commission of the European Communities, (1977a), vol. 2, pp. 279–320.

O'Brien, D. (1976), 'Customs unions: trade creation and trade diversion in historical perspective', *History of Political Economy*, vol. 8, pp. 540–63.

Ohlin, B., Hesselborn, P. and Wijkman, P. M. (eds) (1977), *The International Allocation of Economic Activity* (London: Macmillan).

Ørstrøm-Møller, J. (1982), *Member States and the Community Budget* (Copenhagen: Samfundsvidenskabeligtforlag).

Ørstrøm-Møller, J. (1985) 'Budgetary imbalances', *Journal of European Integration*, vol. VIII, nos 2–3, pp. 119–38.

Oudiz, G. (1985), 'European policy coordination: an evaluation', *Centre for Economic Policy Research, Discussion Paper 79* (London: CEPR).

Oudiz, G. and Sachs, J. (1984), 'Macroeconomic policy coordination among the industrial economies', in *Brookings Papers on Economic Activity* vol. 1, pp. 1–75.

Owen, N. (1983), *Economies of Scale, Competitiveness, and Trade Patterns within the European Community* (Oxford: Clarendon Press).

Padoa-Schioppa, T. (1985), 'Policy co-ordination and the EMS: experience in economic policy co-operation', in Buiter and Marston (1985), pp. 331–59.

Padoa-Schioppa, T. (1987), *Efficiency, Stability and Equity: A Strategy for the Evolution of the Economic System of the European Community* (Brussels: The Commission).

Parkin, M. (1976), 'Monetary union and stabilisation policy in the European Community', *Banca Nazionale del Lavoro Quarterly Review*, no. 118, pp. 222–40.

Pelkmans, J. and Gremmen, H. (1983), 'The empirical measurement of static customs union effects', *Rivista Internazionale di Scienze Economiche e Commerciali*, vol. XXX, no. 7.

Pelkmans, J. (1984), *Market Integration in the European Community* (The Hague: Martinus Nijhoff).

Pelkmans, J. and Robson, P. (1987), 'The aspirations of the White Paper', *Journal of Common Market Studies*, vol. XXV, pp. 181–92.

Pelzman, J. (1977), 'Trade creation and trade diversion in the Council of

274   *The Economics of International Integration*

Mutual Economic Assistance, 1954–70', *American Economic Review*, vol. 67, pp. 713–22.

Petith, H. (1977), 'European integration and the terms of trade', *Economic Journal*, vol. 87, pp. 262–72.

Phillips, A. W. (1958), 'The relation between unemployment and the rate of change of money wages in the United Kingdom 1862–1957', *Economica*, vol. 25, pp. 283–99.

Prewo, W. E. (1974), 'Integration effects in the EEC: an attempt at quantification in a general equilibrium framework', *European Economic Review*, vol. 5, pp. 379–405.

Ricardo, D. (1817), *The Principles of Political Economy and Taxation*; ed. P. Sraffa (Cambridge: Cambridge UP, 1951).

Riezman, R. (1979), 'A 3x3 model of customs unions', *Journal of International Economics*, vol. 9, pp. 341–54.

Robertson, D. (1971), 'The multinational enterprise: trade flows and trade policy', in J. H. Dunning (ed.), *The Multinational Enterprise* (London: Allen & Unwin), pp. 169–203.

Robinson, J. (1983), *Multinationals and Political Control* (Aldershot: Gower Press).

Robson, P. (1968), *Economic Integration in Africa* (London: Allen & Unwin; Evanston, Ill: Northwestern UP).

Robson, P. (1970), 'The distribution of gains in customs unions between developing countries', *Kyklos*, vol. 23, pp. 117–19.

Robson, P. (1971), *Fiscal Compensation and the Distribution of Benefits in Economic Groupings of Developing Countries* (New York: United Nations).

Robson, P. (ed.) (1972), *International Economic Integration* (Harmondsworth, Middx: Penguin).

Robson, P. (1975), 'Examen de las últimas propuestas relativas a la compensación fiscal en el Mercado Común Centroamericano', in E. Lizano (ed.), *La Integración Económica Centroamericana* (Mexico: Fonda de Cultura Económica), pp. 164–81.

Robson, P. (1983), *Integration, Development and Equity: Economic Integration in West Africa* (London: Allen & Unwin).

Rollo, J. M. C. and Warwick, K. S. (1979), 'The CAP and resource flows among EEC member states', *Government Economic Service Working Paper No. 27* (London: Ministry of Agriculture, Fisheries and Food).

Rossi, V. *et al.* (1986), 'Exchange rates, productivity, and international competitiveness', *Oxford Review of Economic Policy*, vol. 2, no. 3, pp. 56–73.

Sato, M. and Bird, R. M. (1975), 'International aspects of the taxation of corporations and shareholders', *International Monetary Fund Staff Papers*, vol. 22, pp. 384–455.

Sawyer, W. C. (1984), 'The effects of the second enlargement of the EC on US exports to Europe', *Weltwirtschaftliches Archiv*, vol. 120, pp. 572–79.

Scaperlanda, A. and Balough, R. (1983), 'Determinants of US direct investment in the EEC – revisited', *European Economic Review*, vol. 21, pp. 381–90.

Scherer, F. M. *et al.* (1975), *The Economics of Multi-plant Operations: An International Comparisons Study* (Cambridge, Mass: Harvard University Press).

Scitovsky, T. (1958), *Economic Theory and Western European Integration* (London: Allen & Unwin; reprinted 1962).

Scully, G. W. and Yu, E. S. H. (1974), 'International investment, trade diversion and trade creation', *Economic Record*, vol. 50, pp. 600–4.

Segré Report (1966), see Commission of the European Economic Community (1966).

Sellekaerts, W. (1973), 'How meaningful are empirical studies on trade creation and trade diversion?', *Weltwirtschaftliches Archiv*, vol. 109, pp. 519–51.

Sheffrin, S. M. (1983), *Rational Expectations* (Cambridge: Cambridge UP).

Shibata, H. (1967), 'The theory of economic unions: a comparative analysis of customs unions, free trade areas, and tax unions', in C. S. Shoup (ed.) (1967), vol. 1, pp. 145–264.

Shoup, C. S. (1953), 'Taxation aspects of economic integration', *Travaux de l'Institut International de Finances Publiques*, neuvième session (The Hague: W. P. van Stockum & Zoon); reprinted in abridgement in P. Robson (ed.), *International Economic Integration* (Harmondsworth: Penguin), pp. 197–218.

Shoup, C. S. (ed.) (1967), *Fiscal Harmonization in Common Markets*, vol. 1: *Theory*; vol. 2: *Practice* (New York and London: Columbia UP).

Smith, A. (1776), *An Inquiry into the Nature and Causes of the Wealth of Nations*; ed. R. H. Campbell, A. S. Skinner and W. B. Todd (Oxford: Clarendon Press, 1976, 2 vols).

Sobell, V. (1984), *The Red Market: Industrial Co-operation and Specialisation in COMECON* (Aldershot: Gower).

Spaventa, L., Koopmans, L., Salmon, P., Spahn, B. and Smith, S. (1986), *The Future of Community Finance*, CEPS Papers no. 30 (Brussels: Centre for European Policy Studies).

Spraos, J. (1964), 'The condition for a trade-creating customs union', *Economic Journal*, vol. 74, pp. 101–8.

Statistical Office of the European Communities (1986). *Eurostat Review, 1975–84* (Luxemburg: European Communities).

Stopford, J. and Turner, L. (1985), *Britain and the Multinationals* (Chichester: John Wiley).

Strauss, R. (1983), 'Economic effects of monetary compensation amounts', *Journal of Common Market Studies*, vol. XXI, pp. 261–81.

Streeten, P. (1964), *Economic Integration: Aspects and Problems* (Leyden: Sythoff).

Sumner, M. (1976), 'European monetary union and the control of Europe's inflation rate', in M. Parkin and G. Zis (eds), *Inflation in the World Economy* (Manchester: Manchester UP; Toronto: Toronto UP), pp. 97–112.

Swan, T. W. (1955), 'Longer-run problems of the balance of payments', paper presented to the ANZAS; reprinted in H. W. Arndt and W. M. Corden (eds), *The Australian Economy: A Volume of Readings* (Melbourne: Cheshire Press), pp. 384–95; reprinted in R. E. Caves and H. G. Johnson (eds), *Readings in International Economics* (Homewood, Ill: Irwin, 1968) , pp. 455–464.

Taylor, P. (1983), *The Limits of European Integration* (London: Croom Helm).

van den Tempel, A. J. (1969), *Corporation Tax and Individual Income Tax in the European Communities* (Brussels: Taxation Directorate, Commission of the European Communities).

Thirlwall, A. P. (1974), 'Regional economic disparities and regional policy in the Common Market', *Urban Studies*, vol. 11, pp. 1–12.

Thomson Report (1973), see Commission of the European Communities (1973a).

Tinbergen Report (1953), see European Coal and Steel Community (1953).

Tinbergen, J. (1952), *On the Theory of Economic Policy* (Amsterdam: North-Holland).

Tinbergen, J. (1965), *International Economic Integration*, 2nd edn (Amsterdam: Elsevier).

Tindemans, L. (1976), 'European union: report by Mr Leo Tindemans to the European Council', *Bulletin of the European Communities*, vol. 9.

Tironi, E. (1982), 'Customs unions theory in the presence of foreign firms', *Oxford Economic Papers*, vol. 34, pp. 150–71.

Truman, E. M. (1969), 'The European Economic Community: trade creation and trade diversion', *Yale Economic Essays*, vol. 9, pp. 201–57.

Truman, E. M. (1972), 'The production and trade of manufactured products in the EEC and EFTA: a comparison', *European Economic Review*, vol. 3, pp. 271–90.

Truman, E. M. (1975), 'The effects of European economic integration on the production and trade of manufactured products', in B. Balassa (ed.), *European Economic Integration* (Amsterdam: North-Holland; New York: American Elsevier), pp. 3–40.

Trzeciakowski, W. and Mycielski, J. (1976), 'Comment on Bogomolov's paper', in F. Machlup (ed.), *Economic Integration: Worldwide, Regional, Sectoral* (London: Macmillan), pp. 325–9.

Tsoukalis, L. (ed.) (1979), *Greece and the European Community* (Farnborough: Saxon House).

United Nations (1974), 'Economic co-operation for ASEAN', *Journal of Development Planning*, no. 7, pp. 1–261.

United Nations (1979), *Transnational Corporations in World Development* (New York: United Nations).

United Nations Conference on Trade and Development (1972), *Review and Analysis of Trends and Policies in Trade between Countries Having*

Different Economic and Social Systems: Report by the UNCTAD Secretariat (Geneva: UNCTAD).

United Nations Conference on Trade and Development (1985), *Handbook of International Trade and Development Statistics* Supplement (New York: United Nations).

United Nations Economic Commission for Africa (1981), 'Report of the ECA Mission on the evaluation of UDEAC', mimeo (Addis Ababa: ECA).

United Nations Economic Commission for Asia and the Far East (1973), *Asian Industrial Survey for Regional Co-operation* (New York: United Nations).

Vaitsos, C. (1982), *The Role of Transnational Enterprises in Latin American Economic Integration Efforts: Who Integrates with Whom, How, and for Whose Benefit* (New York: United Nations).

Vanek, J. (1965), *General Equilibrium of International Discrimination: The Case of Customs Unions* (Cambridge, Mass: Harvard UP).

Vaubel, R. (1978), *Strategies for Currency Unification* (Tübingen: J. C. B. Mohr).

Verdoorn, P. J. (1949), 'Fattori che regolano lo sviluppo della produttivita del lavoro', *L'Industria*; translated by G. and A. P. Thirlwall in *Research in Population and Economics* (Autumn 1978) and circulated privately.

Verdoorn, P. J. (1952), *Welke Zijn de Achtergronden en Vooruitzichten van de Economische Integratie in Europe en Welke Gevolgen zou deze Integratie Hebben, met Name voor de Welvaart in Nederland?* Overdrukken no. 22 (The Hague: Centraal Planbureau).

Verdoorn, P. J. (1960), 'The intra-bloc trade of Benelux', in E. A. G. Robinson, *Economic Consequences of the Size of Nations* (London: Macmillan).

Verdoorn, P. J. and Meyer zu Scholochtern, F. J. M. (1964), 'Trade creation and trade diversion in the Common Market', in H. Brugmans (ed.), *Intégration Européene et réalite économique* (Bruges: de Tempel), pp. 95–137.

Verdoorn, P. J. and Schwartz, A. N. R. (1972), 'Two alternative estimates of the effects of EEC and EFTA on the pattern of trade', *European Economic Review*, vol. 3, pp. 291–335.

Viner, J. (1924), 'The most-favoured-nation clause in American commercial treaties', *Journal of Political Economy*, vol. 32, pp. 101–29.

Viner, J. (1931), 'The most-favoured-nation clause', *Index*, vol. 6, pp. 2–25.

Viner, J. (1950), *The Customs Union Issue* (New York: Carnegie Endowment for International Peace; London: Stevens & Sons).

Viner, J. (1965), 'Letter to W. M. Corden dated 13/3/1965', *Journal of International Economics*, vol. 6, pp. 107–8.

de Vries, B. (1951), 'Price elasticities of demand for individual commodities imported into the United States', *International Monetary Fund Staff Papers*, vol. 1, pp. 397–419.

Wabe, J. S., Eversley, J. T. and Despicht, N. S. (1983), 'Community regional policy in changing economic conditions', *Banca Nazionale del Lavoro Quarterly Review*, no. 145, pp. 185–209.

Wallace, W. (ed.) (1980), *Britain in Europe* (London: Heinemann).

Wallace, W. (1983), 'Less than a federation; more than a regime: the Community as a political system', in H. Wallace *et al.* (eds), *Policy Making in the European Community*, 2nd edn (Chichester: John Wiley), pp. 403–36.

Walters, A. A. (1963), 'A note on economies of scale', *Review of Economics and Statistics*, vol. 45, pp. 425–7.

Webb, C. (1983), 'Theoretical perspectives and problems', in H. Wallace, *et al.* (eds) *Policy Making in the European Community*, 2nd edn (Chichester: John Wiley), pp. 1–41.

Werner, P. (1970), 'Report to the Council and the Commission on the realisation by stages of economic and monetary union in the Community', *Bulletin of the European Communities*, Supplement, vol. 3 (Werner Report).

Whalley, J. (1979), 'Uniform domestic tax rates, trade distortions and economic integration', *Journal of Public Economics*, vol. 11, no. 2, pp. 213–21.

Whalley, J. (1981), 'Border adjustments and tax harmonisation: Comment on Berglas', *Journal of Public Economics*, vol. 16, pp. 389–90.

Wilczynski, J. (1965), 'The theory of comparative cost and centrally planned economies', *Economic Journal*, vol. 75, pp. 63–80.

Wiles, P. J. D. (1968), *Communist International Economics* (Oxford: Blackwell).

Wilford, W. T. (1970), 'Trade creation in the Central American Common Market', *Western Economic Journal*, vol. 8, pp. 6l–9.

Williamson, J. (1971), *On Estimating the Income Effects of British Entry to the EEC*, Surrey Papers in Economics, no. 6 (Guildford: University of Surrey); revised version 'Trade and economic growth', in J. Pinder (ed.), *The Economics of Europe: What the Common Market Means for Britain* (London: Charles Knight Ltd., for the Federal Trust), pp. 19–45.

Williamson, J. (1975), 'The implications of European monetary integration for the peripheral areas', in J. Vaizey (ed.), *Economic Sovereignty and Regional Policy* (Dublin: Gill & Macmillan), pp. 105–21.

Williamson, J. and Bottrill, A. (1971), 'The impact of customs unions on trade in manufactures', *Oxford Economic Papers*, vol. 23, pp. 323–51.

Winters, L. A. (1984), 'British imports of manufactures and the Common Market', *Oxford Economic Papers*. vol. 36, pp. 103–118.

Winters, L. A. (1985), 'Separability and the modelling of international economic integration', *European Economic Review*, vol. 27, pp. 335–53.

Winters, L. A. (1987), 'Britain in Europe: a survey of quantitative trade studies', *Journal of Common Market Studies*, vol. XXV.

Wonnacott, P. and Wonnacott, R. J. (1967), *Free Trade between the United States and Canada: The Potential Economic Effects* (Cambridge, Mass: Harvard UP).

Wonnacott, P. and Wonnacott, R. (1981), 'Is unilateral tariff reduction preferable to a customs union? The curious case of the missing foreign tariffs', *American Economic Review*, vol. 71, pp. 704–14.

Wonnacott, P. and Wonnacott, R. (1984), 'How general is the case for unilateral tariff reduction?', *American Economic Review*, vol. 74, p. 491.

Wood, G. E. (1973), *European Monetary Union and the UK: A Cost–Benefit Analysis*, Surrey Papers in Economics, no. 9 (Guildford: University of Surrey).

Wooton, I. (1986a), 'Preferential trading agreements: an investigation', *Journal of International Economics*, vol. 21, pp. 81–97.

Wooton, I. (1986b), 'Towards a common market: factor mobility in a customs union' (draft).

Yannopoulos, G. (1979), 'The effects of full membership on the manufacturing industries', in L. Tsoukalis (ed.) (1979), pp. 47–64.

Yannopoulos, G. (1986), *Greece and the European Community: Integration and Convergence* (London: Macmillan Press).

INDEX